Luther's Theology

Luther's Theology

A Translation of Hans Joachim Iwand's Posthumous Works

Hans Joachim Iwand

Translated by
Roy A. Harrisville
and *Randi H. Lundell*

with a Foreword by
Johann Haar

and an Introduction by
Karl Gerhard Steck

☙PICKWICK *Publications* · Eugene, Oregon

LUTHER'S THEOLOGY
A Translation of Hans Joachim Iwand's Posthumous Works

Copyright © 2025 Randi Lundell. All rights reserved. Except for brief quotations in critical publications or reviews, no part of this book may be reproduced in any manner without prior written permission from the publisher. Write: Permissions, Wipf and Stock Publishers, 199 W. 8th Ave., Suite 3, Eugene, OR 97401.

Pickwick Publications
An Imprint of Wipf and Stock Publishers
199 W. 8th Ave., Suite 3
Eugene, OR 97401

www.wipfandstock.com

PAPERBACK ISBN: 979-8-3852-0899-9
HARDCOVER ISBN: 979-8-3852-0900-2
EBOOK ISBN: 979-8-3852-0901-9

Cataloguing-in-Publication data:

Names: Iwand, Hans Joachim, 1899–1960, author. | Haar, Johann, foreword. | Harrisville, Roy A., translator. | Lundell, Randi H., translator.

Title: Luther's theology : a translation of Hans Joachim Iwand's posthumous works / Hans Joachim Iwand; foreword by Johann Haar; translated by Roy A. Harrisville and Randi H. Lundell.

Description: Eugene, OR: Pickwick Publications, 2025. | Includes bibliographical references and index.

Identifiers: ISBN 979-8-3852-0899-9 (paperback). | ISBN 979-8-3852-0900-2 (hardcover). | ISBN 979-8-3852-0901-9 (ebook).

Subjects: LSCH: Luther, Martin, 1483–1546—Theology. | Theology, Doctrinal—History—16th century. | Reformation—Theology.

Classification: BR333.3 I96 2025 (print). | BR333.3 (epub).

VERSION NUMBER 01/07/25

Scripture quotations are taken from the New Revised Standard Version Bible, copyright © 1989 National Council of the Churches of Christ in the United States of America. Used by permission. All rights reserved worldwide.

Contents

Foreword by Johann Haar | vii
Translator's Preface | xi
An Introduction to the Volume by Karl Gerhard Steck | xiii
Abbreviations | xxiii

1 Introduction | 1
2 Luther's Doctrine of Justification | 31
3 Christology | 65
4 Church, State, and Society | 162

Appendix: Supplemental Literature | 229
Bibliography | 231
Name Index | 235
Ancient Document Index | 239

Foreword

THE PUBLICATION OF THE fifth volume of Hans Joachim Iwand's "Posthumous Works" (NW) containing "Luther's Theology" was undertaken by Professor Dr. Ernst Wolf in Göttingen. Much to the regret of all of the co-publishers of H. J. Iwand's works, the culmination of the intent to complete the work by the highly regarded scholars and friends of Iwand did not occur during Iwand's lifetime. On September 11, 1971, Ernst Wolf died at age 69, leaving his many areas of responsibility unfinished. After a while, it was decided to finish the work with the support of Dr. Helmut Gollwitzer, Dr. Walter Keck, and Dr. Karl Gerhard Steck, and not least with the help of the publishing house of Chr. Kaiser in Munich and its CEO, Mr. F. Bissinger, in concert with the heirs of H. J. Iwand. Contributing to this decision was the fact that H. J. Iwand and I were colleagues, connecting through seminars, lectures, and the theological work of the late Prof. Dr. Rudolf Hermann (d. 1962), most recently at the Humboldt University in Berlin, not to mention our many letters and discussions over the years and during our year-long work on the "Göttingen Sermons."

The publisher sent me about 680 pages from the posthumous works typed by Prof. Dr. Ernst Wolf that included some longer and shorter sections from lectures given by Dr. H. J. Iwand on "Luther's Theology" over a period of several years, containing the hand-written note "unedited raw manuscript." I also received an additional typed manuscript from Prof. Steck containing lectures on the same material that had previously been in the possession of Prof. Helmut Golwitzer of Berlin. All of these sections on similar themes were made available during the summer semester of 1956 and were recorded on tape in the following winter semester 1956/1957 at the University of Bonn. Unfortunately, the tapes had gaps in several places and the typed manuscripts contained empty places or additions from notes of the hearers. In general, the material contained repetitions and overlaps. Here and there are even some glaring omissions. For example, H. J. Iwand, as was told to me by those closest to him, had carefully arranged his lectures and completely worked through them and edited them to the end. Using these artifacts, I was able to piece together the entire thing into a complete whole, arranging the manuscript into single paragraphs and subsections which now gives the impression of a united whole as was told to its original audience and now, I hope, will benefit the current reader.

I was careful to shorten the material wherever there were repetitions or where the connections were not clear, and I have referred to other places in the works where themes are covered comprehensively. The entire series of lectures is divided into four main parts: 1. Introduction, II. Luther's Doctrine of Justification, III. The Christology, IV. Church, State, and Society. The fact that part IV is shorter than the others is because anything more reliable was not available from the typescripts. In addition, H. J. Iwand's view of Luther's teaching on these questions is also available in other sections of the lectures.

I strove not only to seek out theological scholars, but others who sought a correct understanding of Luther's teaching, to offer a carefully worked out representation. Luther's Latin citations have all been translated into German. In places where the Latin formulation was important to retain, I have rendered it in sentences, phrases, and occasionally retained specific terms. Where in the German text Luther's expressions, or phrases or even entire sentences are not very understandable in today's language, I have substituted obvious similarities using current linguistic expressions. I hope through the comprehensive "apparatus" of notes, that the reader will have welcome information about individual historical dates and facts, as well as theological and philosophical concepts, not least also insights into the individual personalities, their teaching, and writing.

The entire work should convey some of H. J. Iwand's impulsive thought and temperament in his representation of Luther. H. J. Iwand felt drawn to Luther's personality and always learned something new from him. At the middle point of his theology is his Christology, which he otherwise often referred to as "Christ and His Own." In a letter to Rudolf Hermann on July 30, 1925, Iwand writes "It is not the case that the Christology is the precondition and justification the consequence of this precondition—one must also remember that Luther's justification is not a consequence, but a conclusion. That is why the relationship cannot be turned around; one cannot make Christological statements on the basis of justification" (NW VI, 97–98). The internal, hidden core of Iwand's Theology of Luther lies, in my opinion, in the idea of rebirth: in the concept of the new person. From that point Luther's Doctrine of Justification acquires a new dimension, as does that of God's New Creation. This makes the contents of the book, in my opinion, very exciting. The reader is confronted at every turn with a very personal question which demands a personal answer: What is your stance on Christ? The question of confessing Christ is current in every age. In the first thesis of "The Barmen Declaration" of May 1934, it says: "Jesus Christ, as He is testified to us in Holy Scripture, is the one Word of God whom we have to hear and whom we have to trust and obey in life and in death." H. J. Iwand lived by this statement. His lectures on "Luther's Theology" emerge from the spirit of this confession of Christ.

At the end of this Foreword, I would like to thank all of those who have helped me with this edition. Most of all, I would like to thank Herr Prof. D. K. G. Steck, who has also written the introduction to this volume, and his assistant, Frau Dr. Dorothea Demmer, for proofreading the citations. Further, I would like to thank the Director of the Library, Herr Prof. Dr. Kelmens Honselmann, who was helpful to me in researching places in the scholastic literature in the Library of the Priesterseminar of Paderborn. In addition, I thank Frau Erika Hieronymus, the Director of the Theological Library of the Landeskirchenamt at Detmold, for her tireless help in finding the necessary literature and to my wife, Ingrid Bublitz, who carefully assembled the manuscript from often complicated notes.

Thanks are due to the Hans Iwand Stiftung for making the printing of this volume possible, as well as to the Evangelical Church in the Rhineland and the Union of Protestant Churches (EKD).

Lic. Dr. Johann Haar
4943 Horn—Bad Meinberg 1
May 1974

Translator's Preface

OF ALL THE VOLUMES written on Martin Luther's theology, this volume by Hans Joachim Iwand of Göttingen and Bonn Universities must be one of the very best. In a sweep through the Weimar Ausgabe of Luther's works it describes the Reformer's work according to its principal themes. The author proceeds by interpreting and analyzing a principal theme, then supports it by referencing it in the Weimar Edition of Luther's works.

Iwand's analysis does not leave it to the reader to surmise how or in what way Luther's theology relates to modern thought but makes clear its application to current theological and philosophical reflection. For example, Iwand indicates how Luther's thought impinges on modern Protestantism, Catholicism, the Enlightenment, and idealism. Where there may be question concerning Iwand's analysis, he makes clear to the reader where he may be interpreting on his own. The result is an analysis free of the author's bias, and as close to the Reformer's original thought as such a dedicated and seasoned master can get.

Application or relevance to the present reader cannot be overlooked "in, with, and under" the analysis and interpretation. The quotations from Luther, whether calculated by our author or no, call to faith, to hope and confidence in God. Portions of the volume could easily serve as directions in pastoral care.

Altogether, this volume has to do with Luther's preoccupation with God, with God's word, with God's self-revelation in Jesus Christ, with God and those who are "his own." There is more light shown on the first person of the Trinity and his activity interwork than in many other volumes on the subject.

The number of footnotes referencing the Weimar edition as well as nineteenth and twentieth century theological and philosopher thought suggest a career of reflection on the life and work of Luther the Reformer, and its applicability to modern thought and life. The fact that the volume is introduced and edited by two noted systematicians, Helmut Gollwitzer of Bonn and Karl Gerhard Steck of Münster, is a witness and tribute to the analysis and interpretation contained in this volume.

This translation has been the happy collaboration of father and daughter. Dr. Harrisville has translated the majority of Luther quotations as cited in the WA for this volume. His daughter, Dr. Lundell, has translated the Foreword, the Introduction, Chapter I, and Chapter IV of the volume, while Dr. Harrisville has translated the core theological Chapters II and III. The entire volume has received the *imprimatur* of the more senior translator.

Dr. Roy A. Harrisville
& Dr. Randi Lundell
St. Paul, MN
2024

An Introduction to the Volume

"HISTORY DOESN'T ALWAYS MEAN distance, objectivity, relativity. Of course, it can mean these things, but there is another kind of historical encounter that allows for closer proximity. Here the chain of centuries recedes into the background as if we've been transported back in time and distant times emerge in such close proximity to us that we think they are our own time period." Hans Joachim Iwand undertook to move Luther's theology into today's world and placed it in a perspective that is fascinating for us, even now. Those of us who are older still operate under the assumption that any interest in Luther's theology belongs only to the theologians and is inviable. However, opinions have changed over time. Luther's theology is now no longer of any interest and Luther research is regarded as just one more special area of research among many others which, moreover, is not even a very attractive topic. The "recent centuries" that appeared to have receded for Iwand and his colleagues—and that we likewise ignored—have resurfaced once again. We don't mean that Luther's time is our time, or that Luther's theology should be ours, chapter, and verse. Under these circumstances it would be presumptuous to assume that the publisher and editor of Iwand's posthumous works have published his lectures on Luther and with them, accordingly, filled in the last gap of the Iwand collection. But who is there now to consult this volume? On the basis of these lectures, is Luther thus authorized as the original publisher? Admittedly, the content is more shocking than appealing. Dr. Johann Haar himself reviewed the posthumous material of Iwand's lectures on Luther as well as his foundations for the edition (in the Foreword to this volume). I have nothing to add to this, except for thanking the readers who undertook the difficult and often thankless task of pulling together the unorganized raw material, making it suitable for publication into a book. Naturally, the character of the lectures has been retained, although the chapters of the book are not always arranged in way so as to suggest uniformity and balanced content. In addition, the results of the Luther research of the last 150 years are not included in the original Iwand texts. However, whoever is interested in Luther research will now have a wealth of material at their disposal, from which I mention here only the collection of P. Althaus and the volumes of the Luther yearbooks. The work and meaning of Iwand's lectures lie elsewhere.

The End of Protestantism

The difference between Iwand's representation and other Luther publications is based in Iwand's view that we have arrived at the end of Lutheranism. By this he means that earlier generations had a deep primary interest in Martin Luther the Reformer and viewed his theology as more than just a supplement to his work. Iwand says, "Previous generations stood much more firmly on the foundations of the Reformation than is possible for us today or ever will be possible" (p. 4). Iwand speaks of the end of Protestantism in terms of its various associations, including the rise of the question of theodicy, which was already there in Luther's day but did not define thought as such (i.e., Leibnitz s. 96); of the "ethic of conviction" (German: *Gesinnungsethic*) which emerged from "a Protestant type" that "harks back to the Middle Ages" (p. 90); of false statements about an "existential understanding" which can only hinder a true understanding of Luther (p. 66); and of the "end of the 'protestant' person" in Freud and Nietzsche, "who doesn't understand anything about Christ, and does not abide in Christ, but whose "conscience" has given him a new existence and a new "self-understanding" (p. 128). Iwand is even more pointed in his judgment that, "National Socialism was certainly no creation of Catholicism and not of Socialism, but it was a creation of Protestantism. It derives intellectually from this root, is intellectually its result, so that today we are asked again: Who are Christ's "own"? What does the Reformation mean by "his own"? It should be clear: As Protestants, we are not his, nor have we been for a long time, heirs of the Reformation. However, from such a distinction much good can still come" (p. 87).

Interest in Luther's theology grows out of the radical criticism of the development of Protestantism as a whole and, indeed, from its rejection. Whoever has read Iwand even marginally knows that this rejection does not stem from ignorance. Since the 1920s, as his published and posthumous works show, and primarily under the influence of Rudolf Hermann, Iwand consistently studied philosophy and theology and became well acquainted with modern times. We will run across several points in his Luther studies where his judgments and conclusions come into conflict with modern ideas. Even Iwand's studies and judgments of earlier Luther research is impacted by this. Unfortunately, he did not engage in the view of Luther and Protestantism resulting from the great fight between Mohler and Bauer, although he did give lectures on Mohler's symbolism. The most important influence or "forerunners" for Iwand, after both Seebergs, are Theodosius Harnack and Karl Holl. His view of Holl is very positive: "Here is also the great point of Holl's book on Luther: that one must simply read him to know him. Holl learned from Luther that at the center of his Doctrine of Justification is not mankind and its sin, but central is God and his justice" (p. 20). However, Iwand did not subscribe to Holl's axiom of Luther's religion of conscience (on the *punctum indivisible* in W.A. 40 I, 21, 12 compare pp. 122–25) and Iwand also did not agree with the definition of Luther espoused by W. Elert. A comprehensive report on the research regarding Luther is not within the scope of this work because Iwand only addressed and highlighted what for him were the most important and essential issues.

Plan and Structure of the Lectures

Before I discuss the individual elements of Iwand's lectures that are of most interest for us today, I will outline the overall plan and structure of his lectures. Following upon the introduction, his works can be divided into three main chapters: the Doctrine of Justification; Christology; and Church, State, and Society. The three main chapters are not equal in size. The chapter on justification is only thirty-four pages (pp. 31–64), whereas the chapter on Christology comprises the main section (pp. 65–161). The final chapter, which is of most interest for us today, comprises pp. 162–228. One should not, however, make assumptions about the length of the sections as to their importance since the editors in their selections and work took into account Iwand's writings on Luther elsewhere on the subject. In any case, it is significant to note that the bulk of the lectures included here are on Christology. "There is, if we pursue the genuine origin of Luther's theology, a deeper layer which cannot be simply reduced to the question of a "gracious God," or to the question of "my salvation," or to "soteriological" interests" (p. 55). Iwand says, "that Luther's theology is falsely understood where it is limited to the forgiveness of sins because, accordingly, then it must be subjectified and related to the conquest of the consciousness of guilt" (p. 132). Iwand's emphasis is, as we shall see, on power and death.

Whoever notices that some main concepts are missing in Iwand will find that they appear as subthemes: the themes of law and gospel appear often, as do the themes of faith and works. A short section is devoted to the interpretation of Scripture (section 2 of Christology). A longer section is comprised of the lectures on the Last Supper and Baptism (in the last main chapter!). Iwand does not specifically address Luther's "Anti-Catholicism," but it is evident in the background. As for the reason for the split, Iwand says, "it means that Luther, with his teachings, simply could not continue to remain in this Roman church" (p. 174). Iwand does not mention a "Catholic Luther," which representatives of opposing interests have not failed to notice.

Luther's Realism

For many reasons, Iwand's writings on Luther do not comprise a system, something that perhaps many readers will find disappointing. However, this impression is false. Iwand is very aware of Luther's main motif and identifies it at the very beginning of his lectures:

"What Luther did with the opposition of faith and works is connected to what he sought to find in the "real" man and the "real" God and that, as a theologian—finally for all time and as someone very isolated—he is a "realist."[1] Luther does not look for God and His kingdom in the world of imagination, in the spiritual world, in the world of values, but

---

1. Here as before it is noticeable how strongly the idea world of Luther is rooted in the scholastic debates on universals (Nominalism and Realism), in which the question was raised whether the *universalis* (concepts) arise before (*ante*) or after (*post*) the *res* (things). From this we have the opposition of "nominalism" and "realism." Trans. R. Lundell.

in reality, as such. He does not seek God and His kingdom behind the world, but in the world. But this makes him a Hegelian long before Hegel because he knows that the world is perverse; that its understanding of religious questions tends to legalistic, active, and works-based righteousness, and so the reality or actuality of God is only apparent in a perverse way; that is, it is turned on its head in the negative. Only as the negation of that negation can we understand God's truth and righteousness. The *Deus manifestus* can thus only appear as the *Deus absconditus* to the action oriented person: as the Not-God, as something other than a theoretical, but as a practical irritant (p. 10).

Luther's realism is expressed in many ways and not always sympathetically. For example, Iwand says the core motif of his theology is based in the "great mistrust of people and their internal religious motives" (p. 29). More important than the statements and reflections on ethics is what appears in Luther as something very particular and unique to the definition of Christian existence; namely, that "Christian life is not demonstrable . . . ," yet "each person in an inexplicable way nevertheless understands and knows himself to be a Christian" (p. 87). "Faith leads to the deed, to doing, but this doing is no longer determinative" (p. 99). Here we come up against the detail of the new foundation for morality—in terms of K. Holl—which I can only partially highlight here in terms of how much attention Iwand pays to Luther's criticism of the effects of the monastery. Luther's essay "On Monastic Vows", which is only seldom referenced, but receives a closer look from Iwand, that, "in dismantling the monk's oath, the understanding of God's commandment arises in a new way" (p. 101).

Understanding the World

For Iwand, Luther's realism can be divided into three basic parts: understanding the world, understanding the church, and understanding death. "Nowhere else could Luther have expressed his understanding of the world, as did Idealism, as if the availability of the world's material, the matter afforded to us, by which we understand ourselves in spiritual terms and as free agents to do with as we wish in actual practice. The worldview of German idealism cannot be reconciled with how Luther understood the world. One might even go so far as to say that (for Luther) the world is a great historical variable, even a variable of fate. Human existence in the world means in effect that one is always subject to powers which define and rule against one's will" (p. 139). This realism Iwand places in contrast to the reality gap experienced by the everyday person:

> The attempt by Kant to posit the "thing in itself" (German: *Ding-an-sich*) as a generally valid and extremely necessary premise by which to introduce the historical perspective, arose from factual ignorance by the middle class about the actual roots of its existence. As a result, people never encountered historical reality but were thrust into a world of abstractions, always looking through a telescope. This type of thinking belongs to a particular method that attempts to separate things from the physical. (p. 164)

The much touted "real temporality" in Luther is, according to Iwand, the result of the condition of having faith in Christ. To the extent that Luther wants to liberate Christ, His reign must consequently be the result. Accordingly, "we have the entire problem of what is genuinely worldly. It is made worldly without having the state, the authorities, marriage, or society revert to heathenism. Not worldly, however, in such a way that Christ is Lord but in such a way that the world ceases to be the master of Christ" (p. 69).

The Understanding of the Church

It may therefore be surprising to learn that, according to Iwand, Luther's understanding of the church is only "realistic" where, in his early lectures, Luther emphasizes the hiddenness of the church. Here Iwand makes a clear case: "My thesis was and is that Luther begins with the philosophical concept of the invisible church and ends with a biblical one. The fight against the thesis of the visible church in Rome could only be led by Luther after he came to realize the true nature of the invisible church" (p. 183). In fact, he said, the reality of the church is determined by its invisibility. "As long as the church seeks to manifest itself as visible, the true church cannot be there. That is why the true church is invisible, because it is not visible and exists only as such. The invisible church is not remote but is the immediately present church" (p. 179) For Luther, these statements do not mean, "a step backwards into uncertainty but a step forward to certainty. When Luther speaks of faith which lives in the certainty of salvation, we cannot expect a concept of the church from him that is cloaked in uncertainty" (p. 180). "Accordingly, Luther was not successful in giving the church an external representation, not because he couldn't, but because he was basically of the opinion that it wouldn't work because people always tend to pervert what is internal when making it external" (p. 220). "The concept of the invisible church in Luther is thus so formulated that he could not, and dared not, try to make it visible" (p. 181).

Understanding of Death

In Iwand's view, Luther's realism gains weight and impact by the way in which he handles the problem of death. Limiting himself to the subjective can only be avoided, "when we proceed from that point to the question of the conquest of death. I believe that the entire problem of the 'last things,' and perhaps also the problem of demythologization, needs to be grasped on the basis of the idea of death." "However, everything that we have heard about conscience is only properly understood when we go further from that point to the question of the conquest of death" (p. 132). Only then can we press on in view of the modern suppression of death, which has made it into an isolated large specter, to a proper understanding of reality. And also, there is the obverse, when we "in the moment, in which we skip over death and ignore the horrors of death, and overlook its enmity towards God, then we have misconstrued the reality of the world" (p. 136). Even Heidegger has not gone far enough in his understanding of death. Iwand refers to that part of his philosophy which "is bracketed by a fact that was not there for Idealism, nor for Marxism, that is—by death" (p. 137).

On the other hand, everything hinges on a right understanding of the resurrection.

> The resurrection is thus not simply an isolated event in which we have to believe—whoever will actually force us to believe in such a fact—but that God *is* (German: *etwas sei*) something for which the resurrection is a sign. We could say: If there were no resurrection, then God would be an idea, then we will have to fight with the atheists of today as to whether we will live in the modern world with such an idea of God or without it. And one does, indeed, often have the impression that the battle today is really a battle over a phantom. Some say, "Behind your idea there is nothing," and the others say, "There is something behind our idea," and the others say, "Certainly, there is something behind our idea." "These, then are two world views and for these world views living persons are sacrificed. However, for the living

> God only one person was sacrificed: He, himself. The resurrection is thus as certain as God is God. If God is only an idea one forms for oneself, in order, by way of it, to have a concept of order for the existence of the world, or a guarantee for the moral law, or a judge over good and evil, or to have comfort for one's inner conflict—if God is merely that, then in fact we need no resurrection. (p. 143)

All of this Iwand collects by highlighting the evidence in Luther. "Luther saw very clearly that the denial of the resurrection of the dead is ultimately the spiritualizing of God" (p. 138). Iwand very clearly here sees Luther in contrast to ideas of the Scholastics and we must add, also in contrast to Catholicism: "The atheist—who stepped onto the world stage during the Renaissance—this person meets us in Luther's theology. He is not shut out but is included in the Doctrine of Justification. The difference between Luther's theology and S

cholasticism, which people originally were accustomed to saying that he possessed a (naturally Christian soul) *anima naturaliter christiana* (p. 13). Today, we speak of Christians anonymously. "Luther says, rather, that people bring nothing but *rebellio* (rebellion) in response to the invitation of grace" (p. 13)

Political Themes

We approach the political theme separately from the other themes to do justice to the evidence in Luther and in Iwand. As everyone knows, Luther did not benefit much personally from politics and Iwand would be the last to overlook the ambivalence of Luther's theology of politics.

> One could also believe it possible to understand the peasant's rebellion as something other than a diabolical confusion of God and the devil, and to view the matter very empirically and from a non-theological viewpoint. Every matter takes on the viewpoint of its beholder. The view of the peasants' rebellion in Germany is defined through the concept of the Two Kingdoms and through the construction of the concept of the state during the period of the early reformation territories. Since that time, we can see how it has been adopted in this form and fixed point in history. (p. 164)

With such subtle distancing, Iwand has perhaps contributed more to the solution of the clichés that have been handed down as many others have with their lauding of Thomas Müntzer (1489-1525).

Here as elsewhere, Iwand takes up the political roots in Luther such that

> it is a hallmark of the order of church and society that in the context of Lutheranism all social problems should be handled by the state. Basically, there is no social doctrine, since society is immediately connected with the church, where the church itself is the *societas* or social arena. This still only occurs in Anglo-Saxon and North American areas, or in sects. The church cannot be directly associated with society because there is no Christian social organization. If so, then it would fall under the auspices of the state. The state is the transgression of the internal over into the external. It is therefore the kingdom of God on the left; that is the core of this teaching. The state also realizes—rather, it alone actualizes—God's reign over external things, but in the sense that it has allowed itself to be realized on earth while remaining invisible (*incognito*) in a lesser sense, as for example, in rare cases where a noble might serve heaven by the shedding of blood. (p. 219)

Iwand also explores the much asked question of why Luther required the Christian state to support church reform (see p. 215). But more important for today's reader are the questions of resistance and revolution in Luther. He summarizes it this way:

> Luther's warning against rebellion is to hold the field open for God's upheaval, so that the Word of God can move freely and has room to spread. The Word of God is not a blessing on the *status quo*; it does not justify the order of the world but engages it and purifies it. The freedom of the Word is established by the subordination of Christians to the state. Even here there is a certain order of internal and external. Thus, the fog is lifted, a delusion vanishes, and the view of God's truth becomes sharp, for that is what the Word does: Its teaching makes things happen—it is on the move. (pp. 225-26)

The Question of Today's Readership

"In short, Luther's conception does not mean to parrot his doctrine literally, but rather to follow its intention—to separate from the factual developments those things that are appropriate to the formula" (p. 165). Many questions may trouble the reader in my attempt to quote Iwand for the majority of the time and not Luther. However, Iwand was extremely knowledgeable about Luther, which we know from his earlier writings (had I tried to list all of the evidence in Luther there would be no end to this volume). Has Iwand for the most part done justice to Luther? It has hopefully become clear enough that Iwand is critical of Protestantism and holds views different from what has become the history of Protestantism; namely, that one can study the details and interpret Luther differently. And the fact that perhaps even some things—for the purpose of his lectures—have been somewhat simplified, is no longer disturbing. Still, one cannot fail to see how fragmentary it all is. Even so, with the posthumous publication of these Luther lectures we have, in my opinion, arrived at a critical juncture: Today's development of Christianity is unfavorable toward reformed Protestantism. The unification of confessions seems to be more important and promising to today's church than the knowledge of salvation and truth of the real core of the Reformation. It even appears that we are asked to choose between the two. The Reformation heritage is now only valued as remembrance and celebration. Thus, the influence of the Protestant Reformation is at an end. According to the current "new book of faith" the various historical teachings contain nothing of the meaning of salvation anymore and between the confessions now present only predominantly institutional, personal, and economic barriers. However, it goes without saying that they will ultimately be deposed for newer ones. Still, it is worth the trouble, in view of such developments, to orient ourselves on Iwand's portrayal of Luther. It does not make today's challenges any easier, but it prevents us from forgetting too quickly the heritage of the Reformation and especially Luther's insights.

Karl Gerhard Steck
Frankfurt am Main

Abbreviations

BoA	Bonner Ausgabe. Bonn edition of Luther's works
DB	Deutsche Bibel. German Bible
D.H.	Dr. Haar
EKG	Evangelische Kirchliche Gemeinschaft
Fi	J. Ficker, ed. and trans. *M. Luther, Vorlesung über den Römerbrief*, 1515/1516
GW	Gesammelte Werke. H. J. Iwand, Collected Works/Papers
MPL	Petrus Lombardus. *Migne, Patrologiae cursus completus series Latina*. Vol. 192
NW	*Nachgelassene Werke*. H. J. Iwand. Gütersloh: Kaiser, 2000
RGG	*Die Religion in Geschichte und Gegenwart*. Edited by K. Galling, Tübingen 1957–1965
WA	Weimarer Ausgabe. Weimar edition of Luther's works

1

Introduction

The Early Luther

1. Discovery of the Early Luther

IN CONTRAST TO EARLIER generations, Luther, especially the early Luther, has become problematic for us today. However, this does not mean that the impression that he makes on us should be called into question. On the contrary, it means quite the opposite: that the former established and familiar versions under which we viewed the man and his work no longer suffice to adequately convey his work. In the interim, he has become more approachable through the discovery of the early or young Luther. The young Luther allows us to understand the Reformer more clearly, closely, and theologically. History does not always mean distance, objectivity, or relativity. Of course, it can mean those things, but there is another kind of historical encounter that allows for closer proximity. Here the chain of centuries recedes into the background as if we've been transported back into time and distant times emerge with such close proximity that we think they are our own time period, while the struggles of the period are so clearly evident to us that they reveal the truth with deliberative and exhilarating evidence. The past is, as it were, right there. It is as if a rediscovered treasure, a cornucopia, had been waiting from the faraway, spiritual, and deeply related historical past to be rediscovered and understood anew. History is never self-evident, though it can be, or it can glide back into an objectivity, which mirrors the silent cosmos when we try to deduce from it obvious, supposed eternal laws. This does not necessarily have to be the case. History can also speak and make itself present today. It can speak to us so that we wake up and find ourselves and our task anew.

2. Luther's Lectures on Romans

The influence of this transition occurred during the middle of WWI (1914–1918) and beyond such that suddenly the Reformation and especially its internal theological tones sprang to life in a new way, and one might even say they were viewed in a light not seen in the past four hundred years. Suddenly, it was as if a new stream permeated all of theological and church reflection of our epoch, so that we would be remiss if we were to understand things entirely in light of the theologians of liberal persuasion as was the case in the 19th century. Today we think differently, very differently about our relationship to the Roman Catholic church than did our enlightened Lutheran grandfathers of the 19th century who understood the problem to be much more about the contrast between Geneva and Wittenberg than between Wittenberg and Rome—all this is already evident in the early Luther. This is because, as is born out primarily in the research, but also in all of theological understanding, that boundaries were broken which the established Luther research had erected up until then: the boundary of the year 1517! We should remember that it is really not all that long ago that the fight over indulgences was the basis for the break and the emerging Reformation, and that the celebration that occurred during and after WWI was influenced by this tradition, one might even say by this new Protestant view of Luther's. Up to that time it was the view that Luther's theology was essentially confessional, a view that was based primarily on the standard volumes of Köstlin-Kwerau, published in 1875 and influential until 1919, containing the epoch making lectures of Karl Holl who inaugurated a new era of Luther studies. Of course, there were further formulations and transitions. In 1904, Carl Stange had already discovered the meaning of the early ethical disputations, as he named them, clearly a misnomer.[1] In the first volume of his 1908 publication of Luther's reformed biblical interpretations, including a heretofore unknown account of Luther's lectures on Romans recorded only in a student notebook, Johannes Ficker succeeded, by means of a new publishing technique, to publish a version of the early lectures of

---

1. Stange, *Die ältesten ethischen Disputationen* Vorwort.

Luther that widely surpassed those of the original Weimar Version.[2] It was thus from the Ficker school that we have the first attempt to present the exegetical method of the early Luther as a Bible interpreter. All of this came into a new light as the Great War, the tremors of war, and the collapse of the world of the middle class with its view of Christianity as having moral autonomy, broke apart and exposed the area—the inner area of life of an entire generation—allowing one to comprehend what the impetus had been for theology of the early/young Luther and what underheard of fracture had occurred in his early theological study over a period of eight to nine years.

3. Luther's Early Writings

Of course, there are always new attempts to draw a picture of Luther's theology that has no relation to the early Luther; that ignores it and relies on the old traditional opinions, since the early writings of Luther reflect such unclear views and allow for a lot of grey area. There is still a lot of "Catholicism" during this period. Luther's belief in church authority is unbroken so that one might readily assume that his early lectures and sermons do not form the root and beginning of Reformation thinking. This view may relate to the fact that the old Luther himself did not value his beginnings very highly because they contained too little about his fight against the papacy. In the Foreword to Volume I of the *Opera Latina* of the Wittenberg Edition of 1545, Luther says: "But above all I pray you, dear readers, and I pray for the sake of our Lord Jesus Christ, that you would read this with critical reflection and indeed with great compassion. And that you might know that I was then a monk and an ardent papist when I began this study, so moved and so deeply immersed in the doctrines of the pope, that I was only too ready to kill anyone who opposed it if I could have . . . who the pope only with a syllable had hesitated to obey. In fact, I was such an ardent Saul as we have yet to see today . . . At first, I was alone and certainly for such a weighty task very unable and

---

2. See J. Ficker's careful edition of the lectures in WA 56, published 1938 (=BoA 5 1955, ed. E. Vogelsang, o. 222–304, i.A.) and the two volume Latin-German edition, also by J. Ficker. H. J. Iwand cites mainly the first edition in his lectures, J. Ficker *Luthers Vorlesung über den Römerbrief 1515/1516*, (cited here: Fi). A good German translation by Eduard Ellwein appeared in the series of the "Munich Edition" of selections of Luther's writings in Vol. 2 of "Ergänzungsreihe" 1965. On the entire work see also H. J. Iwand, NW IV, 258ff.

very unlearned and mixed up in an unlucky circumstance, not willingly nor with premeditated zeal, in this confusion: as God is my witness."[3] Thus have the succeeding generations seen the "beginnings" of Luther.

Nikolaus von Amsdorf, the Gnesio-Lutheran,[4] compares Luther's early writings to the sunrise that heralds daybreak but is still hidden behind the fog in the valley. That is an accurate analogy, and it is understandable that the generations after Luther show interest in his theology only to the extent that it was clearly codified and formulated, as in the Formula of Concord[5] which succeeded in holding to the terrain that Luther had taken from Roman Catholicism. But today we are not just interested in the theological developments of the momentous eruptions of an historical and ecclesiastical movement, but rather we are interested in the theologian Martin Luther who stands behind the reformer and who alone justifies his Reformation, while earlier generations main interest in Martin Luther the reformer and his theology were as a by-product of his work. This can be explained thusly: previous generations stood more firmly on the foundations of the Reformation than is possible for us today or will ever be possible. They can be divided into groups: those with W. Elert and R. Seeberg who view Luther as the right doctrine and are able to save orthodoxy; and another group, with the philosopher W. Dilthey and the theologian and philosopher E. Troeltsch, who saw in him the founder and beginnings of the modern age, but also saw his theology as the weak link in his work, as the place where he was still most deeply chained to the old. So, the contrast between orthodoxy and liberals muddies the true view of things.

The young Luther teaches us to see his theology in action and in its abiding worth. The movement will no doubt continue, though the results may not be conserved. But it will continue in a different way than liberalism thinks with its humanist idea of progress since the movement

---

3. The entire "Preface" to the German edition is provided by: K. G. Steck, *Luther für Katholiken*, München 1969, 43–56. The original Latin text is in WA 54, 179, 22ff. = BoA 4, 421, 26ff.

4. "Gnesiolutheraner" taken from the Greek work "*gnesios* "= true, pure (see also 2 Cor 8:8), are the theologians whom Luther knew at the beginning of his teaching and who later (after Luther's death) referred back to this early acquaintance. Among them were Nikolaus von Amsdorf. See F. Lau on him and his works in *RGG* I, 333–34.

5. The Formula of Concord "is by intention and expectation not entirely the result of numerous attempts after 1555 to unify and secure the "pure teaching" in the Lutheran territorial churches against the background of internal Lutheran conflicts in the interim." (ed. Wolf in *RGG* III, 1777ff.)

does not lie in the world of ideas or intellectual history, but in theology from which comes the unrest of the Spirit, which also lives and works in the world. That is the most important contribution of K. Holl's book on Luther, because in it he placed the theological and historical motifs of the Luther research in a correct relationship to each other. He wanted to do this because for him it was important to connect the meaning and content of the sources of Luther's early theology. E. Seeberg followed after Holl with his unfinished book on Luther. Seeberg realized that if one wants to truly understand Luther's theology one should not bypass his early writings—or one will not understand the older Luther! Both the late and the early Luther are consistent in their ultimate motifs and in their theological formulations. What has thus been brought to light is from a richer and much more solid, more organically theological body of work than what sprang from the anti-Catholic complex and its resulting polemic.

4. The Effects of Scholasticism and the Apostle Paul on Luther

So, there is a kind of stillness if one presumes the "Catholic" era in Luther's theological work as the fundamental era from which all others proceeded. However, herein lies the particular excitement for us regarding Luther's earlier lectures. It is also true that it was not indulgences, not the Pope and not the ecclesiastical administration or other *"nugae"* (unnecessary things) that led him to break with Scholasticism and its piety, but it is the theology as such: It is the new, inspired by Paul, "entirely different" way to see the Word of God and to seriously understand theology, that led Luther down a different path. It is during this early time of beginnings that his teachings began to take shape. Without knowing what he was doing, Luther broke away and denounced the alliance that High Scholasticism (main representative is the Dominican Thomas Aquinas) had made between Christianity and philosophy, between nature and grace. He saw himself as a "modern," as an Ockhamist, as one who completed what been started by Duns Scotus and Ockham, both of the great Franciscan theologians, with their emphasis on the free will of God, the *potentia absoluta*, with the priority of the voluntary power in the doctrine of the soul. But Luther went even further. He did not mainly learn from them, as he did not actually have them as his teachers, but he learned from Paul. He learned from the Scriptures. He is first and foremost an exegete. He is what he aspired to be as a young docent in Wittenberg: a *Doctor in bibliis*. In the attempt he fractured the scholastic system, clearly also the late Scholasticism in which he had been trained, which had held up the unity of thought and being, namely, the "realism" of the Middle Ages. But Luther also broke the system at its roots: with his Doctrine of Sin and Grace. In so doing, he extended his hand to another—or at least intended to extend his hand—to Augustine and his Doctrine of Predestination! When Luther broke with the Doctrine of Free Will,—an exciting moment that we can still place at its source in Rom 8:28,[6] a moment that we can nearly immediately live all over again and perhaps with more knowledge and more completely than the students who experienced it at the time—when he described the *liberum arbitrium post peccatum* as a *res de solo titulo*,[7] then the break was final regarding the synthesis of God's grace and man's works which Thomas Aquinas had previously so artfully developed it. Where one *et* (as well as also) stands, there stands also one *aut* (either or): *Lex et voluntas sunt adversarii duo sine gratica Dei implacabiles*.[8]

Luther knew well what Frederich Nietzsche (1944–1900) later confessed in his dream of the Übermensch: "If there are gods, then I am certain, that I am not one."[9] Luther knew this well because he knew, and from the Word of God, that next to this self-activating, entirely in-and-of Himself existing God, that people might be able to think about God, but they can't become Him. Existence is not a matter of thinking but of willing: of validating by way of extinguishing! The moment I think I have comprehended God and wish to have him, I abolish him. The God of my own conception and making, who conforms to me, to my analogue, that God is a Not-God. To think about God in this way means to obliterate him. Religion in this sense is an *annihilatio Dei* (destruction of God).[10] Luther knows that in the movement between God and man one of them must go and must be destroyed: either God rules and the person lets God be God, or the person rules, in which case the person remains himself

---

6. See WA 56, 83, 5ff. (Glosses) and 381–88 (Scholien) = BoA 5, 265–71 = Fi (Glosses) 77, 11ff. and Fi (Scholien) 208–15.

7. "Free will in the wake of sin is something in name only." WA 1, 354 (*Heidelberg Disputations*. 1518. These 13) = BoA 5, 378. See also H. J. Iwand on the Disputations in NW II, 383ff.

8. "Law and will are two opponents that are irreconcilable apart from God's grace." WA 1, 227 (*Disputatio contra scholasticam theologiam*. 1517, Thesis 71) = BoA 5, 325 (here: Thesis 72). H. J. Iwand cites the same place in a lecture on "Law and Gospel" (Introduction to the Theology of the Reformers), see NW IV, 258.

9. F. Nietzsche, *Also Sprach Zarathustra*, Part II (On the Happy Island).

10. See also H. J. Iwand, NW IV, 44.

and then God must be changed into an image of one's own imagination and wishes. The theology out of which Luther came, however, assumes the similarity between God and man and the spiritual relationship becomes real in the encounter of the two. Not primarily in the encounter as such, because here it is not primarily Grace that situates the community, but rather the similarity between God and man is the ideal—the *apriori*[11] religious pre-condition for the encounter. This pre-condition is something Luther regards as a pagan fantasy and is something he calls *concupiscentia spiritualis*.[12]

5. The Beginnings of Luther's Theology

When it came to the question of God, the Middle Ages asked the question: *an Deus sit?* (Does God exist?). To that end, it asked after the roots of God's being and the origin of all that is, so that one might ask about God's existence in accordance with every living thing. However, Luther did not begin with the question "Does God exist?" but he begins with the thesis: "God is God."[13] Luther's theology begins here! His teacher, Beil,[14] had already proposed this formulation, but more as a negation of a rational concept of God than as a theological position. Luther used his formulation as a formulation for the First Commandment: I am the Lord your God! From this point of view man cannot refuse to acknowledge the God of, "I am, who I am!" He cannot, because if he did, he too would cease to exist since man's existence—his "I am who I am!"—is from God.

The early Luther is filled with striving to understand the reality of human existence and to bring to light the actual relationship between God and humankind: its true reality! He does so, even if it means sacrificing an entire safety system of reliable concepts and dogmas. He calls this breakthrough to the reality of human life *magnificare peccatum* and says at the beginning of the lectures on Romans: "The chief purpose of

---

11. Under this would be understood a generally valid and strongly necessary intellectual legalism pertaining to all religious experience. See also H. J. Iwand, "Immanuel Kant als Theologe und Philosoph," in NW II, 321–37.

12. This means, as kind of "spiritual greediness," which for Luther is completely absurd.

13. WA 1, 225 (*Disputatio contra scholasticam theologiam*. 1517, Thesis 17) = BoA 5, 321: *Non potest homo naturaliter velle deum esse deum, Immo vellet se esse deum et deum non esse deum*" (A person cannot by their nature will that God is God. They would rather have it that *they* are God, and that God is *not* God. Trans. R. Lundell).

14. On Gabriel Biel (1410–495), see *RGG* I, 1267.

this letter is to break down, to pluck up, and to destroy all wisdom and righteousness of the flesh. This includes all the works which in the eyes of people or even in our own eyes may be great works. No matter whether these works are done with a sincere heart and mind, this letter is to affirm and state and magnify sin, no matter how much someone insists that it does not exist, or that it was believed not to exist."[15] There has seldom been such an introduction to a lecture which is so openly programmatic in its goal of destruction as this one. Look at how things really are, he says. The slogan *"ad res!"* is Luther's motivating lament: *Theologus crucis dicit id quod res est* (English: "The theology of the cross dictates how things are").[16]

Accordingly, we have called the theology of the young Luther a "theology of the cross" with all due respect. But perhaps we have only partially understood it, since at closer glance the phase of his declared *theologia crucis* is that of his second lectures on the Psalms, his development phase of 1519–1521, a period which is clearly his theologically most mature and creative. However, the theology of the cross is the core concept of Luther's entire theology. So it is perhaps for this reason, due to the late pietistic misunderstanding of him, that he was placed in such proximity to mysticism and the theology of the cross was relegated to the later form of empathy with the suffering God. But the cross is ultimately something entirely different for Luther because it stands in direct relation to the *magnificare peccatum!* The cross is God's reality in and of itself. It is the reality of God upon which all false, lacking, and half-formed images of God are shattered. The cross means: "Because man misinterprets the knowledge of God from works, therefore God will only be known through suffering."[17] Here we already find the opposition between works and suffering! And between ethics and grace. This is something that pietism forgot when it took up the theology of the cross. Rather, it reconciled it with natural theology and ethics. "In the crucified Christ we have true theology and the knowledge of God."[18] That is Luther: *Cognitio Dei*, the knowledge of God! There is no forgiveness without that knowledge that it is the true and just—not conjured or felt—God who testifies to

---

15. WA 56, 157, 2ff. (Scholien) = BoA 5, 222, 1ff. = Fi (Scholien) 1, 1ff. Also: *Luther's Works*, 135.

16. WA 1, 354 (Heidelberg Disputations. 1518. Thesis 21) = BoA 5, 379. See on the theology of the cross also H. J. Iwand, NW II, 381–98; more in NW IV, et al p, 247.

17. WA 1, 362, 5ff. (Heidelberg Disputations. 1518. Thesis 20) = BoA 5, 388, 16–17.

18. WA 1, 362, 18–19 = BoA 5, 388, 29–30.

Himself (in Christ): He only forgives. *Magnificare peccatum* also means to proceed from the magnitude of one's sin to see oneself in one's entire and full reality which is hidden and obscured by a false means of salvation! The first and most false means of salvation is the *opus* = the deed! The person intent on doing good deeds is judged by the Cross when he is promised help by his deeds and when, in seeking after God, the person is oriented by way of works. The man of works and the god of works are both judged, and rightly so: "Therefore say the friends of the cross, the cross is good, and works are bad, because works are destroyed by the cross and Adam is crucified who would rather be sustained through works. It is therefore impossible for someone not to be arrogant by virtue of his good works, which already beforehand were not humbled and judged as nothing through suffering and troubles, until he realizes that he himself is nothing and his works are not his works but are God's."[19]

This is the place upon which the young Luther stakes his position. Indeed, under the Cross, but different from the place where Bernhard of Clairvaux, Zinzendorf, and a bit differently than where Paul Gerhardt have stood under the cross. Perhaps there is only the Apostle Paul that he can stand beside. The Cross hides God "who is known by His works" (*manifestum ex operibus*).[20] The Cross is the "hidden God" (*Deus absconditus*) and as a result for the young Luther the opposite is also true: *Deus absconditus* is always *crucifixus*! We cannot come to believe in God, to learn of him, to find him, as long as we think we can operate on the same level. That—and precisely that—however, was the *pathos* of the Aristotelian worship of God because the effects and the mediation of action through creation is what Thomas Aquinas sought to merge with Christian sensibilities. Here the concept of passivity—the *passio*—of suffering and pain, is evident throughout. Certainly, God is at work in hidden suffering so that who would dare be able to perceive his works? *Homo operibus aedificatur* (the person is built up by works)—even this false uplifting must be erased from theology. Now we begin to sense what we do not want to let go of: that the problem of works is not bound to time, it is not "Catholic." What Luther did with the opposition of faith and works is connected to what he sought to find regarding the real man and the real God and that, as a theologian,—finally for all time and in a very unique

---

19. WA 1, 362, 29ff. (on Thesis 21) = BoA 5, 389, 6ff.

20. See WA 1, 362, 8 (on Thesis 20) = BoA 5, 388, 19 (also the citations 1 Cor 1:19 and es 45:15) and further to other concepts and phrases pertaining to Thesis 21.

way—he is a "realist."[21] Luther does not look for God and His kingdom in the world of imagination, in the spiritual world, in the world of values, but in (temporal) reality. He does not seek God and His kingdom behind the world, but in the world. But this makes him a Hegelian long before Hegel because he knows that the world is perverse; that its understanding of religious questions tends to legalistic, action oriented and work-based righteousness, and so the reality or actuality of God is only apparent in a perverse way, namely, turned on its head in the negative. Only as the negation of that negation can we understand God's truth and righteousness. The *Deus manifestus* can only appear to the person motivated by deeds as the *Deus absconditus*: as the Not-God, as something other than a theoretical, but as a practical irritant.

However, the *theologia crucis* is not the formula that encompasses all of the early Luther's theology. Inherited from mysticism, the *theologica crucis* is one of the most deep and profound, thoroughly thought-out concepts of Middle Ages pietism. Luther takes this concept and reworks it using anti-idealistic realism and his studies of Paul. It is hardened in the fires of struggle and doubt so that everything that was weak in it is melted away so that only the finest gold remains.

6. Summary

a) The young Luther breaks with the Doctrine of Free Will in the *liberum arbitrium*.

b) The young Luther contrasts the *theologia crucis* with the *theologia gloriae*. Luther's Theology of the Cross not only validates the Cross as an historical fact, not only makes virtually visible God's activity here on earth (the *virtus Dei*, which lies in the forgiveness of sins), but it is a formula for the destruction of the natural man—of his *virtus*, his *sapientia*, and his *iustitia*. Everything is judged from the Cross; namely all that we fundamentally and basically consider to be our own self-consciousness. The Theology of the Cross is essentially anti-idealistic, if under idealism one thinks that one carries the ideas of the good, true, and just in ourselves and find them within ourselves. This idea is judged on the Cross.

---

21. Here as before it is noticeable, how strongly the idea world of Luther is rooted in the scholastic debates on universals (nominalism and realism), in which the question was raised whether the "*universalis*" (concepts) arise before (ante) or after (post) the "*res*" (things). From this we have the opposition of "nominalism" and "realism." Trans. R. Lundell.

Thus, this formula is also anti-empirical! The new life is "invisible" just as the cruciform life is invisible and beyond one's grasp. In this way Luther combines both of the concepts of 1) *fides* (Rom 1:17) which says that justification is only real when works are destroyed, and 2) that faith cannot be perceived, it is *invisibilitate* (Heb 11:1).

c) The third point, in my view, is the most important and without it one will read the early Luther to no avail. I mean the anti-psychological. The formula *theologia crucis* assumes that a person is in fact both: a *sinner*, as someone who is judged in terms of his own justice, and *justified* at the same time, even though this is the same sinner who takes part in the righteousness of God in Christ! Both things happen at the same time. One is therefore not, as in the Doctrine of Justification of the Middle Ages, a sinner in view of the life from which one comes and justified in view of the life to which one aspires, but both together and at the same time so that Luther coins the well-known formula: *simul iusuts et paccator*.[22]

Illustrations of Luther's Theology

1. Luther's Theology as Process

From the middle of the previous century onward, Luther the man emerged and his theology with him. There is still a struggle around his person and his teachings that hasn't ended. Luther belongs to the Greats who broke barriers of convention. He lived by his words and his teaching. He maintained a strict system because his theology was constantly being formulated. In essence, his theology represents a process. During his early years he struggled with the Catholics and the Scholastics, with traditional positions, formulas, and basic doctrines. Luther is nothing if not a revolutionary. However, during his early years he is still a reluctant representative of strict obedience to the church hierarchy and took his loyalty to the Pope very seriously. Later on, as he encountered the Enthusiasts and Erasmus, he was no longer in a fight with what lay behind him but with what lay in his path. His writings on the Bondage of the Will and his interpretation of the Last Supper are focused forward and point to the problem of Humanism's anthropology and (in the fight over the Last Supper) the problem of a philological exegesis of Scripture. He attributes the never ending string of confusion that he encountered—a

---

22. H. J. Iwand refers here to the book by his teacher Rudolf Hermann, Luther's These "Gerecht und Sünder zugleich," Gütersloh 1960.

lesser mind would never have found them—to the work of the devil, who is always on the lookout for new ways to destroy the Gospel. That is why his work was always evolving. Church history for him was not something of the past, but centrally and incredibly present. Wherever the Gospel is proclaimed, something happens in the world. All of secular history is only modeled on Biblical history as an accompaniment to church history. For God and His Word are not dead, but they live and are active in today's world. Therefore, Luther's theology is only one piece of the picture. Piece by piece we begin to see, like Paul (1 Cor 13:12), that we find ourselves on a *theologia viatorum* (theological journey). This places Luther's theology in contrast to the Scholastics who tried to make a system of theology.

2. The Doctrine and the Person

There are two main avenues of representation upon which we can rely for Luther's theology: his teachings and his life. It is often the case with some scholars that they isolate Luther's thinking and try to make a timeless system of his work. That has happened in recent Lutheran confessional circles, even among the best. But here is the problem: there is a fine line between the *pura doctrina* (pure doctrine) and people who, in their attempt to elevate his doctrines, are not up to the task. We only hear the answers, not the questions, and so the paradoxes are lost. These representations all have come to resemble what later on were deemed Lutheran orthodoxies. What captivates us when we see Michelangelo's painting of the creation of Adam, for example, is the fine line between the painter and his subject in which Adam, the subject of the painting, is separated from his Creator. We see the sadness in his eyes—a look of truth and the stark reality of life—and we can't help but recognize this rift in the painting as it attempts to capture the reality. In the same way the best minds have failed to represent the dialectic of Luther's theology: the dialectic between the living God and those who live, as everyone must live, separated from God. Luther's theology calls upon all men through the Gospel: those who are separated from God, the Dionysians as well as the Nihilists, but also those who know nothing of God and who don't want to understand Him. Even the atheist, who came on the modern scene during the Renaissance is included in Luther's theology and is not excluded from, but rather included in his Doctrine of Justification. The difference between Luther's theology and the doctrines of the Scholastics is that Luther does not believe in the *anima naturaliter christiana* (the naturally Christian soul). Luther says, rather, that man brings nothing but *rebellio* (rebellion) in response to the invitation to grace. The notion of rebellion of the old Adam in every encounter with God is embedded in Luther's theology. The righteous-making God encounters man directly without any mitigating element of a *theologia naturalis* (natural theology) between God and the *homo inimicus* (hostile man). This is evident from other studies of Luther by church historians and systematicians. They have portrayed the person of Luther, his development, and his struggles more clearly in their research, but also with the danger of making his teaching an expression of his person as the pious, God-fearing Luther. As a result, they also circumvent the rift, but from a different, psychological viewpoint. Luther remains true to his teaching as a questioning, doubting, acquainted with sin, very real and accessible man. Everything that he has to say about theology stems from his own struggles (German: *Anfechtung*). As an old man, he wrote down his confessions constantly so that no one would doubt his teaching. He died for them. At the same time, his last statement rings true: "We are beggars, that is for sure."[23] Luther did not rest on his works, he rested on the Word of God, which was *extra nos* (outside us). Accordingly, any psychologizing of Luther's works widely misses the mark.

3. Works on Luther's Theology

a) In this section, various traditional large works on Luther's theology are treated. For instructional purposes regarding the various phases and themes of Luther's works there is the still current, and typical for normal Lutheran interpretation, very precise and objective Julius Köstlin's *The Theology of Luther*.[24]

b) Another, very different volume is *Luther's Theology* by Theodosius Harnack.[25] This book has an unusual story: twenty years lies between the

---

23. This last sentence from the "Letzten Aufzeichnung von der Hand Luthers" (the last notes by Luther's own hand) were found after Luther's death on a slip of paper in his bedroom. Particulars are in K. Aland, *Luther Deutsch*, vol. 10, 340–41 and 393–94. See the different versions in WA 48, 241: "Wir sind Bettler (We are beggars): *hoc est verum.*" WA Ti 5, 168, 35: "Wir sind Bettler, *Hoc est verum*: WA Ti 5, 318, 2f." "Wir sein Bettler. *Hoc est verum.*"

24. Julius Köstlin, *Luthers Theologie in ihrer geschichtlichen Entwicklung*.

25. Theodosius Harnack, *Luthers Theologie mit besonderer Beziehung auf seine Versöhnungs- und Erlösungslehre* (2 vols.). See also the section "Die Kontroverse:

publications of each of the two volumes. Th. Harnack, who completed the first volume in 1862 in Erlangen, was forced to move to Dorpat for personal reasons. There he completed his second volume on Luther's Christology. The entire opus was forgotten for a long time because it was "not current" since Ritschl's theology had gained prominence in the meantime in Germany and the Erlangen school had, unfortunately, receded from public prominence. Only a few knew of the Th. Harnack volumes as containing a wealth of information, voluminous citations, and an impeccable systematic penetration of the massive amount of material contained in the two volumes. The first volume essentially contains the theme of law and gospel, of wrath and mercy, and the second addresses Christology. This arrangement reflects how the Formula of Concord transmitted Luther's theology, but it also reflects the living Luther as richly illustrated in his sermons and lectures. Here we hear Luther actually speaking. And now this book has been revived six centuries later as, in connection with dialectical theology, this side of Luther (the dialectic between law and gospel) is being rediscovered. In 1927, Georg Merz re-published Th. Harnack's theology, which was a great success. At last, this book has been successfully received and acknowledged as one of best written about Luther from a confessional point of view. Whereas Ritschl's theology taught that the wrath of God was merely a product of the human imagination and as a rational result of his confused reflections on God, Th. Harnack felt compelled to raise the point that Luther taught that the wrath of God could be most completely illustrated by a world without Christ. Only in Christ is God's wrath abated. Therefore, faith is always found as moving so that it must always be aided by the preaching of the law and the gospel together. Both aspects must be preached—if one is missing then the other is eliminated as well. The first volume ends with an illustration of Luther's teaching on law and gospel, in that order, because the order is also important: first the law, then the gospel, since the law, like the moon, receives its light from the gospel, the sun. The teaching of Christology is arranged in the same way. It is risky to outline Luther's "Christology," since he had one to about the same degree as Augustine did. However, since he held to the tradition of the church's Christology, it is possible to summarize his statements on it. On the topic of Luther's Christology, Harnack again uses the contrast between "God" and the "God of reconciliation." The righteous God must, in His righteousness, reconcile the sacrifice to Himself

---

Theozentrisch–Christozentrisch" in H. J. Iwand, *Rechtfertigungslehre und Christusglaube*, 94–99.

so that we also may be sure of reconciliation. On the cross, God is reconciled with Himself and with the world. Here, and again in contrast to Ritschl's doctrine of reconciliation which places it in the consciousness of man, we have objective reconciliation in that the law is fulfilled in Christ and cannot accuse us any longer. The dialectic of law and gospel thus finds its resolution in God—and only in Him! And only through Him. Jesus Christ is the *hilasterion* (expiation, see Rom 3:25, Heb 9:5); in Him we have peace. That is what Th. Harnack wants to show. He wants to take reconciliation out of the realm of human reason and place it directly with God, so that, as he says, God is "not reconciled with man, but rather man is reconciled with God." Any attempt at understanding Luther's Christology will have to come to terms with Th. Harnack's work.

c) Another remarkable work on Luther is Werner Elert's *Morphology of Lutheranism*. The first volume, and the only volume of interest to us here, contains a study of the theology and world view of Luther in the 16th and 17th centuries.[26] In his, *Decline of the West*,[27] Otto Spengler drafted a morphology of culture as part of his law of how history moves and changes. Perhaps Elert wanted to do something similar when he spoke of a morphology of Lutheranism. For him, morphology meant morphogenesis and Luther is of interest for him only in as far as he is the originator of Lutheranism. Lutheranism represents an enclosed entity that is constantly growing and moving, influenced by external forces to be sure, but nevertheless a unified, identifiable whole as a particular type of spiritual entity. Lutheranism has a particular understanding of the world and thus has a very particular relationship to time, death, and created life. For Elert, Lutheranism is a confession and to that extent it is a church. Elert's picture of Luther is basically affected by Luther's "primal experience" (German: *Urerlebnis*) as it connects with his concept of the *deus absconditus*. Whether or not that is the case we shall see in the following lectures (by Iwand), but that it describes "Lutheranism," is very appropriate. There is no moral autonomy possible, but only a permanent *accusatio sui* (self-accusation). That goes to the root of the Lutheran attitude towards life. However, the fact that this attitude has a dual aspect, which Elert calls the "evangelical" in contrast to Th. Harnack, can be seen by the quotation,

---

26. Elert, *Morphologie des Luthertums*, Vol. 1: *Theologie und Weltanschauung des Luthertums*.

27. Spengler, *Decline of the West*.

> In Lutheran churches we have sinners, not intentional sinners, but repentant sinners, yet sinners nonetheless, who cannot be but anything else in this life. The righteous ones, who determine their salvation according to the rules of Geneva by the cut of their garments, the food on their plates, and who are known by speaking in the "language of Canaan," have fundamentally nothing to offer. Whatever their membership has or has not to offer ethically, belongs to the category of sociology (!) and has nothing to do with the church. The responsibility lies with the evangelical individual, not with the evangelical church.[28]

This citation suffices, and we Germans can only hear it with the deepest emotions because whatever we can offer, or neglect to offer, belongs in the realm of sociology. The church has nothing to do with that since the church only deals with sinners and the forgiveness of sins! And here we see that the doctrine is only an expression of human experience—and indeed an experience that is assigned a false meaning; namely, an experience of the conflict between what is and what should be, of what cannot be overcome in this life. Doesn't this stem from Kantian idealism about the opposition between what should be and what is (German: *Sollen vs. Sein*) which everyone has tackled in the field of dogmatics and ethics, including Karl Heim, Friedrich Brunstad, Paul Althaus, and Wilhelm Herrmann? And don't we have the use of the phrase "primal experience" (German: *Urerlebnis*) as part of this understanding of the world as sinful originally from Luther? As far as I can tell, it's the opposite from idealism: because Christ came, therefore our works are of no avail; and therefore, our righteousness, even "the best in life," is nothing.[29] When the sun goes out, we should extinguish all of our lights because the greatest, brightest Light is there—the "No" to our own righteousness is always and already the "Yes" to God's righteousness. In this regard, let us recall a single verse from Iwand's lecture on Romans: "God will not save us through our own (i.e., internal, inward life or means), but through His external (i.e., condescending to us) righteousness and wisdom; not by a righteousness that comes from us or is born in us, but rather a righteousness from without us that descends to us, that does not originate on earth, but in heaven. Therefore, it behooves us to learn about a righteousness that comes to us as something entirely foreign and alien. And we must also learn to wipe

---

28. Elert, a.a. O. (1931), 317.
29. From EKG 195, 2.

out every self-centered and internal (i.e., lives in us) righteousness."[30] This looks very different from what we might expect: a righteousness from above that wants to win us over (*in nos venire*), therefore we must sweep the house and make it ready for the arrival of immanent righteousness. God wants to make us righteous by virtue of His righteousness and so we must get rid of everything that smacks of our own righteousness! At Advent we say, "The Lord is nigh," which means: "to destroy, dispose of, and annihilate all wisdom and righteousness of the flesh." (well said!)[31] Of course, that is a quotation by the "young Luther," but if one is already talking about "primeval existence" then one must at least give credence to the source of his thinking. That is because it is not at all true that dualistic thinking had made an impression on Luther's thought. In fact, the opposite is true: he tried to interpret the Scriptures, especially Romans with its (core theology) *iustitia Dei* as something "foreign," as an *iustitia extranea*.

If one would like to identify a consistent theme within Lutheranism, then let it be the idea of *extra nos*. And a more precise notion of "external," as it is often quoted, should be—*extra nos, i.e, in Christo*. This doesn't imply external in the sense of space, but in terms of our inner feelings and thoughts. There is always fear and dread wherever God appears external to our own imaginations and desires, but there is also hope that He is who He says He is! The *extra nos* describes the negative side of God's nearness to use, but the *in Christo* describes the positive side of God's nearness to us. Thus, righteousness is attributed to those who believe and have faith and who have let go of the desire for psychological control. Otherwise, we will not be able to come to terms with human experience, even as primal experience, in Luther's schema. His doctrine of a "foreign righteousness" subsequently describes the person whose fear and anxiety has been stripped away from him by virtue of their faith.

d) We have another view of Luther to consider as contained in the book by Karl Holl titled, "Luther," which has placed all of the Luther research on an entirely new level.[32] It contains essays that the editor has centered around Luther's most important and core ideas. Holl asks questions and allows Luther to answer. He asks questions as a modern person who has read the modern research and puts questions to Luther and his theology wherever it is possible to find answers. He asks questions in

---

30. WA 56, 158, 10ff. (Scholien)–BoA 5, 222, 7ff. = Fi (Scholien) 2, 7ff.

31. WA 56, 157, 2ff. (Scholien) = BoA 5, 222, 1ff. = Fi (Scholien) 1, 1ff. Also: *Luther's Works*, 135.

32. Holl, *Gesammelte Aufsätze zur Kirchengeschichte*, Vol. I.

real-time, as if the centuries in between did not exist, and as if no one else had attempted an answer except Luther. He asks questions like a systematician, although he is a historian. He knows and also states that systematics does not exist within an existing closed system, but within a relevant context. He knew that theology, when it first understands a thing and explains it, or is understood by it, as to what it involves, is naturally systematic by itself. And furthermore: he asks about the young Luther and the sources of his development. It is, if you will, a dialogue with Nicodemus; a consultation after the fact between a scholarly old man and this long ago forgotten, for a long-time half Catholic, immature, and pre-Reformation young Luther from the period of his first lectures on the Bible. This is what Holl uncovers. He peeks behind the curtain of the Reformation, behind the open battle of the Reformer with the Roman church and takes a closer look to find the explanation for this fight and his resulting decision. He discovers the true roots of the large tree that one calls the "Reformation" and finds in it already there the theology of the early Luther. Since then, no one has been able to pass over or dismiss the young Luther. Holl was a contemporary and colleague of Adolf v. Harnack and Ernst Troeltsch. Only he took it upon himself to climb any mountain that allowed him a new view revealing that the young theology was indeed, at the time, on the march. Only he (Holl) saw it (coming). He could not see that Barth, Gogarten, Bultmann and others were close behind, but he did help an entire generation of awakening theologians move forward with the early Luther and he made clear that when you read Luther again, if you want to understand him, you will not be able to stand still: *Christianus enim non iest in facto, sed in fieri*.[33] Holl tried to align with this movement in everything he said. He did not make Luther's theology into an arsenal for orthodoxy, and he did not argue with the dictum "Luther says," but he heard him and tried to understand what Luther meant. In short, at every turn he tried to convey the intention of Luther's words.

Regarding the idea of the "evolving Christian" I offer an example: the justification of the sinner does not mean the justification of the sin. This is what Holl means when he talks about the "new morality" in Luther's doctrine.[34] He saw the danger of a basic contradiction in a

---

33. "A Christian is not in a state of completion, but in one of becoming." WA 38, 568, 37 (*Annotationes in aliquot capita Matthaei*. 1538–Comments on several chapters in Matthew. 1538).

34. This title is in the third essay by Holl, (n. 32), 155–287.

misunderstanding of justification as if God had to bend to the fact that we are sinners because otherwise He cannot save us. If that is the case, then there would be an essential rift in Lutheranism—like there is in Catholicism—a contradiction in ethical terms at the base of a theology of justification. Holl argues vehemently against this, stating that you can only find the unity of the sinner with justification in God alone—not in man. Therefore, the person is evolving, growing in faith, growing in his struggle to overcome sin through justification, which is only to be found in God, because the justification of the sinner is achieved in God who is present in the struggle. Holl was thus at odds with Melanchthon who he said had perverted Luther's teachings by weakening the doctrine of the omnipotence of God. Melanchthon did not agree with Luther that our new life in God is a work of God's alone, whose goal is our justification. If you take this out of the equation, then Luther's doctrine falls apart. What Melanchthon contributed from his own efforts was a bad substitute for the internal damage, since his Doctrine of Imputation had the effect of describing faith as something that could be earned.[35] It inevitably leads to the question of why God could allow Christ to atone for only a part of our sin, and not all of it. And the answer is always going to be because one person believes, and the other does not. The result is that the believer has faith in God as the foundation of his belief by which he is justified through Christ and all of his own efforts are laid aside. All of Melanchthon's attempts and those of his "Lutheran" followers to close this gap are futile.[36] Let us remember that Theodosius Harnack strongly supported the systematic difference between Law and Gospel, and of this "Melanchthonian" systematic sense we remember moreover that Elert stated that the church is only a church of sinners—all moral transgressions belong to the realm of sociology—so that we are able to understand what Holl was actually after: he wanted to show that hidden beneath Luther's justification of the sinner is the justification of the righteous since it is God's judgement and action that justifies and makes righteous. Thus, he gave the first actual decisive explanation of the formula: *simul iustus et peccator*, which is not a contradiction in terms, but thanks to the grace of God it is an expectation. From a person who is completely and totally a sinner we have a person who is completely and totally justified. In this regard, Holl understands what he calls "morality"—it is what under God's

---

35. It has to do with the teaching on "imputation" of the merit of Christ for the (repentant) sinner.

36. On Melanchthon see also H. J. Iwand, NW IV, 309–58.

gracious justification becomes a completely new kind of active person. Therefore, the Gospel is both things according to Luther: "Judgment and Promise." He realized that the division between *lex* and *promissio* can only be united in the Gospel and that here is where Melanchthon goes astray, because he placed the *lex* on the front porch of the heathen and the *promissio* in the sanctuary of the believer, and therefore did not raise the curtain to the inner core of justification. This is the main point of Holl's book on Luther: that you must only read Luther to grasp him. Holl learned from Luther that man was not at the center of the Doctrine of Justification, but God and his justice; namely, what is meant by the "God's sole efficacy" as *sola gratia*, or "faith alone!"

Holl also learned a lot more from Luther. When he encountered the early Luther, Holl belonged to the generation of theologians who were influenced by Ritschl and through him, by Kant. He learned from Luther that even Kantianism is not protected from what he called the "eudaemonic pull of pietism." If one proceeds from man and from man's being-in-the-world, in his conflict between duty and inclination, in his apparent freedom but factual bondage, then God will always appear necessary, in fact essential, for one's self-understanding as more free, more moral, more pious, more serious, and more necessary to the doubting person's way of thinking. The person only appears to die, but in truth he lives again in his own thought world. He lets go of that which he truly is in order to assert more firmly what he is in God. He knows that he cannot live without God but needs God only for the purpose of living a more carefree and unencumbered existence. He seeks God as a partner because he realizes that he needs help against sin and the world and that he needs a helper. However, Holl calls this kind of thinking eudemonic because everything revolves around the person: he is the point of reference for his relationship to God, making God into a personal goal for himself for all of his striving and doing. This concept of God is merely a category of something that is in fact purely human in service of the individual self. It does not take God as its center, but rather man is the center and God is conceptualized as a corollary thereof. In this schema, God is a necessary, unavoidable idea if a person is to understand himself correctly. Sure enough, says Holl, when he emerges from this Nicodemus-like discussion with Luther—because even Nicodemus himself, in his sinful state, was savvy enough to realize he needed God. Holl succeeds in taking the position of the idealist in dialogue with the young Luther to the extent that he converts it: "Guilt encounters the 'spirit' while the flesh is still strong ... However, the justification that he relies on is only found in God's grace in Christ and the factual righteousness is therefore always and only one that he has yet to acquire."[37] With this, Holl put his finger on the core of Luther's Doctrine of Justification and let it stay there, similar to Ritschl and the Ritschl school, but he also reformed the Melanchthon approach and thus made the true, young, daring Luther known once again. At the same time, he also showed traditional Lutherans that Luther did not want to start with the "church of the sacraments" in his debates with the church, but with preaching and faith. Therefore, nothing was more characteristic of this in Holl's thinking than the quote Luther gave in response to the "Volkskirche": "therefore there is no better advice to give than to preach the Gospel and to steer people away from the sacraments and anything external, until they feel they are Christian and know it and by themselves come to faith and love and from there are drawn to external sacraments and the like."[38]

e) Here I must mention one more book that is a helpful reference tool namely, Reinhold Seeberg's, *Dogmengeschichte* Vol. IV.[39] The value of this book is that it brings out Luther's theology in connection with the history of dogmatics of the Middle Ages (Vol. III). In so doing, it clarifies the relationships and the contrasts between scholastic use of terms like *gratia, fides, praedestinatio, meritum*, etc. Erich Seeberg, the son of Reinhold Seeberg, started to write a theology of Luther.[40] He categorized the Middle Ages' view of God using four examples, comparing them with Luther: Thomas Aquinas, Gabriel Biel, the mystics, and Erasmus. This compendium of middle age theology is so well done that one can easily understand Luther in context. What E. Seeberg himself says of Luther's concept of God is something that I cannot go into here. In essence, he says it has to do with the history of ideas. And so, it does. Seeberg proceeds beyond the mystics (Jakob Böhme) to Luther. He is most interested in Luther's ideas and to that extent, his theology. His account of Luther's Christology is very comprehensive. The suffering and dying Christ is the origin and the model, *sacramentum* and *exemplum*. This means also that Christ is the model for death and dying. Therefore, in this sense, to be "conformed to Christ" means to acquire true humanity.

37. Holl, a.a.O (n. 32) 141–42 (from: "Die Rechtfertigungslehre in Luthers Vorlesung uber den Römerbrief...")

38. WA 10/2, 39, 17ff. (On taking both kinds in the sacrament. 1522).

39. Seeberg, R. "Die Lehre Luthers," in: *Lehrbuch der Dogmengeschichte*, IV, 1.

40. Seeberg, E. *Luthers Theologie. Motive und Ideen.*

Luther's Catholicism

1. The Juxtaposition of Two Confessions

We cannot omit to mention that the rediscovery of Luther's theology at the end of the 20th century included Catholic theology's renewed and passionate interest in the phenomenon of "Luther" and the Reformation that subsequently followed him. It is perhaps a blessing—if not also a deeply sad thing—for the German nation and the fate of the German spirit, that it had to carry this deep split within Christendom and henceforth maintain two confessions that represented more than just two "denominations." Again and again, the strengthening of one side gave rise to the strengthening of the other. If the fate of the church in Germany is to be different from that in France or Russia, so it may be said that the conflict between the two confessions is closely connected to the beginning of the political independence of the German nation. Just as the Reformation in Germany fed and nourished the Counter Reformation, so later during the Romantic period, the awakening within the Catholic church influenced a Protestant movement and propelled it forward, which we witnessed at the beginning of the 19th century in Tübingen and at the newly founded University of Berlin. In addition, the resurgence of Luther research, the edition of Luther's Works in the "Weimarer Ausgabe" (WA) of 1883, the increasing influence of his theology on dogmatics and the proclamation of the Gospel all awakened the resistance; namely, debates with the Catholics. This can be shown by two examples which illustrate an extreme position and are relevant for illustrating the possible positions taken by Catholicism: those of H. S. Denifle and J. Lortz. The former work is a polemic by a zealous man, who as a Dominican, still carried an element of internal hostility toward it, which Luther himself experiences as a representative of this order (e.g., Tetzel!). It is written in an entirely new spirit and seeks to understand and to make visible again the unity of the church of the period; a unity that broke in the struggles of the Reformation under the extensive involvement of Luther, his theology, and his writings. Denifle's book *"Luther and Luthertum"* appeared in 1904,[41] shortly before the death of the great scholar, who was born in the Tirol, and later worked in the Papal library in Rome. The other work,

---

41. Denifle, *Luther und Luthertum*. Further details on his assessment in E. Wolf (in *RGG* II, 82–83)

"The Reformation in Germany," by Joseph Lortz,[42] appeared a generation later, and addressed the benefits of all of the Luther research that occurred in the interim and succeeds in an appreciation of Luther's work well beyond anything done previously.

Let us briefly note here the importance of the Catholic research on Luther. Holl has shown that the Doctrine of Justification, the *iustitia Dei*, stands at the center of Luther's theology. However, in terms of the theology of the Middle Ages, it also stands at the center with Augustine, Thomas (Aquinas), Bonaventura, and with Duns (Scotus) and Ockham. It is the Pauline theme that Augustine gave to the western world and still continues to comprise the center, albeit an evolving center, of all of western theology. The Catholic Christian and theology have the same question to answer as we (Protestants) do. The question resounds within the church, in its entire life, in the sacraments of confession, of penance, in the mass, not to mention the Divine Office and Catechism are all imprinted by the question: How is man then made righteous before God? Man as a willful creature takes center stage, and not merely as a rational being or one longing for a solution to death. The decision occurs as part of the willing! In other words, how can a person's will be thus directed that it ultimately conforms with the will of God? That is the basic question and task. With the discovery of the theology of the young/early Luther, there is thus a resulting remarkable fact: here we here learn of him as someone who was constantly in dialogue with the Catholic church, who emerged from its lap, who knows its problems, and who is a late product of monasticism. However, Luther fractured the synthesis that Thomas had erected during the Middle Ages; namely, the synthesis between nature and grace, between *ratio* and *fides*, between paganism and Christianity. And in so doing, He broke its attending ideal of holiness and changed the focus to how one should understand living a Christian life. Luther stands at the center of Catholic Christianity's broken circle of Christendom, just as centuries earlier Paul stood at the center of Judaism and Pharisaism. What might happen now if the young Luther, Luther the theologian, suddenly began each discussion on the subject of justification on the basis of documentation that did not reflect the Catholic mindset? One must think that this discussion at that time (at the time of Luther's beginnings) would not be taken seriously and would be viewed by the Curate and the Catholic theologians viewed as immature. In short, when it came to

---

42. Lortz, *Die Reformation in Deutschland*.

the great disputations everything was already decided and theological discussion was burdened by the many results of church politics, even though it stood at the center of the unfolding events of the Reformation. But now (today!), when we encounter this question, one that we must consider in terms of the irreversible fact of two confessions, we risk the strange possibility of a repetition of a dialogue that did not occur back then. Therefore, we must thank the Catholic theologians, both great and small, that they took up this discussion. And it is also remarkable that the young Luther is able to provide the opportunity to participate in such a theological discussion. Perhaps it is also the fact that Karl Barth's theology was able to accomplish something that had not happened in a long time, and to set in motion the ability to measure this discussion from today's perspective, in order to show that this form of dogmatics was in true Reformation style.

2. Heinrich Suso Denifle

For this discussion the book by Denifle is indispensable because he focuses on the early Luther with such intensity as the theology of *simul iustus et peccator* aroused in him. He is angry with the early Luther in a similar way that our liberal Protestant theologians are angry with Barth. Denifle makes exactly the same complaint against Luther that liberal Protestants make against dialectical theology; namely, that this type of theology is the solution to all ethical maxims. Therefore, Denifle does not shrink from exposing Luther's and Lutheranism's moral laxitude, his crassness, his libertine view of marriage, his gluttony, etc. The core issue lies, however, in that Luther, with his Doctrine of Justification, overturns the connection between natural theology and any natural knowledge of God in the same way that we today have broken the connection between Kantian ethics and the Doctrine of Justification.

Here is the core of Denifle's criticism: Denifle basically maintains that Luther is an Ockhamist (William of Ockham) and as such only continues the process that the former venerated scholastic had already begun with his Doctrine of Salvation. Secondly, he maintains that Luther incorporates the final results in his solution to the Doctrine of Salvation (German: *Auflösung der Heilslehre*), since his own personal experience of unquenchable desire (*concupiscentia*) took precedent over "sound doctrine" (*sana doctrina*; see Titus 2:1; 2 Tim 1:13).

What had Ockhamism accomplished? How had it altered the Doctrine of Justification of the Middle Ages? One can perhaps say that through Ockham's pure emphasis on the grace of God, on *acceptatio* (acceptance), as he put it, the material difference between the natural and supernatural acts of God's love are dissolved. Nominalism (as defined by its founder Wilhelm of Ockham)[43] asks the question of the substantial difference between a good, natural rule in man and that of the grace effecting supra-natural rule, and he finds this difference to be no longer objectively discernable. The decision to accept or reject a work or an entire life lies (at least for Ockham) entirely with God. Ockham realizes thus only a basis or foundation upon which God can act, whereby he can "accept" man; namely, that of "the free grace of God." Accordingly, he must also agree that God can also choose not to accept the sacraments and ecclesiastical works(!!). There is more: according to Denifle, Ockham had accordingly refuted the possibility of a contradiction within God himself, a paradox that was taken up by Luther and one that he applied to the moral ability of man. Denifle focuses particularly on the sentence: "The alien righteousness is mine."[44] And he identifies a further contradiction: "I am at the same time sinner and justified; sinner by nature but declared justified despite the fact that I remain a sinner. I am depraved but deemed moral, though I remain depraved."[45] Thus, the central point of Denifle's argument is: "Although Ockham did not write these lines, Luther is in agreement with him to the extent that he maintains the contradiction, completely in line with Ockham's way of thinking."[46]

So, what does Luther really mean? Here we have the well-known formula: *simul iustus et peccator*, which Holl already had in mind when he said that God justifies the sinner as well as the righteous.[47] Denifle thinks this is a contradiction in terms. But what about Luther himself? Is it possible that Luther improves on Ockham? The fact that Ockham does not expressly say, "justified and sinner at the same time," is a sign that he was not prepared to make the final move to the decisive paradox. As a result, he stalls before the final hurdle because here we are faced not with a logical contradiction, but with a theological one. Luther says: "So we are by nature sinner and yet (in that God deems us righteous) and

---

43. Dempf, *Metaphysik des Mittelalters*, 144ff.
44. Denifle, a.a. O. (n. 41) 586.
45. Denifle, a.a. O. (n. 41) 586.
46. Denifle, a.a. O. (n. 41) 586. Denifle uses the Latin pen name "Occam."
47. Holl, a.a. O. (n. 32) 125.

justified through faith. We believe that He promises to free us, if we can just persevere, so that sin does not rule over us, but that we stand firm until He removes it from us."[48] In other words, Luther is saying that the fact that I am a sinful being under the promise of God (grace) means that the person grasps this promise through faith and is therefore justified (*quia credit* because they believe), and from this faith lives, so that the person, as they are, is transformed into a new and different person.

3. Joseph Lortz

In his book, "Die Reformation in Deutschland," Joseph Lortz has written a comprehensive work that covers the Reformation from both sides.[49] It is very valuable as it does justice to the historical context of the time, including the weakness of Catholic theology in Germany during the time of pre-reformation, the lack of decision by Luther's adversaries which accentuated the hesitation and vacillation of the universities, and above all the fall of the Curate and the shameful roll it played in the politics of Clemens VII, who made a pact with the Turks, as well as the collapse of the monasteries, which during the retreat of Ignaz of Loyola (1491–1556) and the movement of the Counter Reformation took up a purification and consolidation of real religious power.[50] Lortz claims that Luther fought against a Catholicism that was already on the verge of collapse, but not against the "true" Catholicism. That he did not have in mind. On the other hand, it should be conceded that Luther wanted a completely new look at the depths of faith and truth. Luther is in no way the start of a new "religious mindset." In his debates with the *Schwärmer* (English: Enthusiasts) one can detect almost hatred toward this type of movement in which he says that "this smarmy type of subjectivism elevates people above the Word. Whereas Luther insists on being a servant of the Word."[51] But next we hear that Luther's objectivity is delusional and inconsistent. This is such chicanery, because there is no such thing as religious objectivity that can be found from case to case through a living person, or through an infallible, living teacher. Only from personal insight and experience can any objective norm be established. And here

---

48. Wa 56, 271, 29ff. (Scholien) = BoA 5, 240, 30ff. = Fi (Scholien) 107, 27ff.
49. Lortz, *Die Reformation in Deutschland*.
50. On Clemens VII., Pope from 1523–1534. See K. G. Steck in *RGG* I, 1833.
51. Lortz, *Die Reformation in Deutschland*, 402.

lies Luther's inconsistency![52] Thus, two central points converge, both of which are concentrated on the representation of Luther's theology and in the form of a paradox! "He fails in his bias or, the opposite, in making a catholic synthesis." And the second: the unity of the church. According to Lortz, Luther claimed to expose the 1500 year-old church, which still ruled the life and education of the entire known world, of making basic and radical mistakes in the realm of the holy; indeed, of open fraud. With the claim, "through God's grace alone," Luther brought forth the true light of the Gospel—the true Christianity—ultimately exposing the anti-Christ. If one asks about the unity of the church, Lortz answers back unequivocally: "One cannot . . . be rid of the consequences, the danger and burden of subjectivity, as long as the one possible correction is missing; namely, that the decision of conscience can be corrected by means of something objective: an infallible doctrine."[53]

As a result, we have a paradox in Luther's theology. This is an astonishing affair, not only in terms of a formula, but in terms of deeply rooted meaning. It is connected to the fact that I cannot be objective regarding Christ and His works in order to decide for myself what it means for me. The history of Jesus Christ is itself dialectical. This also means that here the "I" itself is objective in that it appears in a certain form: "Through His suffering He makes our sins known to us and strangles them, but through His resurrection He makes us righteous and free of all sin, so that we are able to believe it."[54] There is no clear objectivity visible in the institution of salvation (the church) to make salvation a visible fact in which "one" can believe, but where there is talk of salvation and righteousness it must always be the case that: It is clear to me that I am only the sign of my repentance, but not that of any earned salvation, and so must it also ever again be the case. Not I! That is the dialectic by which we can only speak about God's revelation. In a certain way it is subjective, as it is a *fides* which lives from the "for me" (*pro me*) of the promise, but therein it is also an objective *certitudo salutis* (certainty of salvation).

At this point we come to the second issue, the unity of the church. Luther suffered greatly that the visible unity of the church broke apart. However, he also never intended that one would be able to fix the damage with a visible head of the church or an infallible doctrine. Certainly, the

52. Lortz, *Die Reformation in Deutschland*, 436.
53. Lortz, *Die Reformation in Deutschland*, 407.
54. WA 2, 140, 24ff. (A Sermon reflecting on the holy suffering of Christ. 1519) = BoA 1, 159, 15ff.

disputations with Eck at Leipzig were a hallmark on the way to the advancing his teaching out of the realm of the Catholic church.[55] But wasn't it already clear that it is a mistake to try to answer doctrinal questions by means of church authority? Is the conferring of authority of the Gospel not something entirely different, and must not the doctrine to that end—if it is indeed infallible—subordinate itself to trust in the Gospel and the clarity of the Word? Didn't Luther, by calling into question the authority of the church, first break new ground for the freedom of faith? And if, on the Catholic side, it was always that way, as if with the introduction of subjectivity in matters of faith we have found the solution, so then we should also ask whether with regulations on thought and faith—which always happens as a result of any doctrine—we have cut off the freedom of Christian people at the root?!

4. Summary

If now, in summary and in general, we put the question as to the uniqueness of Luther's theology, so we might answer this way: He re-discovered and re-established theology's original mission. In almost all instances, his theology is a reestablishment of theological substance against its falsifications and distortions. The Reformation as an ecclesiastical and world event is secondary only to its effects in the area of theology and the resulting reforms. We have tried to come close to the moment that was very decisive for the discovery of theology. It would not be appropriate if we did not try, as one of the descendants of many such attempts, to demonstrate how to interpret this mighty and astonishing event.

Luther's theology starts with the scholastic question: "*An Deus sit?*"[56] Already the young Luther writes in a letter to Johann Braun that he was searching for the *nucleus nucis* (kernel of the nut) and added the succinct sentence: "*Sed Deus est Deus.*"[57] With this God's existence was no longer put into question, but rather pushed as the thesis to the forefront of all theology: precisely, that God is God. Accordingly, the person

---

55. Johann Eck (1486–1563). On the "Leipzig Disputation" (1519) see H. Boehmer, *Der junge Luther*, ed. H. Bornkamm, 223–42. Further WA 2, 250–383; Luthers theses on the "Leipzig Disputations" in German translation by K. Aland, *Luther Deutsch*, Vol. 2, 92–94.

56. On this question compare especially H. J. Iwand, NW I (Lecture on "Faith and Knowledge", 112–54.)

57. "But God is God." WA Br 1, Nr. 5, p. 17, Z. 44

is confronted with this thesis: as far as God is also in us and with us, He is also in himself and by himself. Is He what we think and learn, preach, and believe, not also *that* which He is in himself!? There is a sentence in Luther's lectures on Romans that illustrates this idea: "For in the inmost (God) His words are just and true. But in us they are not so conceived, because our wisdom weakens them, until faith gives them a place and adopts them."[58] If we believe then God comes to us and makes us to be like Him: "So that He is in us as He is in himself; for in Himself his words are righteous and justified."[59] This theology also has to do with the issue of whether or not, in our thinking and speaking, we allow God to be God, and that we not deal with him like an idol, or a god according to our own making and desires. Accordingly, Luther conveys great mistrust about people and their internal religious motives.

Further, here it is also clear, that Luther gives theology and its expression a strong a-sartorial character. This can be seen in his conflict with Erasmus on the principle theological questions.[60] Here is where Erasmus saw arrogance. He wanted theology to be measured and developed from piety and argued against many of the theses and statements, mainly that of the "bondage of the will," which Luther included in his theology. He asked Luther whether it then meant that to allege such thing, which was interesting and important as scientific problems were interesting, but for the people, for the populace who are pious, would only cause problems. Against this Luther asserted that in all statements that we make about God, God himself is the subject, and that even the spirit of God, who hides the truth, does not sanction skepticism.[61] Theology is thus not lowered to the level of human opinion and experience, but must make a claim that, "is more firm and more certain than life itself and all of experience."[62]

Finally, we come to the point where the certainty that Luther sees as essential for any theological statement, is not to be compared with what we term philosophical principles. The question, however, never goes

---

58. WA 56, 226, 14ff. (Scholien) = Fi (Scholien) 64, 31ff.

59. WA 56, 226, 20–21 (Scholien) = Fi (Scholien) 65, 4–5.

60. Erasmus of Rotterdam, 1466 (?)—1536, published, among others, writings on the freedom of the will ("*de libero arbitrio Diatribe*," (1524), to which Luther in 1525 responded with his treatise "*De servo arbitrio*" ("On the bondage of the will"). For more see II, p. 87ff.

61. "*Spiritus sanctus non est Scepticus.*" WA 18, 605, 32 (*De servo arbitrio*, 1525) = BoA 3, 100, 31.

62. WA 18, 605, 33–34 = BoA 3, 100, 33.

away. The person is continually striving for a truth that eludes them. The truth of theology, however, is that the truth encounters the person in the question of whether or not we trust God. All theological questions are based on the promise of revelation. Wherever a theological statement does not allow for the promises of God, for the "*promissio Dei,*" then one cannot believe it. One cannot believe in the statement, but only in God. Thus, the young Luther did not understand the *remissio peccatorum* (forgiveness of sins) as something by which we can select what is "appropriate." There must be forgiveness of sins, so he taught, in the *habitus*, in the "essence" of our lives—until we grasp that faith is dependent on God's promise and not on our feelings or perceptions.

2

Luther's Doctrine of Justification

Doctrine of Sin

1. The *peccatum remanens*

IN TWO DECISIVE PLACES, a break occurs in Reformation theology that puts it in opposition to the Scholastics: first of all, in the concept of religion. The knowledge of God from his works, the *opera*, which lead up from the creation to the Creator and which bases this ascent by means of Aristotelian philosophy, is rejected, and in its place is the knowledge of God from his *passiones*, that is, from the cross. The result is the *theologia crucis* as thematic of Luther's epistemological approach (cf. I, pp. 34ff and often). The second break occurs in the ethical formation of concepts. Here too occurs an amalgamation of Christian ethics and Aristotelian philosophy in such a way that the work, the *opus* of the person, would be the criterion for the formation of ethical tasks and the distinction between good and evil. And from there, one proceeds to the distinction between virtue and blasphemy. From this "objective" catalog of human moral development—from fall to recovery—the kingdom of God is measured and regulated. We find this approach in Thomas Aquinas, in the *Summa Theologica* where he develops the concept of *virtus* (virtue). The classical definition reads: "Virtue is the good condition of mind by which life is tightly lived, which no one uses wrongfully, which God works in us and without us."[1] What is meant by this is that virtue is an activity, a

---

1. Aquinas, *Summa Theologica*. II/1, 55, 4 according to the *Editio Leonina, Romae*

right position toward virtue, and of course such a definition, which does not swing back and forth, reveals a steadfastness toward the good.² From this virtue as a *virtus infusa* (infused virtue)³ and it then follows that God effects virtue *in nois sine nobis* (in us without us). We see here also how grace and sanctification are thus woven together by way of the concept of virtue. It is precisely this hinge of medieval ethics that Luther wanted to eliminate and had do so on the basis of his doctrine of continual sinning, the *peccatum remanens*, which was not his, but as he continually emphasized, is that of the Apostle Paul.

Let us take a brief look at the scholastic Doctrine of Sin, by which we again make reference to the *Summa* of Thomas. Here we meet the doctrine of sin, as it were, on the basis of the concept of virtue, already marked in a section titled: "*De vitiis et peccatis*" (blasphemy and sins; II/1, 71). Sin and virtue, so it reads here, do not mutually exclude one another but sin brings the *operatio* (uncovering) of virtue to a standstill. The virtues can be hampered in their function by an act of oral sin, but not made inoperative. They are silenced, but not simply set aside. As winter hampers the sprouts of the tree, so mortal sins simply hamper the ethical function of the whole person by repressing *caritas* at the root, in *fide et spe*, and thus in the two other theological virtues. They remain *informes post peccatum*.⁴ It is otherwise with the *peccatum veniale* (venial sin), or a sinful act not directed against "love," which does not make the theological virtue succumb, but can be *simul esse et cum virtutibus infusis, et cum aquisitas* (it can at the same time be both infused as well as acquired virtue).⁵ There is thus a *simul* (at the same time; a "both and") in Catholic theology, and of course based on the question: "Can there be both sin and virtue?"⁶ This *simul* is thus differently limited according to whether a

---

1923 s.: "*Virtus est bona qualitas mentis, quae recte vivitur, qua nullus male utitur, quam Deus in nobis sine nobis operator.*" In the "Paris Edition" (1895) of the "*Summa*" it says: "...*qua recte vivitur...*" (instead of: "...*quae recte vivitur...*"); the meaning and place is m.E. not essentially different. (D.H.)

2. See similar "*finis...virtutis...est ipsa operatio*" (the goal of virtue is works), and also ad 6.

3. See similar "*finis...virtutis...est ipsa operatio*" (the goal of virtue is works).

4. See similar "*finis...virtutis...est ipsa operatio*" (the goal of virtue is works), II/1, 71, 4 ad 3. "They remain shapeless after sinning," whereby the "*peccatum mortale*", the "mortal sins" is meant, as the context indicates.

5. See similar "*finis...virtutis...est ipsa operatio*" (the goal of virtue is works).

6. "*Utrum peccatum simul possit esse cum virtute*," and "*finis...virtutis...est ipsa operatio*" II/1, 71, 4.

venial or mortal sin is involved. A total extinguishing of the (remaining) condition of the one reborn, his *habitus* by which he sins, does not come under discussion, since otherwise one would have to deny the workings of grace evoked in human beings by penitence and baptism!

In this way the background is circumscribed in which Luther's struggle plays out regarding his understanding of "remaining sin after baptism "(*peccatum remanens post baptismum*). What is involved here is a decision of wide-ranging significance and it is really this struggle which, in opposition to the Catholic magisterium during the years 1518–1521, claims Luther's entire attention. Only now it is clear how decisively the first thesis on indulgences from the year 1517 was determined by the sentence *peccatum remanens*: "Since our Lord and master Jesus Christ says 'repent, etc.' he intended that the whole life of the believer be repentance."[7]

Since no one is it without sin (because there is no objective measure between mortal and by nature a venial forgivable sin), for this reason repentance does not denote a sacramental act, but a life-long attitude. It is an interior act. For this reason, in his second thesis, Luther distinguishes his understanding of repentance as it derives from the preaching of Jesus, apart from the sacramental understanding: "This word cannot be understood from the sacramental act (i.e. the penance and satisfaction which the priestly office solemnly effects)."[8] Here we can still go another step further: What Luther effects with his sentence regarding the *peccatum remanens*, is the shattering of the entire understanding of the human being and salvation, as he found it. Now that means specifically that he places any peace and reconciliation between persons outside of the person; in the person there can and will be no peace any longer insofar as he/she is really a penitent. With *poenitentia* (repentance) an *odium sui* (hatred of self) is planted within the person, a "No" to oneself which, like a wound that never heals, stays open for their entire life.

But the struggle reaches its high point in the doctrine of the *peccatum remanens* when the Roman bull of Pope Leo X condemned the Lutheran theses, including the 31st thesis that states: "A devout person sins in all good works,"[9] and the 32nd: "A good work done to perfection is still a daily sin."[10] Likewise the second thesis: "Whoever denies that after baptism sin remains in every child, steps (Latin: *concultat*; tramples)

7. WA 1, 233 = BoA 1, 3.
8. WA 1, 233 = BoA 1, 3.
9. WA 7, 433, 13 (Basis and Reason. . .) = BoA 2, 121, 2.
10. WA 7, 437, 33–34 = BoA 2, 123, 22.

on Christ and Saint Paul."[11] Finally, we have the magnificent theological conclusion in Luther's writing; "Against the Louvain theologian Latomus, 1521."[12] This writing forms the end of the struggle around the question regarding the *peccatum remanens*, the *justitia extra nos*, and the *imputatio Dei* (God's reckoning), who does not reckon to us this remnant of sin, the *reliquum peccati*, remaining in us. Forgiveness of sins denotes something final and absolute. It is not a step in the process of the new life, not a necessary act, with which I take my way to a new, better goal, but something first and last over which we never get beyond. Many quotations on this subject can be cited, which continually witness to this one thing: that the forgiveness of sins is nothing which one gets beyond, but beneath which one remains one's whole life long, when otherwise one lives in faith and from faith. With forgiveness an entire system falls, which means that either the person lives from out of their *opus*, or they live from the *opus* of Christ. The one who is justified is thus both things: from God's perspective his/her righteousness is complete and a total reality for Christ's sake but seen from his/her own perspective totally a sinner and lost soul. Thus, a reality appears before the person's eyes which they should erase because it is long since cancelled by God: *non imputat!* (HE does not reckon it). Something remains—and that which remains is basically the *peccatum originale* (inherited sin).

There are passages in Luther in which he criticizers one thing in particular: that one has made *peccatum originale* into a defect. Here Luther objects: Original sin is not a human weakness, an inclination which continually would like to transform itself anew into an act; it is in fact an inclination in the human being which intends to alter his/her enmity toward God into an act. Luther calls this inclination "concupiscence" (desire). Thereby he returns to Rom 7 and defines concupiscence on the basis of the first commandment. It is incomprehensible that the human should desire to be involved against God's will, *qua* God's will, and to set their will against God's commandment, thus intending to oppose God's will. Concupiscence thus appears as a sign that the person is not free; that they do not eagerly and naturally subject themself to God, but actually give in to a latent strain of their own inner life. Luther calls this concupiscence, because it is factually present and exists in the midst of an otherwise ethical life as the desire to break out and to rebel: in short,

---

11. WA 7, 329, 9–10 = BoA2, 70, 30–31.

12. WA 8, 43–128. Reference to the beautiful translation and explanations of the writings by R. Frick in: *M. Luther, Ausgewählte Werke*, Ergänzungsreihe, Vol. 6.

to make oneself the lawgiver of one's own life. A second is added: Luther does not recognize an ultimate harmony between nature and grace, to which even Augustine was inclined, and which thus became the basis for the Thomistic system. Here, in Luther, we encounter an unreconcilable dualism for which the reconciliation lies solely in the grace of God. It is the reconciliation of the unreconcilable. Nor is there any continuity between creature and creator. Both sides—nature and grace—are sides of a total life. If I really love God, I cannot proceed from self-love and in it find true self-love, that I love myself in God but that I say "No" to myself. This in turn is the deepest meaning of the *theologia crucis*. But from this Luther draws the decisive conclusion that, first of all, "we continually sin, while we act well,"[13] and the other, that the inherited sin is not only concupiscence but absolute *incredulitas* (unbelief). It consists of "unbelief, despising God, and other sins against the first commandment."[14] Only insofar as the *remissio peccati* begins, and insofar as we are, according to the word of James (Jas 1:18), and which Luther eagerly cites, the *initium creaturae Dei*, has a process begun whose object it is to struggle against the ever-remaining sin in us.[15]

2. The Forgiveness of Sins

Here we are confronted with the question: What does *remissio peccatorum* mean? Luther has removed from the "good work," the *opus bonum*, its ethically obvious character.[16] Sin bursts the connection between the work and the person. The work in itself is good, but to want to conclude from this that also the doer is good would be perverse. Thus, the righteousness of God in its actual meaning is something which must be independent and given priority over all action. This is Luther's actual achievement in the teaching of justification, that he does not understand righteousness on the basis of work, but knows of a persons' being righteous, a being-declared-righteous, which occurs in a sphere decreed prior to one's working. One does not become righteous in giving shape to life by the work;

---

13. WA I, 367, 26–27. (*Heidelberg Disputations*, 1518) = BoA 5, 394, 26. Luther often cites Pred (Sermon) 7:20 on this idea.

14. WA Ti 1, 593, Nr. 1193. See also WA 18, 780, 18ff. (*De servo arbitrio*. 1525) = BoA 3, 284, 29ff.

15. Haar, *Initium creaturae Dei*, 99ff.

16. See n. 13; more on the following paragraph "Person and Works" in: H. J. Iwand, NW IV, 56ff.

our works are not the course of our growing or receding righteousness, but we have our righteousness before God in the forgiveness of sins. Sin is not annulled by the *opus bonum* but is annulled by the fact that it is forgiven. God "regards the godless at the same time as unrighteous and righteous. And at the same time their sin is annulled and not annulled."[17] It is annulled in the forgiveness of sins; it is not annulled in reality. When my being righteous or my being a sinner is no longer legible from my *qualitas*, precisely because the criteria which I have in hand, especially the ethical, are deceptive, then it must appear in another dimension, be graspable for me—and just that means the forgiveness of sins. Let us make clearer what *remissio peccatum* does not mean: it is not the assumption for the attaining of true righteousness, as when I forgive someone a debt so that he can now go to work anew and is free of the burdensome pressure of a lingering failing, but forgiveness is something ultimate, not to be surpassed! It is as Luther at the high point of his theological achievements continually says of the exchange between my sins and Christ's righteousness: "When he has made my sins his own, then I have them no longer and am free."[18] Thus forgiveness means: that God appears in my place by taking my sins on himself, and I share his righteousness so that a "happy exchange" appears of which Nikolaus Hermann sings: "He exchanges wonderfully with us . . ." and "He becomes a servant and I a lord, that there may be an exchange . . ." (EKG 21m 4and 5). Then Luther in the "Sermon on the Sacrament of Penance, 1519" says: "There is no greater sin than that one does not believe the article (of the) forgiveness of sins."[19] Forgiveness is thus God's entry into the place of the sinner and entry of the sinner in the place of the Righteous One! Forgiveness is something ultimate, by which we live and die here on earth. To believe forgiveness means to allow this very judgment of God to be valid over against all reality of the sin still clinging and remaining.

From this emerge three elements. First, the decree of the righteousness of God regarding the opus: Forgiveness belongs to the sphere of the first dimension. It is exactly the righteousness of God effectively applied to me. But from this follows the second: that sin remains and yet does not remain, is forgiven, but is not annulled, but only begins to weaken. And third: the decisive sentence relative to this reads: "So I battled with myself and did not know that there is really forgiveness, but there is no removal

---

17. WA 56m 270m 12-13, (Scholien) = BoA 5, 239, 34-35 = Fi (Scholien) 106, 6-7.
18. WA 56, 204, 19-20. (Scholien) = BoA 5, 227, 32 = Fi (Scholien) 44, 7-8.
19. WA 2, 717, 33-34 = BoA 1, 179, 10-11.

(*ablatio*) of sin, except in hope. This means that it can be removed by the gift of grace. This begins (*incipit*) to remove sin so that from now on it is no longer reckoned as sin."[20] The person thus with forgiveness before one's eyes, as a partner of God, now takes up the struggle with remaining sin; but also (the struggle) is *donum gratiae* (a gift of grace).

3. Luther's Formula: Righteous and Sinner Alike

In order to win a starting position in the struggle with sin, Luther makes use of the formula *simul Justus et peccator*, which we encounter very often. In the previously mentioned writing against Latomus,[21] it reads in one place: "Entirely the same motive of wrath and desire is in the devout and the godless, the same before and after grace, just as the same flesh before and after grace, but in (the force field) of grace can do nothing; outside of (the force field) of grace, it has supremacy."[22] Thus this means that of the "nature" of the sinner or, as Luther also says, in its "substance," nothing has changed; it is the same "before "and "after" the reception of grace. But the person is no longer the same, the change called forth in us by the mercy and forgiveness of God is total. Whether up to that point the person is conscious or unconscious under the judgment of his/her works, thus from out of their immanent moral self-consciousness, now the person lives by faith that God is gracious to the sinner. Whereas up to that point the person thought that God is gracious only to those who are good and righteous, they now believe, which means that they now live from out of grace, and thus the sin which in itself is and remains sin, is not sin. "It is sin also after forgiveness, but it is not reckoned."[23] Luther compares this ever present, ever traceable sin, that is ever accusing and judging me, with a chained robber: "But who does not know that a robber who is free is no less a robber as a prisoner? But his power is extinguished; there is nothing weaker than the one to whom death is near, he can no longer do what he wanted as a robber."[24] From this we see that Luther does not coin the formula "both righteous and sinner" in order to level out the seriousness of sin or describe the struggle with and against it as hopeless.

20. WA 56, 274, 8ff. (Scholien) = BoA 5, 242, 4ff. = Fi (Scholien) 109, 10ff.
21. See II, p. 67 (n. 12).
22. WA 8, 91, 37ff. Trans. by R. Frick.
23. WA 8, 91, 8ff. Trans. by R. Frick.
24. WA 8, 91, 31ff. Trans. by R. Frick.

He often indicated what a comfort for the conflicted conscience it is not to fear when this chained robber rattles his chains and shows that even so, his entire, totally wild life still sticks to him: This struggle between spirit and flesh, between the one who really hungers and thirsts for righteousness, and the one who is in agreement with him/herself, does not cease. We are always both, and our works, our good ones as well as our less good ones, our successful as well as unsuccessful ones, are a battle continually won or lost. For this reason, we cannot understand Luther in such fashion as though for him an essential difference existed between inclination and deed. In Paul it reads: "You will not fulfill the deeds of the flesh" (Gal 5:16). For with the sinful deed, say, the sin of David or the denial of Peter, the intention of the fleshly person (*homo carnalis*) is still not affected, this would only be reached when the person, due to a fallible deed, despaired of God's righteousness. The deed still belongs under the sign and movement of my being-a-sinner; something to be annulled, to be conquered by faith. They are precisely signs of the not-entirely-chained robber, as not quite given into my power but the person must not see him/herself ultimately described and established before God with these deeds. The *non-imputjtare* (not to be reckoned) means in the judgment of God, in the verdict handed down by him over us is otherwise than in your conscience: Here you identify yourself with your deeds, but there—before God—you are not identical to them. This is what *non-imputatio* means. Only God can do that. Both, therefore, the judgment that I myself pass, I who feel and experience the chained robber still in me, and the "No" of God, which occurs for me in Jesus Christ, fall in one and he same lifetime, apply to one and the same person, when this one even as a Christian always lives two lives, one of self, as *caro* (flesh), and another which does not derive from oneself, but which he/she, as Luther says, lives as a *Christianus* (Christian person). In the later course of his theology Luther does not retain the formula *simul Justus et peccator*, but he develops the subject to which it refers more and more clearly: namely, the Christian life is the future life which indeed is already here and present but is opposed to my life in the flesh. For the first time we find the formula of the *simul Justus et peccator* in Luther's commentary on Romans: "Therefore, wondrous, and very dear is the mercy of God, mercy which regards us at the same time as a sinner and not sinners. Sin remains and does not remain."[25] Here occurs an act which can never be reached on the level of human *opera*.

---

25. WA 56, 270, 9ff. (Scholien) = BoA 5, 239, 30ff. = Fi (Scholien) 106, 2ff.

Luther calls this act *misericordia*, mercy. There is something ultimate in humankind, something absolute, that cannot be healed by any kind of work or practice: "It is an error (to assume) that this evil can be healed by works, since experience teaches that even when we do ever so great and good works, the desire for evil remains and no one is clear (*mundus*) of it, not even a day-old child."[26] Here then we also find the comparison with the sick person to whom the doctor promises healing. In the hope of healing the sick person holds to everything forbidden him/her by the doctor. So, Luther asks now: "Is this sick one perhaps well now?" And Luther answers: "For sure, he/she is sick and well. In reality he/she is sick, but well due to the sure promise of the doctor whom he believes, who regards him already as it were as well (*reputat*)."[27]

Here would be a good place to recall that beautiful passage (in Matt 13:33; the parable of the leaven) in Luther where it reads that, "The same new leaven is faith and the grace of the Spirit, but he does not do it at all by (and with) the yeast, but fine and tasteful over time he makes us new like him and bread of God. For that reason, this life is not a devotedness but a becoming devout; not a being healthy, but a becoming healthy; not a being but a becoming; not a rest but an exercise; we are not yet, but we will be so. It is not yet done and having occurred, but it is in process and in motion. It is not the end, but it is the way; everything does not yet glow and sparkle, but everything is being swept (clean)."[28] Thus we see that we will not properly understand Luther if we were to understand merely dialectically his formula "righteous and sinner alike" as if no determination were made between grace and sin. With faith there is always the determination, and of course a determination made for life. This faith which clings so to forgiveness, living from out of it, has God on its side. It is the announcement of a new existence, which indeed is still to come, but which already makes itself known by the fact that it pulls one to itself, toward this its future. But faith finds within its own realm, as it were, a genuine and mighty opponent who, from the topsoil of human existence, from the flesh, creates continually new power and truly does not die by itself, and also does not go aground by our good works, but by its contest with faith. In the opponent whom faith discovers in its own realm, living in the existence of faith as such, the enemy grows within him/her, on whom he/she has to exercise faith. The believer has the experience that

---

26. WA 56, 271, 24ff. (Scholien) = BoA 5, 240, 24ff. = Fi (Scholien) 107, 21ff.
27. WA 56, 272, 7ff. (Scholien) = BoA 5, 241, 3ff. = Fi (Scholien) 108, 2ff.
28. WA 7, 337, 28ff. (Foundation and Cause. . .) = BoA 2, 75, 8ff.

in him/her, that is, in their flesh, that which he/she believes *in Christo* he/she is not. Here sin is not yet dead, here death has not lost its terror, here the *infernum* is not yet overcome. Thus, the believer from the height of *certitudo fidei* (certainty of faith) down into the reality of one's life, into one's *opera*, as Luther also says—into the "world"—here finds him/herself involved in a war in which one is more often the vanquished than a victor. But as long as, now, so I might almost say, the believer does not despair in view of this state of affairs, then he/she is still always a warrior. There is a despair which threatens to overwhelm the person, which can penetrate so deeply that the person no longer finds anything good in oneself, that even one's best works appear immoral and useless. On this front Luther's theology reaches the heights of watchfulness and an unimaginable sense of discovery in giving comfort. As one plagued by inner conflict his entire life, he can give comfort as scarcely another could. Here he stands watch. Here he pulls back those who suicidally would like to give up on forgiveness. Here, for that reason, he constructs a further doctrinal piece by which the person makes faith a kind of work or performance with which to encounter the enemy within. Just as the tax-collector (who we are) is declared righteous in the forgiveness of sins, at the same time the Pharisee (who we also are), is judged for his pride. This *simul* which we learn to know at the same time in defining the person as *simul Justus et peccator*, is repeated in the order of Law and Gospel.

Law and Gospel

1. The Order of the Two Concepts

The height which Luther reaches in his teaching on law and gospel[29] lies in the supremacy of Gospel over the Law, which was defended by him and pursued to its final consequence, and with it the limiting of the law, so that the law no longer reaches the person's conscience. Christ appears between the law and what it pursues; namely, the person who is threatened by accusation and death: this is actually his *inercessio* (intercession, acquittal). To this extent, he is the end of the law. Luther expresses this with the phrase *amittit lex ius suum*, meaning that the law has lost its right to judge.[30] This also means that where Christ rules, who died and

---

29. This chapter is treated very briefly here because Iwand's ideas on this important theme regarding Reformation doctrine is covered thoroughly in volume IV of his NW.

30. WA 40/1, 565, 3 (Gr. Commentary on Galatians. 1531. Hs.)

was raised for us, the law is powerless to make any claim on a person, since here God's right of grace rules. But it is essential to realize that we are also entering an area that proves to be the limit of the limitless, the end of the infinite; that thus there is a point where sin, death, and the law—the great threesome—find their end. Only God himself can be the end, so "that . . . you are totally in him, and everything together is one thing: God, Christ, and you."[31] For since the Son comes to us, something indeed occurs on earth: a kingdom, a realm of power is erected within which peace and victory and eternal life rule. For this reason, the word Gospel means "good news" from this divine victory in the midst of us and for us: "For the Son comes down from the Father and clings to us, and we in turn cling to him and through him come to the Father . . . He has forged this link between him and us and the Father and us three so that we are in him and he in us, just as he is in the Father and the Father in him."[32]

2. The Distinction between Law and Gospel

It belongs inseparably to Luther's theological understanding that he emphasizes the difference between law and gospel, indeed more, that he gives prominence to it as something fundamental. Here, at this point, he finds the difference between his theology and Scholasticism fixed and recognizes the mortal enemy of the Reformation in the mixing of the two, in whatever shape this might appear: "Therefore I say that one should rightly learn and properly distinguish law and gospel, for whoever can do so, may he/she thank our Lord God, and may well exist as a theologian. I, of course, in my inner conflicts cannot yet do it, as I really should."[33] And: "But contrary to that, the papists are not able (to distinguish) and have nothing certain to teach, whether of faith or of works, of the sins of this life, or the distinguishing of the spirits, etc. This means that they have mingled the teaching of law and gospel together wildly and disorderly. The same is true of the mobs and the fanatics . . . In all the schools and churches over some hundred years nothing rightly has been taught or preached about the difference between law and gospel, by

---

31. WA 20, 230, 8ff. (Sermons 1526. Sermon on Matthew 3 on the baptism of Christ.)

32. WA 45, 587, 33ff. (Sermons on chapters 14 and 15 of John's Gospel. 1538).

33. WA Ti 6, 142, Nr. 6715.

means of which the poor miserable consciences have come to great danger and injury. For where one does not quite exactly and clearly separate the gospel from the law then it is not possible to be able to keep Christian teaching from being falsified."[34] Luther thought that with the teaching of the distinction between law and gospel he had arrived at the center of Pauline theology and, as it were, to have touched the point from which one arrives at the totality of Pauline theology. For this purpose, he constantly chose the epistle to the Galatians: "The epistle to the Galatians is my epistle, to which I have betrothed myself. It is my Katie von Bora."[35] He regarded Paul as the one from whom he learned this distinction. He saw the apostle in his conflict with Peter and the others in a similar war as he himself was in the struggle with the works righteousness of Catholic teaching. Here he took his position and thought that whoever cannot do so is not a theologian. It is not a matter of an abstract, conceptual "distinction," but of retaining this "distinction" amidst inner conflict. Inner conflict is the mixing of the two. That is Luther's formula for inner conflict. Here lies his pastoral care. And he understands pastoral care on the basis of the doctrine of justification, not the reverse. Thus, just as the Holy Spirit continually sounds the alarm in order for us properly to learn to grasp the distinction between law and gospel, in constant and ever newer practice, because life goes on and always plunges us anew into inner conflicts, errors and dangers, on the other side there stands the devil. We can say there is a demonic power which brings us to the point, in the hour of inner conflict, of grasping what is false, to exchange law and gospel, indeed, even to make Christ a preacher of the law, a "legislator," and a "Moses." Luther, as a theologian, is always on the track of these continual blurring's and mixings: "I have not learned my theology all at once, but have had to dig ever deeper and deeper, then my *tentationes* (inner conflicts) brought me to the point *quia sine usu non potest disci* (because one cannot learn without practicing). This is also what the rabble and fanatics lack, because they do not have the proper contradictor, the devil, who instructs one really well."[36]

Luther saw that the law has the tendency to make itself independent and to appear over against the gospel as a *norma normans*, as the absolute determining norm. He saw the rational root in the law and also saw that humanity, with the aid of their inborn law, strives to set up their

---

34. WA Ti 6, 136, Nr. 6705.
35. WA Ti, 1, p. 69, Nr 146 = BoA 8, p. 24, Nr. 146.
36. WA Ti 1, 146, Nr 352 = BoA 8, 46, Nr, 352.

own worship of God based on it. In this way Luther understood Gal 4:8: "Since you do not know God, you serve those who by nature (Greek: *physei*) are not gods." He adds: "You serve your heart's dreams and ideas, by which you without, indeed, against God's will and command serve such a god who permits atonement by works and worship, chosen from among your own meditations and good opinion."[37] Luther means that a person's natural religion is a kind of legal religion, built on the relation between performance and counter performance, between sacrifice and desert, and thinks that we by nature construct our idea of God from there, "for outside of Christ there is nothing else than idolatry and a vain falsely constructed thing about God; it is like the Turk's Quran, the Pope's decree and command, or also Moses' law when one thinks by this to be righteous and blessed before God."[38] What Paul warns against in his theology is in Luther's opinion the confusion of revelation, which continually refers to the word of God by way of our inborn, natural religion.

Apparently, the best theology and the finest wisdom helps not at all against such inner conflict. They come continually and faith needs to be exercised on them ever anew. Johann Schlaginhaufen told a beautiful story[39] about when he was at Luther's house in Wittenberg with the wife of Dr. Stephan Wild, how he (Schlaginhaufen) was saying that the bodily sufferings and inner conflicts are not as bad as those of the soul, like those of Saul and Esau, and that he could not "separate them from *evangelio.*"— Whereupon the Doctor (Luther) responded: 'Indeed, dear Master Hans, if you can do that, then you are a doctor!'—And stood up and take off his beret and said: 'If you can do that then I will say to you: Dear Herr Doctor Johann, you are learned. Paul and I have never been able to bring it to that point.'"[40] This really means that in our life, in that which we call human existence, we never will have reached the point where we have "firmly" fixed the distinction between law and gospel because it is ever anew comingled, as when one writes in the water: "Therefore it is best that God plays with us in such a way, and we recognize our own poverty and misery and cling to the Man called Christ."[41] The experiential,

---

37. WA Ti 6, 59, Nr. 6587.

38. WA Ti 6, 59, Nr. 6588.

39. Johann Schlaginhaufen was a student in Wittenberg in 1520 and one of Luther's table talk participants from 1531–1532. He was later a pastor and superintendent in Kothen (see H. Ruckert in BoA 6, 448).

40. WA Ti 2, 131, Nr. 1557.

41. WA Ti 2, 131, Nr. 1557.

psychologically accessible "I" is forever the site of the conflicted "I" and can gain from it no certainty. For this reason, Luther placed such value on the doctrine, on the *doctrina*, because it is the point at which I can cling in the hours of inner conflict. We can perhaps say that natural religion makes the mixing of law and gospel unavoidable, that it exists as this mixing, and is uncovered and overcome by the distinction.

For this reason, Luther calls it the art of the devil "to make a law of the gospel."[42] And here now it becomes clear why he so often speaks of the two words of God: "The distinction between law and gospel has an effect, since the devil hits one on the head with the word and if one focuses on the law, then one is lost. It is not conscience that rules, but the distinction, so that you say: The word is twofold (duplex), the one threatens, the other comforts."[43] But also the preaching the distinction between "law and gospel" is twofold.[44] On this subject Luther has something else important to say: "Therefore it is a great misunderstanding, indeed foolishness that one will pretend that it is God's word, therefore it is right, etc. Indeed, God's word is not all the same, but different; the law is another word than the gospel, so the laws or the commandments are also not all the same . . . our fanatics know nothing at all of this distinction."[45] Let us hear Luther further: "So, whoever understands this art of distinguishing law from gospel, set him up and call him a doctor of Holy Scripture, for without the Holy Spirit it is impossible to make this distinction. I experience it in myself, and see daily in others, how difficult it is, the teaching of separating law and gospel from each other; here the Holy Spirit must be the master and teacher, or there will be no person on earth to understand or teach."[46] Or: "In such conflict and anxiety over death it is high time and necessary that faith be up and doing and with all its power break forth, see the law under the eyes and comforting say to him/her: Hey, dear law, are you alone God's word? Is not the gospel also God's word? Then the promise is at an end? Or are the two, law and gospel or merit and grace from now on mingled and cooked together, become one thing? We will not have a God who can give no more than a law."[47] And then finally: "I appeal from the law to the gospel for God has given another word over

---

42. WA Ti 1, p. 276, Nr 590 = BoA 8, p. 76, Nr. 590
43. WA Ti 1, p. 277, Nr 590 = BoA 8, p. 77, Nr. 590
44. WA 36, 9ff. (Sermon for January 1, 1532, on Gal 3:23ff.)
45. WA 29, 18ff.
46. WA 29, 18ff. nn. 32ff.
47. WA 34, 36ff.

the law, which states that is the gospel which gives us its grace, forgiveness of sins, eternal righteousness, and life."[48] The difference between the two words means to separate what is mixed. Contrary to that, the unity of the *verbum Dei* would not be that in which it is spoken as promise from God, but the mixing of faith and work. But with the gospel a boundary is set against the limitless law: the sinner is no longer accessible through the law.

3. The Function of the Law

If we want to see the function of the law in the relation between law and gospel, then we must observe two things: first, that the law is not without meaning when it requires "what is impossible," and second, that it brings knowledge of sin, *cognition peccati*, as Paul says in Rom 3:20b. We must observe that Luther gave great value to this statement and that for him, out of both—out of the thesis of the "impossible" requirement on the one hand, and the other, positive thesis of the power of the law to create knowledge—there results a self-contained, closed, meaning of the law as such. Luther states on Rom 3:20b that this knowledge occurs through the law in twofold fashion, first in the sense of Rom 7:7-8: the law makes me conscious of desire. Here Luther uses the parable of the water which one pours on chalk: "The fire in the chalk sleeps deeply hidden. We do not even know that it is there. But when water is poured over it, then the occasion arises of showing itself. So, the water has not created the fire, rather it has had the effect such that the fire has the opportunity to show itself."[49] So as chalk takes opportunity through the water, *osteandi se* (to sow oneself), so also sin becomes "alive when the law portends! A peculiar desire flames up in a person, the law would not like to be there. A "willing" (*voluntas*) springs up in a person who would rather, "if it were possible that there were no law and one were totally free."[50] This *voluntas* which I did not know before, is "discovered, wakened to life by the "*nomos*." Next to this "speculative" (gained through reflection) knowledge Luther (in the exposition of Rom 3:20b) places a second which he calls

---

48. WA 35, 28ff.

49. WA 56, 67, 26ff. (Glosses) = Fi (Glosses) 63, 14ff. (BoA vac.)

50. WA I, 228 (*Disputatio contra scholasticam theologiam*. 1517, These 85) = BoA 5, 326 (here: Thesis 86).

experiment talis (through experience): *per opus legis*.[51] Here Luther does not have in mind the person as he/she is in intention, not the total contradiction against the law as such, but rather the one who of course actually makes use of the law, but unhappily: "But when one's will acts compelled by the law and does this willingly, then one sees how deeply sin and evil is rooted in one, which one would not see if he/she did not have the law and had not begun to act according to the law."[52]

But when the law does not bring one to the point where one accomplishes a good work pleasing to God, to what purpose then is it there? Is it not senseless to say that the law requires "what is impossible"? Here we must observe two different statements of Luther. First, that we indeed do not have to do with someone who on his/her own recognizes sin and the wrath of God. The law brings such knowledge, and Luther calls it the *lex spiritualis*, the "spiritual law." To know it means thus to be miserable for the greatness of our guilt. If one knew by nature how things are with one, then of course the law in this sense would be unnecessary. So, the knowledge of sin which the law brings to one must be a *novum* in one's life. Second, the other derives from the fact that the *opera* do not fulfill the law, but that the fulfillment of the law effects the *opera*. The Christian stands over against a law fulfilled according to its object, and for him/her the law is now a leader, helper, dear, and comforting.

In ever clearer diction Luther stood for and advocated this thesis that the law works knowledge, cognition. According to him this does not mean that it does not move one to act, but on this way to action it arrives at an act of insight and knowledge, the knowledge of sin which is unique. It is effected in spiritual fashion. Luther can also call that understanding of the law spiritual. But to understand the law spiritually means that under the influence of the word of God something happens to him/her, not only that his/her deeds are improved but that something occurs with him/her, precisely what Luther gladly calls a" killing and life giving" and what he ascribed to the Holy Spirit alone. The cognition worked by the law—with the help of the spirit of God—is thus at the same time the sign of a decisive coming into existence. This person does not remain as is, but by the knowledge of sin (knowledge is to be understood here in this way) he/she recognizes God and him/herself, recognizes both. Like a flash in the night the law sets the person's nature totally free before the

---

51. WA 56, 253, 22ff. (Scholien) = Fi (Scholien) 90, 4ff. (BoA vac.)
52. WA 56, 253, 28ff. (Scholien) = Fi (Scholien) 90, 10ff.

might of God. This knowledge is the horror of death of all that is human in us, of the person who still can hope in some way to live before God with the help of the action of the law, with the aid of some sort of ethical possibilities, indeed, in any event from out of one's own possibilities. For this reason, Luther also calls this knowledge a kind of "killing." One can live neither out from, nor with, this knowledge.

But this knowledge is indeed not only a self-knowledge—it is also that—but where else than in myself should it appear? But it is knowledge of God! Here we meet this continually recurring, selfsame thesis of Luther, that God reveals himself in his true nature, in his grace and mercy only to the humbled and shattered, thus to those who possess that knowledge. Only they believe only they rely purely and totally on his mercy. Only with them can he build a kingdom, only they are "righteous" and now can do the law. Thus, only the gospel justifies, but even with justification or with faith the law too is changed for me. It becomes something which can be realized. Its impossibilities fall away; with that also its merely negative sense. Now the law will be fulfilled in those who live by faith. A genuine "Yes" to the command of God because it is really God's command that struggles its way through in me. Luther writes to Jonas of Coburg in 1530, "Here I have become a new student of the Decalogue, and as one who becomes a child again (*repuerascens*), I learn it word for word and see that he is true and his wisdom is beyond measure."[53] In his draft, "*De loco iustificationis*," 1530, it says at one point that it is another thing "to weigh the work by itself," and "by the favor of grace or the shadows of promise."[54] Here something is illuminated from the fact that according to evangelical understanding the law, under which we also remain as the justified, as to whom for Christ's sake all sin is forgiven, is shadowed round by the *promissio*, that it will be understood from the eschatological future: "You can, for you shall!"[55] That "you shall" sounds to us like a promise, not from our own power, but precisely from the accompanying of the Holy Spirit. The space into which we are redeemed is not a "legal" space. The Christian—as the one justified by grace—is not a superman. The Christian lives in the fulfillment of the law. But Luther also thought of what we term the meaning of life. Grace therefore does not abrogate human existence under the law, because otherwise it would

---

53. WA Br. 5, 409, 26ff. Nr. 1610 = BoA 6, 305, 8ff. Nr. 242

54. WA 30/2, 668, 18–19.

55. See "Xenien von Goethe und Schiller" in: Goethe, *Werke*, 150. Nr. 383. The formula harks back to Kant; see also Akademie-Ausgabe 8, p. 287, Ftnote 35.

totally abrogate its action, its warfare, the giving of meaning here and now to a being "still on the earth." We remain under the *nomos* in the *militia* (service) of Christ. But how then is it with our freedom?

Christian Freedom

1. What Is Christian Freedom?

All the Reformers, not just Luther, created a definite, and theologically precisely formulated idea of Christian freedom. But this has become so foreign to modern consciousness that we will have to clarify its peculiarity once again. For this I first choose from the writing, "Judgment on the Monk's oath 1521,"[56] a portion of which has the superscription, "What Christian freedom is."[57] Here there is a surprising triad. First: Christian freedom concerns the conscience of the *homo religiosus*, thus of the person who believes in God and lives under his commandment. It is not something outside God's will to save, and not simply developed as freedom of the *homo naturalis*. It is, as it were, the question of the "Christian person," whether or not he/she knows that his/her freedom is mediated to him/her through Jesus Christ. Christian freedom is not an "also," but an "only" freedom applicable to the Christian. Therefore, we have the title to the writing, "On the freedom of a Christian, 1520,"[58] in which it says, "That we may know thoroughly what a Christian person is, and what happens with the freedom Christ has won and given to him/her."[59] Now then, what does this freedom consist of? It consists in a delivering of the conscience, as if one is able—only HE is called to do it—to deliver one's conscience from its bondage to the *opera* and in its place "bind" it to something entirely different; so that if one still calls that bondage, then that is exactly this essence of one's *opus*! The bondage that I assume is nothing other than bondage to the deed of the liberator! "Christian freedom or evangelical freedom is thus the freedom of conscience, by which the conscience is freed from works, not that none are done, but that one relies on none." The conscience is not the "power of acting," but a "power of judging," and precisely this is the action of Christ, that he has freed our conscience, "freed from works," and of course by the fact that he teaches

---

56. WA 8, 573–669 (*De votis monasticis iudicium*. 1521) = BoA 2, 188–298.
57. WA 8, 606ff. = BoA 2, 225.ff
58. WA 7, 3–38 = BoA 2, 1–27.
59. WA 7, 20, 25ff. = BoA 2, 11, 2ff.

the gospel (here is the root of the restoration concept of "*doctrina*"!), "not to trust in any works, but only to accept his mercy (*praesumere*)."[60] Here we would have to insert an investigation over the extent to which human conscience is actually always supported by works, to what extent therefore that "power of judging" is always related to what "I have done." That is what is "inborn" in humankind, it is a natural religion. No enlightenment, no levity, no Nietzschean "Beyond Good and Evil" can free one from it. Conscience inclines fundamentally toward the *opera*! To alter this inclination, to produce a change, means to bring one freedom and of course a freedom in the spiritual sense: "Thus we see that a Christian has enough faith, needs no works to be devout. Then, if one needs no works any longer, then one is surely absolved of all commandments and laws. If one is absolved, then one is surely free. That is the Christian freedom, the only faith whose effect is not that we become lazy or can do what is evil, but that we need no works to arrive at devoutness and blessedness."[61] Now conscience in the historical sense means something entirely new and different. It is the ability to "distinguish and to judge between the *opera* Christi and one's own." What is true of it is that *Christi opera apprehendit* (it grasps Christ's works).[62]

Secondly, this freedom is not merely a possibility for people, but a command. "This freedom specifically is of divine right."[63] It is evangelical freedom: "This freedom God has established. He will neither revoke it nor can he allow anything against it (that is, a *votum*!), nor is one allowed to damage it by even the smallest sentence."[64] We are thus not only freed from all "*opera*" in or own existence, that is, from an evaluation proceeding from there, but with this freedom are at the same time "deprived" of all commandments and rules which people have set up as necessary to salvation: the commandments of men (Matt 15; Mark 7) and the "elements of the universe" (Gal 4:3; Col 2:8). God cannot take back this freedom once it is proclaimed by the gospel. From that point Luther breaks the entire system of the *vota* and of *consilia*. They now no longer are needed before God; they are merely to be judged by their use which they have for education and society. The person is thus insofar free as he/she—thanks to this evangelical freedom of theirs—can move around

60. WA 8, 606, 30ff. = BoA 2, 226, 26ff.
61. WA 7, 24, 35ff. = BoA 2, 14, 38ff.
62. WA 8, 607, 4–5 = BoA 2, 227, 2–3.
63. WA 8, 613, 9 = BoA 2, 234, 10.
64. WA 8, 613, 9ff. = BoA 2, 234, 10ff.

with the orders as their lord! "I saw servants going on horses and princes on foot like servants" (Eccl 10:7). It would annul the divine right if one would render binding these orders in the religious sense in addition to the gospel: "It is no less sin to damage the freedom established by God, than to sin against any other kind of commandment of God."[65]

But now, thirdly, appears what is remarkable, not to be missed, that this freedom cannot merely be secularized: "The evangelical freedom rules alone in things which occur between God and yourself, not in what happens between you and your neighbor."[66] Is there here a gap in the Reformation definition of freedom? The neighbor cannot set me as free as God does, "because your neighbor has not committed (awarded) to you to be delivered and free, as God does."[67]

2. Freedom of the Will and the Bound Will

Luther very early on in bold theses attacked and judged the concept of free will (*liberum arbitrium*) that was given special emphasis in Scholasticism. It is not as if he hadn't grown up with it. But also, as usual, with eminent basic theological concepts one day a change appears here with Luther, toward which he never returned. In doing so he waved goodbye to an understanding of the world and life which in itself forms a contained whole. He did not repair one point of the old system, to allow what was left to be improved or retained, as was the object of his later opponents in this matter (Erasmus of Rotterdam), but with it shook the foundation on which the doctrinal system till then was based. It is no accident that among the first theses condemned by the Catholic Church was Luther's denial of the freedom of the will. And it is likewise anything else than accidental that the humanistic wing which formed around Erasmus and first was friendly toward the Reformation sought and found here the decisive point of the disagreement. Already in this conflict between Luther and Erasmus we see the powers of the counter-reformation being raised. For in this war over his doctrine of the "bound will" Luther not only stood in opposition to the world of yesterday, but also with that of tomorrow. Without question he over-interpreted Erasmus; he saw in him the spokesman for a world view which would make the person "lord of lords and god of all

---

65. WA 8, 613, 41ff. = BoA 2, 235, 12–13.
66. WA 8, 615, 28–29 = BoA 2, 237, 13–14.
67. WA 8, 615, 36–37 = BoA 2, 237, 23–24.

gods." There are always great theological decisions made "between the times." They are both revolutionary and reactionary, and thus make clear that for truth there is no possibility of erasure, that the apex on which it becomes visible falls away on both sides and that the way "to hand down" truths in the upper air of revelation is a mysterious and deeply contingent (accidental) process. It is other than one supposes, when one takes in hand a textbook on the history of dogma which resembles a museum of natural knowledge, where one collects knowledge, but not that dogmatic event itself in the open field of battle, where knowledge is the object. Just that was given to Luther in his still ever thoughtworthy and exciting opposition to the head of the humanistic school. At the same time, one has the impression that the reformer detected that Erasmus carried in his loins the Nietzschean-man, the man "beyond good and evil." For this reason, Luther exhibited blitz-like anger, passionately thrusting through all the pretexts and excuses, until he hit the decisive point at which the evil is sitting. He had something else in mind than to break a lance on the "I–Thou Relationship." He just as little wanted to be a stirrup for determinism, as it appeared to theologians of the 19th century who were favorable to him and he would indeed have exercised some reservation toward the honor which Arthur Schopenhauer paid him, when he ranked himself among the witnesses of Luther's concept of the bondage of the will.[68] Luther's doctrine of the bondage of the will (*servum arbitrium*) is not to be detached from the discovery of the grace of God in Jesus Christ. It leaves the way open to it. He had to remove the Doctrine of Free Will out of the way since otherwise the light emanating from Christ would not have reached the true, total person; that is, the lost person. The doctrine of the bondage of the will is nothing else than just that clear and pure mirror of that which God in Jesus Christ has done. Free will belongs to the lanterns with which a humanity, far from God's light, allow a bit of light into the night in which it wanders. To recognize the bondage of the will means that the day has dawned (Rom 3:12) and we see in its light how it is with humanity: it is the day of Jesus Christ in the message of his gospel. Thus, if we isolate the doctrine of the bondage of the will, if we make of it a theory related to determinism, then we lose the most intimate connection of this knowledge with the knowledge of God; we tear it from its theological context like a flower one tears from the root. It will soon wither. In order to break through to Christian freedom, the fiction of

---

68. Schopenhauer, *The World as Will and Representation*, Vol. 1, Chapter 70. On previous paragraph see also Vol. II, Chapter 48.

the freedom of the will must be removed. The freedom of the will—thus the human's freedom of choice between good and evil—is the most basic deception of the person regarding him/herself. The person does not have two possibilities regarding him/herself, but only one reality; that is, of his/her inseparable, factual lostness, to be revised by nothing. Thus, when we cling to the grace of God, when we live from out of it, we cannot at the same time persist further in the fiction of the freedom of the will, as if there lay with us the freedom of decision for or against God. The decision lies not with humans, but it lies with God. To return to God's hand from out of the dream of our possibilities, to step over to the unchangeability of our reality, that means to retreat from free will. Free will is a predicate of God, says Luther against Erasmus; it must be reserved for God. Human will is only "free" when it is a will moved by God and his promise, thus determined in his direction. A self-determining will is actually a will fallen away from God, a will setting to itself freedom as booty. From that point we may perhaps better understand that Luther lets such a will then be determined and led by the devil. The famous picture of the human as a horse which is ridden now by God, now by the devil,[69] can be misunderstood insofar as it could look as if the will were and remained here and there the same, merely the power changed. That is not what is meant. But the devil can only direct the supposedly free will loosed from God; can move the misuse of freedom to sin, which indeed the human at bottom does not want, but the power of God over the will is not punishment and usurpation, but a genuine assignment which also resides in the nature of the will.[70]

Election and Comfort

1. The Revealed and the Hidden God

If ever the freedom of the will is recognized as a fiction, then the way is also free for an understanding of a basic doctrine of our faith, otherwise ridden and obscured: the Doctrine of Predestination. The rediscovery of predestination belongs to the primary elements of the reformation

---

69. On this theme see in Luther's *The Bondage of the Will*, WA 18, 635, 17ff. = BoA 3, 126, 23ff. See also the footnotes in the BoA.

70. See on the above statement also the "Theological Introduction" by H. J. Iwand to the edition of M. Luther's *Werke*, Ergänzungsreihe, Vol. 1: "On the Bondage of the Will," ed. G. Merz et al., B. Jordahn, 253–64.

certainty of salvation. The Doctrine of Free Will has delivered this to a continual uncertainty, made it dependent on doing, on the human's moral progress, thus of something which it only supposedly, but in truth actually does not have in hand. But thereby the certainty of salvation is surrendered to uncertainty. When Luther discovers predestination through Paul this is a result of his personal life. He becomes free of the self-interest of piety and the criterion drawn from it of a judging God. In the Doctrine of Predestination one thing is expressed: That God is God, and, of course, that he is this in his "being gracious!" Here, his being gracious will be discovered, found, and believed. We cannot recognize the primacy with which Luther assigned the first commandment and at the same time deny predestination. For faith in God in his promise, in his "I will be your God," that is faith in predestination. Contradiction of it always comes from the *ratio*, that is, from an evaluation concerning either me or God, which I find in myself and from out of which I form an *a priori* judgment (here: from the very outset). And, of course, either in such fashion I declare my moral striving from the outset purposeless over against predestination, or that I declare I could not understand God who both elects and damns! From this result two main arguments respecting doubt in predestination: a) the question regarding the individual and his/her certainty; b) the question regarding God's decree of salvation involving all humanity. Both are used in relation to faith. Thus, a) is the denial, the *resignation ad infernum* (sending oneself into hell),[71] with Luther no longer a mystical usage but the acceptance of God's judgment, and b) the distinction between the *Deus absconditus et revelatus*, the hidden and revealed God, a necessary distinction in God himself, to protect the freedom of God in the election to grace.

2. Predestination and Grace

Luther's distinction here characteristically ends with Rom 8:28: "We know that all things work together for good for those who love God, who are called according to his purpose." Luther remarks here that he is now nearer to the "matter of predestination and election," which is "not so

---

71. See on this difficult place WA 56, 388, 10–11. (Scholien) = BoA 5, 271, 17 = Fi (Scholien) 215, 8–9. Here Luther speaks of the third and highest level of decision/election which is achieve by those who, "in reality according to God's will are sent to hell." See similar in K Holl, et al. (I. p. 19 n. 32) 149ff. See also the literary references in Johannes Tauler.

deep as is thought, but rather extremely sweet for the elect and those who have the Spirit, but extremely bitter and harsh for the cleverness of the flesh."[72] Predestination and grace basically combine. This means: the grace of God encounters me in a decision withdrawn from my reflection, made over me and totally out of the freedom of God. This is annoying to those would like to see dependent on their will the scope of grace's validity in their life. The call to salvation resulting from God's decree means that in our call there is a necessity, a *necessitas*; not, say, in the sense of a mechanical necessity, but yet in such fashion that the many vagaries involving human beings must be submissive to it. Precisely on the basis of God's call to salvation, human destiny no longer appears inevitable, and so the called and elect are no longer exposed to all the unforeseen external and internal temptations and inner conflicts they could encounter. A new inevitability appears, not based on the strength of our faith, nor the decision of my will, but on the recourse to this "election of God," which precedes all that is temporal with its historical accidents, is the effective basis of our certainty. In relation to this "decree" of God—must "all things work together for good." That MUST before which the deepest need and inner conflict finds its limit, is also one over against which sin and death must set their prisoners free. Thus, for the young Luther predestination is anything but the human being's enslavement; it is rather that higher order of the freedom of God and the certainty of salvation, before which every accidental event, the evil and the good things of the world, stands, as before a higher tribunal. Our salvation thus does not stand on all that we experience or is performed on our own. We already see here why the "work" of the human being never can establish human "being," and not the human being as a person before God: "not accidentally but necessarily (*necessario*) the elect are redeemed."[73] But then also the lifestyle of the "elect" should make clear that they would be a thousand times lost and foundered if God's election were not the basis of their salvation. "For if he would not lead us through a host of monstrous appearing opinions, then he would leave us in all kinds of (false) views of our merits. But now he shows that we are saved by his unalterable love. In doing so he does not indicate that our will is free but is the unbending and fixed will of his predestinating (*praedestinatio*). For how could it be that a person was to break all this, something that he/she would have a thousand doubts

---

72. WA 56, 381, 17ff. (Scholien) = BoA 5, 265, 20ff. = Fi (Scholien) 208, 22ff.
73. WA 56, 381, 28–29 (Scholien) = BoA 5, 265, 30–31 = Fi (Scholien) 208, 33–34.

about, unless the eternal and steadfast loved of God led him/her through all this and the Spirit who is present helped our weakness and intercede for us in prayer with unutterable sighs? In such distress the person does not know what he/she is doing and should pray for."[74] Here it is clear that what in the "election" the eternal and steadfast love of God is involved—not a demiurge's act of choice, as if we had to draw red and black lots which determine the course of our life, and from which, in fatalistic fashion, the course of our life then gains shape. First of all, in Luther there is no talk of such a graceless determination, but it is the eternal and steadfast love of God. It is this which "is strong as death" (Song 8:6). Everything must be allocated to this election, be taken up in it. It is the Good: the power of God making everything good, taking everything into its service and changing everything, and it would be absolutely evil if the person electing him/herself were the person emancipating him/herself from this election of God.

3. Certainty of Salvation and Theodicy

If we ask how Luther comes to see anew the Doctrine of Predestination—so new that the entire Middle Ages did not see it—and from an angle which is simply identical to the Pauline, so we may perhaps say that with him the argument collapsed which most strongly spoke against it. This argument is the personal interest in salvation; namely, the personal question regarding the certainty of salvation. There is, if we pursue the genuine origin of Luther's theology, a deeper layer which cannot simply be reduced to the question of a" gracious God," or the question of "my salvation," or to "soteriological" interests. The clever device of the flesh says: "It is harsh and merciless that God seeks his power in my misery. Hear the voice of the flesh: Mine, mine it says. Take this "mine" away and say: "Glory to you Lord! (*Gloria tibi, Domine!*) and you will be saved."[75] "Take this "mine" away." That is the log in the eye of medieval theology, in the eye of the "devout" of that great Christian epoch, which Luther hindered from measuring the size and width of the Doctrine of Predestination. Luther hits the nail on the head. The question of "mine"—"my salvation, my misery"—must first of all be postponed. The person who, regarding the question of salvation, proceeds from him/herself and his/her interest,

---

74. WA 56, 382, 5ff. (Scholien) = BoA 5, 265, 38ff. = Fi (Scholien) 209, 6ff.
75. WA 56, 386, 14ff. (Scholien)–BoA 5, 269, 31ff. = Fi (Scholien) 213, 19ff.

must die. In this matter he/she may not have a say. We can precisely say that along with it Luther loses the bracket which the Middle Ages had fixed between the decree of God and the human's personal interest in salvation. The will of God and love of self—of course properly understood, not related to the transitory world—have, with this view, the same goal. They meet in the objectives. If, at the very basis of myself, by thrusting through to the actual ground of myself, by thrusting through to the layer where I live "estranged" from myself, then I will also find God there. With his revelation God intends that I thrust through to this essentiality, for which reason no one can find God without being certain of the eternal basis of his/her soul (*anima*), and vice versa. Thus, throughout the entire history of salvation reigns a harmony to be precisely described ontologically. This appears in these few sentences in which Luther develops the antithesis between God and humans, between "thought" about God and humans and we see here how exactly the two things hang together: the election of God on the one hand, and the conquest of works righteousness on the other. Only when one did not understand the doctrine of God's election to grace proceeding all our doing, was the theological theme of "works righteousness" ethicized. Originally the rejection of *opera* depends on the grounding of faith on the election of God; salvation is a process which occurs *extra* as Luther says, thus, in a sphere which our works, whether good or evil, cannot penetrate. Not for the reason it is inadequate, sinful, or because it is hindered by our human condition, but rather because in this sphere of the election of God as such, no "works" defined from the human side can interfere. Here God acts alone. Therefore, the *opera* does not offer enough of a starting point for "dealing with God." As Luther happily states, whoever wants to deal with God can only do this in faith in his word. In the word God elects us. His word is always, where it meets us, a word that rejects or elects. To believe his word means to seize the hand of God with which he elects me in his free, unconditional grace; to grasp his election in rejection. For this reason, preaching appears at midpoint in the worship. God and humans no longer strive—from this new aspect of predestination—by nature with one another. Their striving with one another is not merely hindered by the world as having come "between," and darkened, but two worlds stand over against each other: on the one side God who has decided my salvation totally by his choice, while rejection forms the other, dark, horrible side of his freedom and it is horrible only for the rejected, and on the other side the person who would like to see him/herself as a factor, as co-determining this event.

He/she sees him/herself—that is, his/herself determination, his/her own freedom—excluded in this act of divine election and thinks that by it he/she is excluded. However, the person does not see that it is different with God, that there is a higher, more wonderful, and never an "about me," something for all time elusive in thought; that the *pro me* (for me) in the *sapiential Dei* (wisdom of God) sounds otherwise and is something totally different than the *pro me* in the "wisdom of the flesh." For the person both things cohere. What in the workings of God he/she—from out of his/her well understood, religious-moral interest—cannot conceive, that is what he/she for this reason also cannot regard as godly. Such a person thinks wherever he/she (the person) cannot in freedom decide, cannot be the activity of God. So, we will best understand Luther's "discovery" when he/she sees that all his/her motivations for the Doctrine of Predestination are at the same time arguments against human wisdom. *Electio* means: "You have not chosen me, but I have chosen you" (John 15:16). Here the Why question toward God falls away. There remains God's mystery and in truth his absolute mystery; why he then choses the one and rejects the other. It is typical and reveals the modern, middle-class period that begins with the puritanism of the Enlightenment, with the thesis of the "best of all worlds" in Leibniz' question of theodicy, that is, the question of the righteousness and goodness of God in view of the evil in the world. It can only occur where the question of Why over against God is seen as legitimate. It is naturally also present earlier, also with Luther, but does not define theological thinking. And it receives—no answer as it, indeed, also receives no answer in Job. And as it receives no answer with Jesus on the cross. Whoever in faith lives by God's godhead, whoever truly lives in faith, must let the Why-question be underfoot. Only beyond this question does the way of true freedom begin.

4. The Question of the Meaning of Suffering

Here we must observe something further: in the medieval "system" the Christian was raised to carry out such ethical activities as were according to the (mediated by the church) reception of grace. It was a matter of the correct *opera*. However, with Luther activity no longer stands in the foreground in terms of the Greek ethos, but rather suffering. All genuine work derives from the fact that I suffer on account of God's activity in me: "See, this is the way of the cross, which you cannot find, but must lead you as one blind. Therefore, not you, not a human being, not a creature, but I, I myself, through my Spirit and my word, will show you the way you should walk. Not the work which you choose, not the suffering which you conceive, but what is against your own choice, thoughts, desires, follow there; there is where I call you, there be a disciple, there it is time, your master is coming there."[76] And further: "Have you not read, 'The eyes of God are open over the devout" (Psalm 34:16) and Mount Moriah is called "the Lord sees" (Gen 22:14),"because I alone shall see it... Therefore, the words—faith, hope, humility, and patience—are not mentioned by name, but what is expressed in their actual nature. There are many who write of things known but hail the names more than display their nature."[77] And on Psalm 32: "Be not as the horse and mule which have no conception and understanding," it is stated most characteristically: "They are those who will not let me reign but just as the beasts with any sense follow as so soon as they feel (something) and where they do not feel or trace anything, they do not follow... Thus, also people who will not allow or suffer anything further than what they can measure and conceive, feel, trace, are not able to measure my understanding. There are with their reason like horses with minds: both walk no further than according to their feelings... In this way God compels the resisting horse when it does not allow what is wanted (and, of course), just like those who go around crisscrossing in the path of God as do the overly proud horses, until they finally begin to trot, and come to understand that it must be endured and does not go according to our will."[78] This last piece is from the "Exposition of the Penitential Psalms 1517," which Luther published as the first practical result of his new theology of God's election. The persons described by Luther here as those who "have no conception and understanding" are a very definite type of person who is not living outside of the church but in the church—just as indeed also the Psalm itself is directed against the false "devout" among its own people. "They are those who rule themselves," they are the defenders of the *liberum arbitrium* (free will), who "will not allow God's reign, do not walk other than according to their opinion, who can compel God neither with sweet or sour, neither with attractions nor threats, who tear apart reins and bit, and yet suppose they regard and honor God best; they are the most obedient, devout, the most upright because they have a good opinion and

76. WA 18, 489, 21ff. ("The Seven Penitential Psalms." Second edition, 1525.)
77. WA 18, 489, 21ff. nn./line 33ff.
78. WA I, 172, 20ff.

what their good opinion gives is right. These God always resists."[79] From these citations which would allow for any number more, this one thing is clear: the discovery of predestination is not a theorem, but that the reality of God will be endured. It is never conforming to what we imagine in our best opinion about ourselves. It is a process of enduring the *mutari*, of the being changed, of encounter with that which is *extra:* God is the external which can never be changed to an internal. And thus, predestination for Luther has a dual aspect: it offers to the one who sees it only with the natural eye, the picture of a horrible God, blindly handing persons over; a God who, without feeling, allows the one to slip, the other to rise. Whereas, on the other hand, it opens to the one who encounters it in faith and allows to enter in its inmost mystery and then uncovers it—precisely as the mystery of the election of God in Jesus Christ: "But Christ, the crucified, brings all this with himself and just as totally that wisdom among the perfect (1 Cor 2:6) and there is no other wisdom to be taught among Christians than that which is hidden in mystery and applies to the perfect."[80] But when we observe the omnipotence (all powerful nature) of God by itself, then it is clear that all unbelievers are caught beneath it, without being able to avoid it. They are all "imprisoned under sin" (Gal 3:22) for the sake of Christ so that, "The omnipotence of God has the effect that the godless cannot avoid the one working and acting, but forced to be subservient to him and must obey him. But the depravity, or turning away of self from God, has the effect that he/she cannot be moved toward the good and can be torn away. God cannot give up his almighty power and have regard for the descent from it. The godless cannot alter his/her falling away. So it happens, that he/she continually and compulsively sins and errs, until pointed to the right way by the Spirit of God."[81] What does this statement mean? The godless cannot be converted, says Luther. From that point he also understands the raging of the world against the gospel as something unavoidable. But who is this "godless one"? Luther answers: "The godless one is as his prince, Satan, totally directed toward self and possessions, he/she does not ask about God and does not ask about God and does not bother with who God is. He/she will rather restfully enjoy his/her treasures, glories, works, knowledge, ability, and in general his/her kingdom."[82] Luther will thus state what

---

79. WA I, 173, 17ff.
80. WA 18, 639, 1ff. (*De servo arbitrio*, 1525) = BoA 3, 129, 25ff.
81. WA 18, 710, 3ff. = BoA 3, 204, 35ff.
82. WA 18, 710, 11ff. = BoA 3, 205, 3ff.

follows: the person must be as he/she is. He/she cannot avoid the fact that just his/her inclination becomes a deed, an act, because there is a movement that is living and mighty in him/her, which cannot be avoided. Rudolf Hermann[83] has always related the Doctrine of the Bound Will to the idea of the totality of our life, and indeed that is what Luther means here. The life of the godless is a whole, total life. And the evil belongs totally and wholly in that life; they are no less subject to the omnipotence of God than those who believe in him. Otherwise, there would be no cross. They must hate it and flee. They cannot do otherwise. But insofar as the godless is a creature, a nature and has a will, he/she is subject to God's working. Such find themselves in an ultimate contradiction, insofar as they know only themselves and theirs, and yet do not exist by themselves or are free. Also, the evil one is entrapped, held, and moved by God. And of course, precisely by the same God who has revealed himself in Jesus Christ. To this extent there is a tragedy in all our human existence, for wherever we live, thus would grasp the fulness of life, there we are inevitably driven by a power which we cannot escape. Thus, that by the working of God evil becomes a reality in us, is not God's but our guilt. And why does God not slacken in his working? "That means to wish that on account of the godless God would cease to be God, since you have the desire that his power and activity would cease to be good, so that they would not be more evil. But why does he not at the same time alter the evil willing which he still motivates? This belongs to the mysteries of the majesty where his judgments are incomprehensible" (Rom 11:3). "It is not our affair to explain this, but it is fitting for us to hallow his mysteries."[84] Even the evil one is accordingly understood from passivity; from a being carried away into the suffering to which he/she is captive. The bound will make excuses—not before God, but before ourselves—him\her as well, for we should know that he/she cannot do otherwise. All genuine guilt is based and born from this not-able-to-do-otherwise, when otherwise I am who I am. So, there is always in it something tragic, something human at the deepest level, and something unavoidable. While the moralist conceives guilt under the schema "It could also have been different," and "Why have I not behaved otherwise?" But the theologian knows that a necessity rules in it all, which the human cannot escape. And since he/she sees the person, the one fallen, the godless

---

83. Rudolf Hermann (1887–1962, ultimately at Humboldt University, Berlin) had influenced and inspired H. J. Iwand theologically. See Vol. VI NW.

84. WA 18, 712, 22ff. = BoA 3, 207, 29ff.

under God, under his omnipotence, that one knows that God can also change this person. The change, of course, is by faith, and by faith absolutely alone.

5. Summary

Here we can summarize what Luther says of the Doctrine of Predestination:

a) Doubt—Luther is serious about the fact that we have to do with God and his activity, with God and his will. In this way he meets up with the fact determining his entire life, that there is no norm, no law for this will of God, that rather God is the good. But then there is the doubt concerning predestination. Luther continually engaged it and, if I see correctly, in three phases: In his youth he found comfort and help in the *resignation ad infernum*. In doing so he could think of Tauler and the "Theologia Deutsch;"[85] of the best German mysticism had formulated from the depths of self-examination, namely: Even in eternal death and hell they do not oppose God's will and make no attempt at change or revision when God wills it, but simply say "Yes" to his will. Whoever in this manner engages the will of God, which is possible only through the Spirit, the "roaming of the Spirit" (Rom 8:26), is always a man of God, even in damnation (cf. p. 91). This is the one, the first path which Luther takes, in order to conquer his doubt in predestination. A genuine and more difficult path, which is precisely the path of Christ, his true "imitation" (discipleship) in suffering, not in his works, is a path that I think Luther never totally gave up on.

b) Hope—Added to this, as far as I can see, is the "*Operationes in Psalmos*, 1519–1521," a second path applied to this doubt concerning predestination in more analytic fashion. The magnificent piece I know from Luther in this respect, is his exposition of the fifth Psalm: "All rejoice who hope in you . . ."[86] Here the question of hope is at issue. For Luther, the first commandment belongs to faith, in which for him so much was contained, because hope may not be put to shame. A hopeless faith, a *fides sine spe*, is for him an absurdity. Luther now sees this hope threatened by the doubt over predestination. He objects: Does not the Doctrine of Predestination make our Christian life fatalistic? Our

---

85. Tauler, *Theologia Deutsch*, is a mystical writing that appeared at the end of the 14th century and was published by Luther in 1516. On the topic, see Chapters 10 and 11 (J.H.)

86. WA 5, 156ff.

Christian life fatalistic, hopeless? The question tortures and unnerves him that I "could hope in vain, if I am not predestined (for salvation)."[87] Here Luther consciously strides the path by resolving the motivation for this putting of the question in order to bring the person out from inner conflict. That is, he means that this question does not stem from us, that we are not the questioners, but that an evil spirit insinuates (gives) in us such a question, and, of course, according to him this question is clearly "from then devil."[88] This is Luther's consistent opinion of inner conflict: It is something which comes over the believer "from the outside," but still in such a way that it appears to him\her to come from within him/herself. Everything that God is moves us "to keep the commandments and to do his will."[89] Thus, only such a question concerning God's will which relates to the deed, to carrying out his command, is from God, not "anxious concern over your predestination."[90] Of course, even the "devout" are anxious about their predestination, and ask about God's will, but only apparently. "For concerning this will, I can only ask when I try to do it, but not only to know it." Thus, when we are anxious about our destiny, we neglect doing God's commandments. But that is exactly the intention of Satan and therefore the commandment of God is afforded us here as an aid and means of salvation. We should care that his will is done, and this care should allow us to forget about caring for ourselves. But that one, the great tempter (*perversor!*) turns the series around: "He wants you first of all to be anxious about ourself and then about God's instructions."[91] As a second proof that this question does not come from God and therefore can find no answer in God, which Luther calls the second temptation of Christ (Matt 4:5–7).[92] The question concerning predestination implies the question concerning a *signum* (sign). But the doubt regarding predestination issues from the fact that we cannot bear "the uncertainty of the divine decree." Here the person encounters just that fact that in truth the *skandalon* (offense) for him/her means: Briefly, one loathes that God is God because he/she does not will that one (God) knows otherwise than what he/she knows."[93] But God's being God meets one in the *praedestina-*

---

87. WA 5, 172, 1–2.
88. WA 5, 171, 24.
89. WA 5, 172, 8–9.
90. WA 5, lines 10–11.
91. WA 5, lines 29–30. "*Ille vero perversor . . .*"
92. WA 5. See also 172, 36–37.
93. WA 5, 173, 5–6.

tio Dei. He/she, the person, stumbles at the mystery of God, stumbles at the fact that salvation, justification, should be a mystery of God—and not the mystery of one's own. And again, Luther says: "But when you accept in love the will of his hidden decree, then you are already predestined."[94] Behind this attitude is the wisdom of the preacher Solomon, who teaches that wisdom of life that fears the Lord—but in a specific way that voids "being bothered by" that "care" which is not our care. Here it is shown that the *fiducia*, the trust, is the proper attitude which leaves it to God how he will lead me.

c) Promise—It was already shown in the struggle with doubt concerning predestination that God has a double face: God as he shows himself to us in the word of his promise, and as God "in himself." Very early on, Luther already worked out the difference between the "revealed God" (*Deus revelatus*) and the "hidden God" (*Deus absconditus*). There is a time in which both coincide for him and the *Christus crucifixus*, the crucified Christ, is the *Deus absconditus*. But the understanding that remains is this: there are manifestations of God which are such that we cannot tell whether God or the devil is standing behind them. All deeds and appearances ascribed to the *Deus absconditus* are ambiguous "revelations;" they leave it to the person, so to speak, what he/she makes of it, to our interpretations and opinions. In these events God stands "behind." In doing this Luther also happily uses the concept of the mask, the" larvae," or the disguise. In this regard the *Deus absconditus* is a limiting concept; it removes, as it were, from the *Deus revelatus* the question whether God exists and where he is at work. This question reaches further, is darker and more horrible than can be gathered from the concept of the *Deus revelatus*. But it is the reason why we hold to the *Deus revelatus*, to reason and abyss alike. Whoever does not hold to the *Deus revelatus* is left to the *Deus absconditus*, which means they are left with horror, judgment, and deep despair. Why then for Luther does God have this Janus face? Evidently because the God who is Father of Jesus Christ, is at the same time the one who has all that happens in the world in his hands. Perhaps most beautifully Luther described this in that scene in which Jesus weeps over Jerusalem (Luke 19:41ff.)[95] If there were only the *Deus absconditus* then we would not be in possession of the revelation in Jesus Christ. If there were only the *Deus revelatus* then we would no longer cling to him as

---

94. WA 5, lines 9–10.

95. WA 36, 224–28 (Sermon on August 4, 1532, for the 10th Sunday after Trinity. In Rörer's Afterward.)

believers, but just as those who know. Hence both must be seen alongside each other, because not everything is revealed. Hence, God must have a dark, enigmatic aspect in the life of human beings and retain the history of the world as "framework" of the revelation, because the resurrecting of the dead and the total victory of his kingdom are still to come.

3

Christology

Christ and His Own

1. Christ Is Never without His Own

THIS PRELIMINARY REMARK PROCEEDS from the thesis that Christ is never without his own. We will never be able to develop a Christology by separating Christ from his own. And we will never be able to separate him from his own since they are always conformable to him. In 1519, in his writing on the Lord's Supper, "A Sermon on the sacred sacrament of the holy, true body of Christ and the brotherhoods," Luther says, "The meaning or the work of this sacrament is the fellowship of all the saints, for which reason we also call it by its daily name *synaxis* or *communio*, that is, fellowship. *Communicare* in Latin means to receive this fellowship, which we express in German as 'to go to the sacrament,' and derives from the fact that Christ is, with all the saints, a spiritual body, just as the people of a city are a community and body, each one a citizen of the other in like measure and of the whole city. Thus, all the saints are a member of Christ and of the church, which is an eternal city of God, and whoever is accepted into this city, that is, is taken up into the community of saints and incorporated into the spiritual body of Christ, is made his member."[1]

This means that just as little as I am able to see Christ as he is, I cannot see his own without him. I will not understand Luther if I assign

---

1. WA 2, 743, 7ff. ("Zum Vierten") = BoA 1, 197, 13ff.

to him a modern concept of Christ, be it an historical or a critical one. There is thus no "existential understanding" of the Christology of Luther, that proceeds, say, from human existence in the world, but the total understanding of existence which we encounter in Luther's description of human being is always and already determined by the fact that we are his own—we are in his Church. The Church defines the understanding of existence, not mere isolated human existence. In Luther there is no Christology from an abstraction by which we could observe Christ, say, in isolation. And here lies the root of the "*pro me*" (for me) in Luther. True faith in Christ does not leave us as we are but creates a new existence. Just as Christ, who meets us as the Lord of sin and death, is the living Christ, so also the one whom he encounters is not a fixed creature, a being that is such-and-such and not some other, but one who is changed. Those who are his are similar to him in movement, in becoming, just as Christ is in movement, the Coming-to-us-of God, the Entering-for-us of God. With Christ and his own an event is always involved. So, due to Christ, it is made clear who are his own and who are not. Those who merely hear of it, without accepting him with outstretched arms, and without receiving life, righteousness, and salvation, find nothing; those who merely hear of it are not his own. Luther is not of the opinion that Christ is there for all. Naturally, he is there "for all," but Luther has continually said: The All are the believers. He is not there for us in the sense that this "*pro nobis*" follows without further definition, or without election by him. He is not simply there so that one can come and receive him: He is not open to call.

2. Election in the Cross

His own are already determined by the call of Jesus and only because I am the one called by Jesus as his, do I belong in this *communio*. In other words: The relation of Jesus to his own is that of election. Here the element of the crucified, the *crucifixus* has definitely to mean something. In the *crucifixus* his own are elect; namely those who do not rely on their own remorse and repentance, but know they are called by his suffering. If that is so, then from that point on we gain an entirely new aspect of the doctrine of "law and gospel." The law with its "No" rejects those who are not his own. Thus, all those who trust in their own righteousness, their own wisdom, in their existence, in their acts, in their humility, all these are rejected by the "law," by the *nomos*. The gospel is not simply so available that everyone can come and take it, but it is shielded, protected. The Pharisees must remain outside. The law belongs under the election of Christ, by which his own truly remain his own; they are the poor to whom the gospel is preached. The law is then a kind of fence set up against the *iustitiarii*[2] *as* Luther says. And that is so because his own are actually determined—not in terms of actual predestination—but in this divine election to grace, which results in Jesus Christ and is issued to the poor (Luke 6:20), to the heavy laden (Matt 5:4), to the bruised reed, to the smoldering wick (Isa 42:3), to the people who walk in darkness (Isa 9:1). From that point it would be understandable that the Doctrine of Law and Gospel is, for the most part, connected with particular persons. The law is directed toward the *superbi in sua iustitia* (the proud in their righteousness). The law does not simply say something into the empty wind but has its addressees; it has a people, and it is directed to these people. These people must take care that they do not appropriate for themselves what is the Lord's. And conversely it says to the *humiliate in sua paupertate* (the humbled in their poverty) who long to have Christ, that Christ is here. This is what the gospel says. I do not believe that we can, say, simply trace Luther's early period back to the *humiliatio*. The *humiliatio* is not a human condition, but the *humiliatio* are his own. They are those who belong to Christ by virtue of his election. If he did not come with the call: "Come unto me, all ye that labor and are heavy laden" (Matt 11:28), then being heavy laden and laboring-while-weary would not be near to Christ. He comes for these people. If there were no longer such people, then he would no longer be there for anyone. So he is, the crucified, the *contradictio* (the contradiction) of God against all who would dictate to God their own righteousness, their own wisdom, and their own goals. The *crucifixus* is the protest of God, the sign that God is the Lord. It is the defense against all those who are not his own, the judgment of all false piety, for in him the *crucifix* stands for everything that would be lofty, noble, pious, and true in this world without Christ. Ultimately, Luther is concerned that God is the Lord who divides the *superbi* (proud) from the *humiliati* (the humble) between his own and those who regard themselves as his own and are not his own. To the extent that this *Christus crucifixus* is the *signum contradictonis*, the "sign spoken against" (Luke 2:34), it is the judgment which follows from God over all our piety

---

2. Under the *iustitiarii* we understand custodians of justice and law, like the Pharisees in the NT.

and righteousness. Through this proclamation Luther frees Christ from human hands. Christ is the Lord.

3. The Antichrist in the Church

Then there is the opposite: Christ in human hands has been depicted in frightening pictures. It must have been one of the most fearful realizations for Luther when it slowly became clear to him that the Antichrist is in the Church itself. Naturally, to a great extent the Middle Ages had already known that, but not to the extent as with Luther. Luther drew these things out in his explanation to the 22nd Psalm. He interpreted it entirely in terms of the passion of Christ. He explains it from that perspective and then comes to speak of the *regnum*, of the kingdom, and says: "This seems to me to be an excellent work of the Antichrist, with the cooperation of Satan, to have the Pope restore the declining empire of the Romans."[3] Luther sees Christ captive in this empire. Christ and his own are so captive just as he, in his time, was captive by the synagogue and was clothed in a purple robe by Roman soldiers. Now the Church in the place of Christ is clothed with the glory of the empire; she supports herself not by the word and the scripture, but puts her trust in the worldly and the bloodstained empire: "Christ is not derided, except one throws a purple robe around him."[4] Thus the Church is forced to allow itself to be garbed with the glory of this fictive empire in the most disgraceful way and to allow itself to be derided, and sits in the midst of the empire in a shape that produces a shudder. Thus, Luther also sees Christ and his own raped by the empire. The cross therefore has a double significance. On the one side, it is the sign that the man of God is overpowered, and in just this way Luther can say this also of the Church: So, Christ remains in the Church but is poured out like water. His bones remain, but in pieces. His heart remains, but it is wearied. His power remans, but it is dried up. His tongue remains, but it cleaves to the gums.[5] Then to the end of the world Christ and his own must suffer. Conversely: As soon as the question arises who then are now his own, there the figures become clear to us that encounter us in the story of Jesus: the poor, the

---

3. WA 5, 649, 24–25 (*Operationes in Psalmos*. 1519–1521); the citation is translated by H. J. Iwand.

4. WA 5, 650, 3–4.

5. All of these images by H. J. Iwand relate to Psalm 22.

lame, the sick, the sinners. These are his own. His own would not at all know that they are his own if there were not the gospel: It says "No!" to all our own righteousness, worth, majesty, and wisdom. So, just as in the Gospel itself, Jesus fends off the Pharisees in order to hold space open for the tax-collector, so the law fends off the self-righteous, who live from the law, from their *opera*, and holds the space open for his own. By this means the criterion is given by which Luther will move to the question of the Church and everything that belongs to the Church. Thus, the Church will clearly always be a site where the "truly believing," the *vere credentes*, his own, who are at war with those who would make him their own. And it will not be otherwise with the world, which girds him with the royal robes. Just as Luther would set Christ free, so must the empire deliver the Christ. In a certain respect it is made worldly. Here we have the entire problem of what is genuinely worldly. It is made worldly without having the state, the authorities, marriage, or society revert to heathenism. Not worldly, however, in such a way that Christ is Lord but in such a way that the world ceases to be the master of Christ. These are the sections we must look at carefully; namely, the Doctrine of the Church and the preserving of the Christian in the world. Christ is the crucified for human beings, insofar as they are human, not for those who regard themselves as gods. Those who build on their own spirit, and their own self-confidence, who thus do not want to be genuinely human, are thrust into God's judgment. The call of the gospel must encounter specific persons because God made himself specific on the cross. Only those who are truly his will not take possession of God, who reveals himself in the crucified. The *crucifixus* is the elect of God since he elects all those who do not regard themselves as elect and rejects all who regard themselves as elect.

The Question of Scriptural Exposition

1. The Understanding of Scripture

We must first say something regarding the question of hermeneutic (scriptural exposition) if we want to understand the problem of the theology of the *Christus crucifixus*. In the Middle Ages there was, among other things, the fourfold sense of Scripture which nevertheless was in no way (!) schematically applied by all medieval expositors. It was divided into the literal, the allegorical, the tropological or the moral, and the anagogical (the higher, and mystical) sense. The early Luther still resorts to this division. The division itself has its roots in Origen (185–254) who (corresponding to 2 Cor 3:6) draws the distinction between *litera and spiritus* (literal and spirit). The literal and philological understanding always has behind it a pneumatic (spiritual) understanding, and of course the *spirituale* (spiritual) is the only genuinely theological. To have a spiritual understanding of a scriptural passage one must be illumined by the Spirit. Like is only known by like.[6] As long as Luther thinks in this fashion it is naturally the humanity of Christ, his sensuousness which the senses grasp; the *nudus homo* (naked man), something external. The Jews saw him in this way. But we must also have the spiritual understanding. To see him "spiritually" means to see God behind the man—to this then is added the Church in which we live with its earthly, visible aspect, on the one side, and on the other side its history in heaven as that of the *ecclesia triumphans*. In this way, we are able to categorize the fourfold sense of scripture in the Middle Ages. The literal sense, the *sensus literalis*, is Christ; the *sensus allegoricus* concerns the Church; the topological sense concerns the individual in the Church; the anagogical sense concerns the Church as it is redeemed (i.e., the *ecclesia triumphans* in its relation to the *ecclesia militans*). In this way (according to Luther) we are able to read every word of the Psalms; first of all, as the word of Christ, then as the word of the individual who prays the Psalm today, including the Psalms of revelation and glorification, as the word of the Church which is saved.

2. The *Christus Crucifixus* as the Point of Relation

In a "*Fragmentum Sermonis*" (1515), Luther says: "Whoever wants to read the Bible, must take care that he does not err, for the scripture can expand and lead, but no one leads it by his own affect, but is lead to the fountain, that is, to the cross of Christ."[7] And there is a beautiful passage in the exposition of the twenty-second Psalm, in which Luther paraphrases the text: When we pray: "My God, my God, why have you forsaken me" (vs 2),[8] that cannot occur without sin, for it is the expression of unbelief, but as the prayer of Jesus it is without sin. And to the extent that what is

---

6. Since the *Porentheorie* (*Theory of Elements*) of Empedocles (495–44 BC) the teaching of the recognition of "like by like" was constantly repeated in philosophy and later on also in theology. See W. Capelle, *Die Vorsokratiker*, 236; also on the topic see Goethe „Were the eye not of the sun," *Collected Works*.

7. WA 1, 52, 15ff.

8. See WA 5, 601, 5ff. (*Operationes Psalmos*. 1519–1521), esp. 602, 13ff. and 4ff.

expressed in the "I" of the Psalms is merely related to existence and to the understanding of human existence, it is never without sin. But insofar as it is related to Jesus, it is something new. For—and now we come to the meaning Christology has for Luther—Jesus does not suffer on his own account, but because he assumes our nature. Related to Jesus the verse "My God, my God, why have you forsaken me" is to be understood that here Jesus suffers the God-forsakenness of us all, thus a *passio*. So, as a person, (we can only say that analogically) he takes on the inner life of a fellow human who suffers what this person is going through. So, all human sufferings and inner conflicts are in Jesus because he has assumed human nature, because he is the love of God for humans. So, the love of God for us in Jesus Christ is the reason why nothing human is foreign to him. And insofar as the "I" of the Psalms (for Luther the Psalms have a very special meaning), the human in his/her humanity is open before God, it is also at the same time related to Jesus. The actual human being thus stands in an overarching tension with Jesus, not because Jesus is also a man, but because he has assumed human nature: he is the point of relation, the new Adam, toward whom all human existence, not by itself, but by him, is related. The true human does not exist in us in this way; we are always in the last analysis only on the way to it. But whatever a human truly is, we do not have what is truly human.

Of course, we can say I think of the truly human when we say "You," but we must admit that it is never entirely accessible to us. This human, whom we never arrive at in ourselves, who is always the "transcendent," has become human in Jesus. And this is the presupposition for understanding Luther's hermeneutical method. We will never understand this if we do not begin with the fact for Luther Jesus is defined by the Doctrine of the Two Natures. It is the word of God that has become human, not an historical person in the sense that we are historical, but exegesis gains its order from the fact that it arranges the figures from the concept of the *corpus Christi*. Thus, from that point the *sensus literalis* gains a totally new meaning. It means: If you will understand one word of scripture, then you must hold to the *historia*, to the story of Christ. What you interpret in the Psalms regarding the psalmist must be in an inner relation to the history that occurred with the incarnate God and bears the name Jesus. So, for Luther the allegorical exposition of scripture is the application of the word which he binds, to the Church, to his body. Thus, the understanding we would denote as the historical, is thus secondary, and the Christological the primary. But then a third thing is still lacking. The third thing is the tropological sense. But for Luther it is not what precedes but what is subordinate. Thus, it is a matter of the *sensus literalis* and of the interpretation of the Church as the *membra Christi*, the members of the Church of Christ, which precedes. The tropological sense of scripture now means—on the basis of the Christology—that I cannot understand what is occurring here when I interpret a word of scripture without a decision occurring in my own existence; without this understanding taking me into the opposition of flesh and spirit. Accordingly, Luther can also say that the cross is decisive for the entire Bible.

With the *census literalis* there thus occurs a movement, not merely in the ethical sense, but also in the *noetic* sense of the Spirit. We can only interpret when the interpretation itself is an event in the sense of being led by Christ out of the "flesh" and into the Spirit. In this way Luther took up the tropological sense. The Spirit who is at issue here is God's Spirit and means this: that based on the resurrection, on the new life, it will be grasped what first of all lies before us in the sign of the "flesh." If I cling to the *caro Christi*, then this *caro* pulls me into the Spirit, for this flesh of Christ now has this primary tendency. With this Christological method the others fall away. Thus, those people are correct who say that the old method of the fourfold sense of scripture is abandoned by Luther. It is striking that later, as a rule, Luther still recognizes a threefold sense of scripture: the *literari*, which is Christ; the allegorical, which is the Church; and the tropological, which is the movement in the one who understands, or being taken up into the Spirit—we can also say being taken up into the community of the Church through Christ. However, the anagogical sense of scripture is lacking, so that we may ask whether it is rightly lacking.

3. The Hiddenness of God

When Luther talks about what it means to believe in Christ, he develops it on the basis of the cross. Whoever removes the cross, has no access to Jesus. Luther says that he understands nothing at all in the scripture unless it is the Crucified One. He finds him everywhere. The cross of Christ is thus not a single historical event, but a key by which the entire holy scripture is unlocked. If we see the *passiones* and the cross of Christ behind all of the Psalms, then we understand them rightly. Christ for him is the inwardly conflicted man absolutely; the man of God, who cannot help himself (Luke 23:35). The *Christus crucifixus* at the same time is the revelation of humanity before God—as we actually stand before God—and is God's judgment on humanity.⁹

What is new, what is radical in Luther's theology of the cross, is that both the content as well as the form of the revelation are derived from the *Christus crucifixes*: "*Ego in Christo crucifix est vera Theologia et cognition Deo.*"¹⁰ At the same time, the theology of the cross for Luther denotes the *extra nos*, that we are saved: "*Non in nobis, sed in Christo, extra nos in Deo.*"¹¹ According to natural thought, God is hidden here. We can also speak in terms of a double hiddenness of God. In the Middle Ages the hiddenness of God is his "invisibility" in the metaphysical sense; we cannot grasp him with our senses. At this point there appears in Luther the *Deus absconditus*. He is visible in Jesus. He denotes something totally new. He is an historical reality; he is in our midst. He, the *Christus crucifixus*, as God's own presence among mortals. He is not only present in the *kerygma*, but he is first of all present *per se*. Without the Spirit of God, we cannot grasp the cross. Without dying and rising with Christ we cannot have this gift. What does the *extra nos* in Christus mean? What we today call the historical world would best apply to it. The fleshly human being, proceeding from his/her world, cannot know God's reality. It is *extra nos*. Christ's story as human is both typical and exemplary. Here all the laws collapse by which humans think they find God. As long as the human relies upon him/herself, God must be given up. If we do not allow God to be God here, then he must show himself here as the One he is. In *Christus crucifixus* God is truly the One he is. More than all the saints, Christ has been damned and forsaken. He offered himself totally to God. Christ elects his own predestination on the cross. Thus, Luther does not understand the suffering of Christ as analogous to our own sufferings. No one has suffered as Christ did. Christ makes clear what sin is; the death of Christ is a death no one has ever suffered. *Christus* tastes the wrath of the law. We scarcely sense it in our inner conflicts. Christ's suffering is the real suffering and the real dying. In Christ, death and sin, as real power, have found its end. Luther explained this in the "Sermon on Preparation for Dying, 1519:" "This grace and mercy is that Christ on the cross takes

9. See III, 111 (Note 7).

10. „Therefore: In the crucified Christ is the true theology and the knowledge of God." WA I, 362, 18–19 (*Heidelberg Disputation*. 1518, on Thesis 20) = BoA 5, 388, 29–30.

11. "Not in us, but in Christ, external to us in God." WA 1, 139, 35 (Sermon 1517).

away your sin from you, bears it for you, and strangles it. To steadfastly believe this and have it before our eyes, not doubting, means: to see the portrait of grace and form it in oneself; likewise, all the saints in their suffering and dying also bear in themselves your sins . . . as it is written, 'Bear one another's burdens and so fulfill the law of Christ' (Gal 6:2) . . .'" So, he himself says in Matt 11:28: 'Come unto me all ye that labor and are heavy laden, and I will give you rest.' See, so may you surely regard your sins beyond your knowing. See, here sins are no longer sins, because they are conquered and swallowed up in Christ. For just as he takes your death on himself and strangles it, that it may not harm you, if you only believe that he does this to you, and regards your death in him, not in you, thus also he takes your sin on himself and in his righteousness out of pure grace to you (for you) conquers it; if you believe it, thus they (your sins) no longer harm you."[12] Where Christ encounters sin and death he is victor.

4. Knowledge of Self under the Cross

This *Christus crucifixus* is also the source of self-knowledge. On this topic a passage from the "Sermon on Observing the Sacred Suffering of Christ, 1519:" "Those rightly think of Christ's suffering who see him in such fashion that they fear it from the heart and their conscience sinks into despair. That such fear should come from seeing the severe wrath and unchangeable seriousness of God over sin and sinners, that he did not want his only dearest Son to be free of sinners, to the extent that he paid such heavy price for them, as it says in Isaiah 53: 'For the sins of my people I have struck him.' What will happen to sinners when the dearest child is stricken so? There must be an unspeakable, unbearable seriousness here, that such a great immeasurable person intervenes and suffers and dies for it. And if you really think deeply about the fact that God's Son, the eternal Wisdom of the Father himself suffers, then you will surely fear and all the deeper."[13] This recognition is the knowledge of the human in the eschatological sense. What has become evident in Christ will one day be evident to us all; that is what is significant about the *Christus crucifixus* and the person who feels this finds refuge here. If we feel it only on the last day, we will still feel it, but it will help us no longer. The cross is not an impersonal thing nor is it a mechanical event, but the fact that Christ

---

12. WA 2, 689, 30ff. ("On the Eleventh") = BoA 1, 166, 2ff.
13. WA 2, 137, 10ff. ("On the Fourth") = BoA 1, 156, 5ff.

reigns on the cross as high priest who enters it in his person and as he does, the cross first becomes redemption. In Christ sins, "are surely no longer there, but only were so, for they are in Christ, in whom is all that is. And by these gifts you will be saved, and indeed in such a way that you always know yourself as the one whom Christ says you are, and thus flee from yourself to him in true faith."[14] Here Luther speaks of a particular "affect." Whoever will hear of the passions of Christ must "put on" this condition of suffering along with it, as if he/she were actually conformed to the passion.[15] For, because Christ has borne our person in the passion, therefore he is ours, and therefore that (the passion) is ours, because we are such as he himself wanted to appear to us before humankind. Thus, in Christ something has happened; what we actually are is brought to light, and what we are not in our historical, earthly, temporal existence, hidden by our own untruth, but what we are in truth before God. We could also say we are what we yet will be—toward that which our life moves us. Here it is clear how strongly Luther continually emphasizes the two sides in his Christology: on the one side, in Jesus Christ God's grace has appeared, God's reality, the Godhead itself, and on the other, our reality.

It is not entirely easy to say what Luther understands by "affect." It is not simply what we understand by the term "experience" but what is meant by this is a knowledge that overwhelms us, toward which we are passive. And this will agree with the fact that the truth of God, if it dawns on us, will never stand before us in such a way that we are still free to decide for or against it. Rather: when the truth of God dawns on us, it will always overwhelm us. Then we must admit—it is so. This is what we will understand by affect: it is a truth concerning which we need first of all to prove nothing, where we also need take no pain in believing it and are not free to lay it aside again. The proper doctrine of Christ is precisely a power and not merely a theory—because He lives.

---

14. WA 1, 339, 11ff. (Sermon I. The Passion of Christ. 1518).
15. See also 336, 26ff.

The Humanity of Christ

1. The Incarnation of God in Christ

What is at issue is to make intelligible what Luther means by the sentence, "We cannot drag Christ deeply enough into the flesh ."[16] We will be able to determine that Luther often links together the theology of the cross, the *theologia crucis,* and the *Christus crucifixus* with the theology of the incarnation of God. For example, in the introduction to the series of lectures on Galatians (1531) he says: "But in the matter of righteousness toward sin, death and the devil, or for the satisfaction and the forgiveness of sins, for the atonement and our salvation, it is simply to refrain from all ideas and speculations over majesty and simply to cling to the man Christ who has set himself before us as mediator and says: Hold on to me."[17] In this passage Luther does not say what he often says, "Here we must cling to faith," but he says, "Here we must cling to the man Christ." In such passages it is clear that the *humanitas Christi* or the *homo Christus* is not an indifferent matter for his Doctrine of Justification. But we may not overlook the fact that Luther then immediately follows with: "Then I will see his majesty as suited to my ability to grasp it."[18] So the *maiestas Dei* remains in the *homo Christus*. It is not a "*kenosis* theology," a theology of the self-emptying of Christ that we find here, as if the incarnation were the surrender of the majesty of God, and as though we find here only the simple man. Luther adds that this man is the revelation of God, in whom are hidden all the treasures of wisdom (Col 2:3). However, the suitability to my understanding of the revelation of God does not mean, say, that in it God subjects himself to the criterion of earthly knowledge. For the world, this is not just the revelation of the wisdom and the treasures hidden in God: "The world does not see it, for the world despises the man."[19] We have before us the very remarkable fact that on the one hand, regarding

---

16. H. J. Iwand refers here to the Luther quote that is highlighted in the highly praised theology of Theodosius Harnack (see p. 42) in his work, *Luther's Theology*, among others volume 2, p. 107, with particular focus on parallels in Luther. The places are: WA 10/1/1, 68, 6–7 (Church Book/Postille 1522. The Gospel in the story of Christ's birth in Luke 2, 1–14). It says: 'We cannot pull Christ so deeply into nature and into the flesh; it is still for us much more precious."

17. WA 40/1, 78, 8ff. (Gr. Galatians Commentary. 1531, Hs.)

18. WA 40/1, 79, 31–32. The Latin original says: "*Tum videbo maiestatem meo captui attemperatam.*"

19. WA 40/1, nn. 5–6.

the question of justification, Luther says that we may not proceed from the majesty of God but must stop looking for the majesty of God and direct our gaze toward the man Jesus. But then he says further that the majesty of God is also suited to my ability to grasp it. And lastly, he adds that this ability to grasp it is not an ability that I bring as a creature of this world, for the world does not understand it. This means: Christ does not suit himself to human conditions of experience, to history, or to sensuality. If that were so, then the question regarding the incarnation of God for Luther would be very easy, because then we could establish the historicity of the revelation from the incarnation of God. This too is continually attempted, but is false: *Mundus non videt, mundus respuit hominem* (the world does not see it, the world despises the man). In other words: The revelation of God in the man Jesus is at the same time his deepest veiling. And if he here is adapted to my ability to grasp, then my ability must mean something else than the disposition which I, as a man of this world, have for God. Luther never recognized such a disposition. We will rather see the reverse, that the fact that God becomes man, first of all, gives to me this ability to grasp. Human nature, which in this way is set in the situation of knowing God and understanding God, is not something to be derived from the concept of world. In a relatively singular passage on Genesis 2:7, Luther says: "Because man has been created in the image of the invisible God, so through this is described as hidden how we will hear that God will reveal himself to the world in the man Christ."[20] We will probably not be allowed to understand Luther in such a way that he gives a natural point of contact and would mark our sense and our flesh as the condition which God had to undergo if he wanted to reveal himself to us. Our sense, our flesh grasps nothing of this. On the contrary, the result of our natural experience is that God must be abstract; that is, that he does not appear in this human person. And when he does appear in this person, then we will continually have to go beyond this person, to find God behind him.

2. The Believers' Understanding of Existence

What is decisive for the incarnation of God is just this, that we do not go beyond this man Jesus; that he is the point beyond which there is nothing beyond; that here the man stops short, that thus the humanity of Jesus

---

20. WA 42, 66, 24ff. (Lectures on Genesis 1 1535–1545).

Christ is given by God, which we no longer transcend, while reason and rational religion continually aspire to transcend this humanity. This is first of all what is decisive in Luther's doctrine, that with the humanity of Christ a point is reached to which we can cling in faith. Whoever goes beyond this, whoever would come behind it, falls into an abyss. From this point we could unroll the entire problem of modern Christology. It was characteristic that the Enlightenment wanted to get behind the man Jesus. The entire quest for the historical Jesus is an attempt to do so. Luther always understood the Doctrine of the Two Natures in such fashion; namely, that this doctrine forbids our coming behind it. That is the rule. Only when one laid this doctrine aside did the question emerge in an entirely new way: Who stands behind this man Jesus?

I could also formulate the question this way: Is it decisive for faith that God became man, or can the faith that we have become righteous by grace alone also be assumed when this statement that God has become man, is more or less a dogmatic, metaphysical construction? Then, essentially, it would amount to nothing for the believer's understanding of existence. Faith's understanding of existence could then take comfort that the natural person thinks they become righteous before God by their actions, by their moral efforts, while the Christian knows that Christ has intervened for us, and we are blest by grace alone. By virtue of the Doctrine of Justification could we not simply lift all of Christendom from its artful base of dogmatics, from the Doctrine of the Trinity, the Doctrine of the Two Natures, and in this way transform it into the simple human understanding of existence? Then I need to bring nothing else to an understanding of Christian faith than the moral questions regarding my own life.

Luther was clearly from the school of thought that made an attempt to fathom the attributes and the nature of God, apart from the incarnate Son. In a theological supplement to a letter to Spalatin in the year 1519 (Letter No. 45), there is a famous testimony about this. In response to Spalatin's question regarding theological method Luther says," There is only the single path to knowing God, from which the doctors of the sentence commentaries have long turned away, who have fallen into speculations over the Godhead in the absolute sense, by leaving aside the humanity of Christ."[21] By this *humanitas Christi* Luther is not thinking,

---

21. WA Vol. 1, 328, 45ff. (translated by H. J. Iwand). With the *Doctores Sententiarum* Petrus Lombardus (1100–1160; see *RGG* V, 253) and his followers are meant. The decisive place in the letter is: "*omissa Christi humanitate*" (also 329, 1). To G. Spalatin

say, of historicity, but by the *humanitas* he is thinking of the form of God's revelation. The *humanitas Christi* remains in the *potentia Dei* (power of God), even where it is subject to earthly conditions of existence. In this way God will reveal himself. Thus, there are these two paths of the revelation: On the one side, the attempt to know God as he is, and on the other, to know God there where he became man. Prior to this passage, Luther says in the letter, "In all that we see having happened in Jesus, he leads us—that is Christ—leads us to love, to honor, and to glorify the Father, so that we do not, say, stop with the *humanitas Christi* by which the mercy of God is offered for us."[22] In the *humanitas Christi* we grasp the *misericordia Dei*. This does not mean that we can conclude from the *humanitas Christi* that God is merciful, but that here we meet the mercy of God. In the *humanitas Christi* the mercy of God is in our midst: "But by it we are then drawn into the invisible Father, since we marvel at him whom we see doing such a great thing with us through the humanity of Christ."[23] God is the one acting with us in this humanity. Thus, we see that what is at stake in the question of the *humanitas Christi* is the problem of the revelation. On the other hand, we could say that what is involved in the *crucifixus* is the problem of justification. Indeed, we are also justified by the incarnation of God, but the decisive theological element here is the concept of revelation. And naturally God also reveals himself in the *Deus crucifixus*, but the decisive theological element that developed from this is the element of justification.

3. The Antithesis of Reason

Now what does it mean that with regard to incarnation, we continually meet the antithesis of reason, the continual polemic against reason? This polemic is coherent with the fact that in scholasticism the attempt was made to assign to reason an immediate knowledge of God, while Luther recognized that we can no longer grasp the incarnation of God from such a concept of God. If, first of all, I have developed a concept of God independent of the incarnation of God, I thus believe I know who God is, and if I have developed this knowledge in detail, then it is with great difficulty that I find what it means that God has become man. I must

---

(1484–1545), a friend of Luther's, see *RGG* III, 221.

22. WA Letter 1, 328, 40ff.

23. WA Letter 1, nn. 43ff.

sacrifice *one* concept of God. Luther said that the concept of God that is innate in my reason is what I must leave outside if I want to enter the stall of Bethlehem. In rationalism it indeed was shown that with one's own concept of God one can only ethicize the incarnation: "So it is an art to know this king, that he is true God and man. But, as I have said, begin first at Bethlehem, and say: 'I know a king born of a virgin, who is truly of my flesh and blood.' When you have grasped him by the humanity, then go on to believe, then indeed the text will be found that the one born of a virgin is also born of God in eternity. Thus, you will indeed be safe among the hovels of the flesh and blood of this man. In summary: There is one single person and two results. The mother has given birth to a man, but not only a mere man, but she has also given birth to God." At this point Luther speaks of the fact that this man is twice born, from God and from the virgin: "So, whoever blasphemes this man, he blasphemes God; whoever prays to him prays to God, whoever believes in him, believes in God, whoever touches him, touches God, whoever strikes him strikes at God, whoever hears him hears God, whoever sees him sees God, whoever honors him honors God."[24]

From this point it is also clear why Luther places the scripture in the foreground, for this Jesus Christ in whom God has become man, is testified to us only by the scripture. He is not to be grasped by speculation. We always meet him *a posteriori* (in experience), never *a priori* (in reason). In another version of the sermon cited above, from January 6, 1532, it is clear what Luther means by his "beginning—from-above:" "But if you invert and begin with God, how he rules the world, how he burned Sodom and Gomorrah with hellish fire, and have inverted whether or not he was mistaken (explanation by H. J. Iwand as "predestined"), you will begin with the works of majesty on high and in this way want to know God and come to him, but then you will soon break your neck and be thrown down from heaven as happened in Lucifer's fall. For this means to begin from above and build the roof before you have laid the ground. So, if you want to proceed correctly, then you must begin from below and let God do what he does and say: 'I will not know him unless I have first known this Son of the virgin, both his person and office.'"[25] So, it means there is no concept of God which preceded this revelation of God in Jesus Christ, by which we can measure whether it is a revelation that we have in Jesus

---

24. WA 36, 79, 5- 18 (Sermon of 1532. January 6, on Micah 5:1).
25. WA 36, 78, 25- 35.

Christ. The revelation of God in Jesus Christ appears so authoritatively that it can be measured by no other concept of religion or morality. Here God has been revealed and nowhere else. For that reason, this concept of revelation dominates the entire scripture. Thus, what is at issue regarding the knowledge of God in Jesus Christ is that God will be known here; that in doing so he has defined his own revelation. Our knowledge of God shatters on the fact that we do not ask where God will be known, but we suppose that we could penetrate the mystery, the sanctuary of God, wherever we want, and that reason is a means toward knowing God whether he will be known or not. With this rational knowledge of God, we forget that we have to do with a God who goes his way with us, and that we first of all we must see and ask where his way goes. God is not simply a quantum, a being, as if this quantum had no way with us and the world. This is what Luther means when he speaks of the *maijestas Dei*. We are shattered on it because God is God. The *maijestas* first of all means that we must recognize the inaccessibility of God. Reason must understand that if God will not reveal himself, we would never be able to come to him. He is in heaven—and we are on earth.

It is necessary at this point to ask how far Luther has foreseen that rationalism and speculation about God necessarily turns into radical atheism, since he continually says, "We will fall into an abyss." From this point is exposed the problem of atheism: that the attempt to lay hold of God from God's point of view must be shattered and the person asking after God in this way wanders into nothingness, and that reason, which inquires in this way about the maiestas *Dei* must assert that God is nothing. God and nothingness are interchangeable concepts. This is the essence of atheism, by which the disobedient inquiry about God is punished. God and nothingness are such interchangeable concepts that conversely the one who encounters "the nothing" does not know whether or not he has encountered God (cf. the fever fantasies of the atheist Ivan Karamazov).[26] These "nothings," this nothingness, is a force injecting itself into one's spirit. And from that point one can only understand what the incarnation of God means.

---

26. Dostoyevsky, *Brothers Karamazov*, Part 4, Book 11, Chapter 9.

4. The Concept of Personality

In response to the question regarding the incarnation of God in Luther's theology we need to observe and consider that what is at issue here is not a concept of personality introduced by later "Protestantism." In his writing 'The Eternal in Man,' the Catholic philosopher Max Scheler says, "With the assumption of the personality of God, however, the manner is already determined by which a divine mediation (revelation) can only occur to humans: that is, through the agency of human persons."[27] The basic view that all religion grows in its history, and also decreases, and is purified and ruined according to the rule of personal example, and of the succession of leaders and followers—this basic view is essential to every theism. However, precisely this does not provide access to what Luther understands by the incarnation of God. It does not mean that here God meets us as a person and in Christianity we have a personalized religion (a notion common in modern thought), and it is not the antithesis to what Luther understands by incarnation. When we proceed from personalism we can naturally understand Christianity in terms of a founder's religion. In this way Schleiermacher (1768–1834) saw Jesus as a founder of religion. In this way the entire 19th century saw the history of revelation under the aspect of personalism, say, of prophetic religiosity, and in this way Julius Wellhausen (1844–1918) saw it in his description of the Old Testament.[28] In this way, also, the Quest for the Historical Jesus[29] saw it in its view of the New Testament. For this reason, it is with difficulty that we understand what Luther means by his idea of the incarnation: "So I take hold of God where he is the softest, and think: Oh, this is God's will and good pleasure, that which the Christ has done this for me. And at the sight, I experience the high, inexpressible mercy and the love of God in this, that he has put his dear child in disgrace, shame, and death for me. This friendly regard and lovely sight lift me. So, God must be known in Christ alone. For this reason, Christ himself says to his disciples: No one knows the Son but the Father, and no one knows the Father but the Son (Matt 11:27)."[30] Here it is very clear that Christ is

---

27. Scheler, *On the Eternal in Man*, Vol. I, 693. M. Scheler (1874–1928), famous philosopher, similar to E. Hüsserl's *Phenomenology*, rejected Kant's "formalist" ethic and supported a "material work ethic."

28. Wellhausen, *Israelitische und Jüdische Geschichte*, esp. Chapter 23 "The Gospel," 342–56.

29. Schweitzer, *Geschichte der Leben Jesus Forschung*, Vol. 2, 77/78 and 79/80.

30. WA 10/1/2, 277, 29ff. (Summer Book/Postille 1526. Gospel on Ascension

the place where God will give himself to me to know. Thus, if I wish to know God, I must also ask the other question about what, from his side, are the assumptions given that I can know him. My knowledge of God must at the same time be so led that it is obedient; that is, that I with my knowledge of God follow the will of God. If God were not willing to give me to know, then I could never know him. The fact that I make the attempt to know God from the notion that I am of one spirit with him (this is the basic idealistic position, that we are related to God, that he is spirit, and we are spirit), this old Gnostic thesis, the "enthusiasms" as it is called in the Smalcald Articles, "instituted in men by the old dragon,"[31] is reduced to the absurd by the incarnation of God in Jesus Christ. It is no accident that Luther develops in their entirety all these statements about the knowledge of God in his Son, Jesus Christ, in the incarnate one, as an exposition of the Gospel of John. Perhaps by doing so he has in his own way taken up the antithesis of John's Gospel to Gnosticism; that is, a knowledge of God which proceeds from and is based on the idea that we as spiritual creatures are related to God, and that as soon as we hark back to our spiritual relation to God, we have access to God. If this was the antithesis of the Johannine Gospel in its understanding of the incarnation of God in Jesus Christ, so in similar fashion is the antithesis in Luther's theology regarding a sheer knowledge of God by virtue of reason, as was usual in the general doctrine of God in high Scholasticism.

It is noteworthy that at the same time, Albrecht Ritschl ((1822–1889),[32] in taking up this thesis of Luther and understanding it as an anti-metaphysical thesis, holds firmly to it, and, of course, in the area of practical reason; namely, that we as moral-religious personalities have an original knowledge of God. Accordingly, he basically misunderstood Luther's position. For Luther it is not a matter of making impossible metaphysical statements about God, especially not Trinitarian and Christological statements. For Luther the issue is not to see the contact point in an inborn condition of reason, whether theoretical or practical, or whether it is speculative or has its effect in an ethical respect. For Luther what is at issue is something totally indifferent: that no one can fathom the mystery of God except that God will reveal himself, and of course

---

Sunday, John 15:26—16:4).

31. *The Smalcald Articles* 1537. 1538 Part III, Article VIII, "On Confession," last paragraph (WA 50, 246, 20ff; compare BoA 4, 317, 3ff.)

32. Ritschl, *Die christliche Lehre von der Rechfertigung und Versöhnung*; compare Vol. I, 164–65 and Vol. III, 6ff.

will reveal himself in such a way that in the revelation he remains the One he is.

The attempt to know God as he is on the basis of the human rational state can, as already mentioned above, turn into radical atheism. This means that one retains nothing in oneself but "the nothing;" that the nothing, as it were, is the reverse side of the *maiestas Dei*. Luther called this phenomenon *Deum annihilare*: to make a "nothing" of God. There is a capacity of the human to come near knowing God, which God reduces to nothing. We have an example of this from the effect of world history, that is, the end of the Hegelian philosophy. When Friedrich Hegel (1770–831) died, an atheism arose in German philosophy such as one to that point had never seen before. From this epoch of reversal of the Hegelian attempt to know God by virtue of reason, to address reason itself as divine, emerged a radical atheism which now understands God only as a human hypothesis—as the object of the human to come to oneself. The human had to think God's thoughts in order to be conscious of one's divine rationality (see also Ludwig Feuerbach (1804–1872), David Friedrich Strauss (1808–1874), Karl Marx (1818–1883) and Friedrich Nietzsche (1844–1900)). And against this background we must understand our German destiny of the last century.

Luther says, "If you do not want to fall into the net of the evil enemy, then let go of cleverness, conceit and subtleties, and cling to the divine word. Crouch in there and stay there like a rabbit in its hole in the wall. If you go out and engage in human chatter, then the enemy shall lead you and you will finally fall so that you do not know where reason, faith, God, and you yourself are. Believe me, as the one who has experienced such and has understood."[33] Here we see that in this question as well, Luther regards the human as subject to inner conflict, and that clinging to the word and the humanity of God in Jesus Christ is the refuge that the person seeks, which God has prepared for one against one's own ideas and doubts. Here one is saved from oneself, from one's own reason. Here is the point where one is no longer made captive to one's own reason, or to one's own opinions and judgments about God. The result of the new thought and understanding Luther describes as follows: "See, when the light, the reason, the old conceit, is dead, dark, and been changed into a new light, then must follow and be changed all of life and all human powers. For where reason goes, the will follows; where the will goes, love and

---

33. WA 10/1/1, 193, 11ff. (Postille 1522. The Christmas Gospel of John 1:1–14).

desire follow. And so, the whole person must creep into the Gospel and there become new; remove the old skin, as does the serpent when its skin becomes old. It seeks a narrow hole in the rocks, there it creeps through and removes its skin itself and leaves it outside in front of the hole. So, one must make one's way to the Gospel and God's word, and in comfort follow his promise. He will not lie. So one sheds the old skin, leaves one's light outside, one's conceit, one's will, love, desire, speaking, acting, and so becomes an entirely other new person who sees everything differently than before; who directs differently, judges differently, conceives differently, wills differently, speaks differently, loves differently, desires differently (what is meant is, perhaps, "gladly to do something with a new joy" J. Haar)."[34] Luther means that to know God is thus a process by which the person is not only conscious of themselves as a spiritual creature, but by which the person becomes another; also with respect to one's reason, becomes another. This means, at bottom, Luther appears to have been of the opinion that it is no paradox that God becomes man, for human nature can accommodate to God. It is thus not so that we would have to say God is hidden in this human nature. Human nature can, for its part, reveal God. And when Luther says that one cannot draw Christ deeply enough into the flesh, then he means just this: that here the flesh, human nature, becomes a bearer of the revelation, naturally, only by the fact that God condescends on behalf of God. To "draw Christ into the flesh" thus not only means to humiliate Christ, but at the same time also means to exalt him.

5. The Incarnation of God is no Paradox

In conclusion it may be said that what is decisive is that we make it too easy to understand Luther's description of the incarnation of God by using the modern concept of personalism. It is not so that God becomes a person here, that the absolute God meets us here in personalized form (thus, all liberalism). In himself God is a person but does not first become a person in such fashion that his absolute idea is concretized in a person. I am always suspicious of people who speak of the "historicity" of the revelation and what they mean by it. At bottom I believe they think Christianity is a personalistic religion in contrast to the pantheistic. However, in so doing, something foundational in Luther's understanding

---

34. WA 10/1/1, 23, 7ff.

of the incarnation of God is overlooked, which is this: that God assumes human nature, the *humanitas*. And, because we ourselves are all bearers of this nature, for that reason we are together ennobled, dignified, and bestowed with grace together with him. That God becomes man and does not appear to us as an angel, that he makes use of the revelatory of a human in order to reveal himself to us, as if he were mute in himself, and needed human nature so that he could make known his mystery—all these are modern reinterpretations. This has nothing to do with Luther's doctrine of the incarnation of God but comprises an entirely different understanding of *humanitas*. The *humanitas* as such is suitable as a nature for God to assume; yet God does not break nature apart but makes use of his creation. It is no paradox then that he appears to us in a man. What is wonderful is that this man in whom he appears to us is without sin; that in this man God is present, that he puts an end to sin and death. We are included in this human destiny. The other is that we must be on our guard against thinking that in this way God has accommodated himself to our capacity for understanding; to our sensuous nature, to our historical-temporal existence. As though now our senses were suited to lay hold of God! Here, of course, we speak of a paradox. For this reason, it will always be a paradox that God encounters us as man, because reason always expects that God meets us as spirit. Reason always wants to seek God behind the man.

Who Are His Own?

1. "His Own" and the "Protestants"

Luther again asked: "Who are his own?" I believe that the Reformation arose from this question. This question became the criticism of the Church and led to the thesis: Those who regard themselves as his own are not! Once more we will have to ask how Luther defined "his own." Is there a real human life behind Luther's teaching? Are not "his own" also the "Protestants?" Are they not, or were they not, in orthodoxy, in fanaticism, in pietism, and further in idealism and in the nationalism of the 19th century? In the years after 1933, when the "Confessing Church "reflected on word and scripture," we have all been able to speak with less concern about these questions. At that point in time, we were still somehow proud of this "Protestantism." In an essay by K. Holl titled, "The cultural significance of the Reformation," it appears as if a line leads directly from the Reformation to the "Protestantism" of the 19th and 20th century. Here Luther acts as a forerunner of Kant, as a forerunner of "practical reason," and of the moral-religious personality.[35] But here we must draw a thick line. The opinion that we can identify Protestantism with what Luther called "his own" was a deception. This deception brought National Socialism to light. It is an historical phenomenon of special significance that precisely the theology coming from Luther was especially susceptible to National Socialism. National Socialism made something evident that is ultimate. National Socialism was certainly no creation of Catholicism, and not of Socialism, but it was a creation of "Protestantism." It derives intellectually from this root, is intellectually its result, so that today we are asked again: Who are his own? What does the Reformation mean by "his own"? It should be clear: As Protestants, we are not his, nor have we been for a long time heirs of the Reformation. However, from such a distinction much good can still come.

2. Christian Existence according to Luther

What is peculiar or unique in Luther's definition of Christian existence? I would offer two characteristics: a) the one characteristic is that for Luther, Christian existence has been made unobservable; and b) the other characteristic is that each person in an inexplicable way nevertheless understands and knows him/herself to be a Christian.

With the concept of the unobservability of the Christian life, there still is, of course, not much said, since the Middle Ages had also known this unobservability. The Christian lived in the unseen, in the world to come, in hope. It is the metaphysical world in which the Christian lives, in which one also has one's "being." But that is not the unobservability as defined in Luther's theology. And here emerges what is specific, as perhaps not at all yet defined, which awaits an entirely new analysis and definition, namely, the fact that the being of the Christian cannot be measured by his/her action, because being is absolutely decreed ahead of action: "Not that we do what is righteous are we righteous, but by the fact that we are righteous we do what is righteous."[36] This formula is often

---

35. Holl (I, 47, n. 32) 468–543, especially the explanations on page 528 where Holl on the concept of "community" (as a deeper definition of society, which was up until then a "leading concept within western philosophy") suggests that Kant's "moral imperative" has its roots in Luther.

36. WA 56, 255, 18–19 (Scholien) = Fi (Scholien) 91, 26–27 (translated by H. J.

applied, but when we are clear that with this formula what was new in Luther's theology began, then it becomes clear what this theology has meant and should mean within the space of Christianity: Am I not then by nature, or am I then not at all, what I do? This does not consider that I do something not "natural" to me; that I do external, ceremonial, traditional things. And when, as Protestantism has often thought, an attitude is involved, where the issue is that which I do comes from the heart and is noble, then by this nothing at all is added. This would be a radicalization of the ethical. It would be precisely the same as Kant expresses it: that not legality, but morality, decides.[37] Then, at best, Protestants would be those people whose intentions are more noble than, say, the Catholics. Rather what is at issue is the action in which I would seek and find my own life. What is at stake is that one stakes one's being in particular deeds, in action as such. "Do it and you will live!" (Luke 10:28). Luther understood Paul in such fashion that this sentence is no longer practicable. We do not gain access to life by way of the *opera*. For that reason, too, is the denial of freedom. The *opera* comprises the area of human possibilities. In this area there is no life for you any longer—this is what Luther means. As a result, every definition of holiness falls. The *sanctus*, the holy one, is now no longer to be specified objectively. When in the area of particular *opera* Christian existence becomes objectifiable, then we can say in the practice and imitation of these *opera* I arrive at Christian existence. Then this Christian existence has a visible form, a distinguishable form of existence, and of course must not always be like the existence of other people; but it can, of course, be my own existence by which I distinguish myself. And here Luther maintains that every conclusion that a person draws from "doing" to "being," is a failure. He sets the works, the *opera*, under entirely new categories, and does not see in them a criterion by which to judge one's own being. In this way one ceases to be one's own judge: "What will the devil do where he finds such a bare soul which will answer him neither regarding sin nor holiness. There one must let go all one's cunning, that is, both puffing up sin and scorning good works,"[38] are two mutually corresponding sides. By "scorning good works" Luther means that the devil leads one to the assumption that one has done nothing good; that everything good one had done in life is lost and appears

---

Iwand).

37. Compare I. Kant, *Critique of Practical Reason*, Part I, Book 3, Section 3 (Akademie Edition Vol, 5, 71ff.) etc.

38. WA 31/1, 150, 11ff. (Lecture on Psalm 118. "Das schöne Confitemini," 1530).

in vain. By no means is it so that from the outset a radical consciousness and feeling of sin derives from God. It is precisely the reverse. With "puffing up sin" Luther means that one has no criterion for the size or the smallness of guilt. When we deal with such things one is a great fool and falls into the devil's hand. Of course, we also know this Christian devil; he often actually speaks from the chancel, and then leaves people with nothing good. And many people find that to be correct.

What is special about the Reformation is that in it the recognition dawns that the entire concept of the *opus* fails over against the reality of death and sin. Luther says," So you see now, who are the greatest enemies of the gospel, that is, the work-sanctifiers. They want to be rich in works. But the gospel intends that they should be poor."[39] This means there is no peace between the Gospel and the work-sanctifiers, no grace, no atonement! "But Christ must let himself be crucified beneath it; for he and his own must stick in the squeeze." "His and his own" continually appears in Luther. "He and his own must stick in this squeeze between the Gospel and works. And so is pressed down and ground like wheat between two millstones: The stone below is the quiet, peaceful, and immovable Gospel, the stone above the works while the masters rage and wreak havoc."[40] So, this means for humans that works are continually an inner conflict. What Luther achieves is that here is a certainty that cannot be cancelled. That is what is incredible in the theology of Luther: where this is understood, there one is blessed. It is the final certainty when works no longer make up the definition of my existence, but what is determinative for my existence is that Christ is for me. "Christ and his own"—then Christ himself would have to be lost if I am lost. The identity of myself with him over against sin and death is so secured, that the person stands in superiority over against these realities which, according to psychological or human criteria, do not exist at all. Luther says, "Now whoever is under this heaven cannot sin or be in sin. For there is a heaven of grace infinite and eternal. And if anyone sins or falls, they do not fall from the same heaven, unless one would not want to remain beneath it, but rather go to hell with the devil, as unbelievers do. And whether sin can be felt right away, or death blackens its teeth and the devil howls, then here there is much more grace which reigns over all sin, and much more life which reigns over death, and much more of God who reigns over all devils; that

---

39. WA 10/1/2, 160, 22ff. (Advent Book/Postille 1522. Gospel for 3 Sunday in Advent, Matt 11:2–10).

40. WA 10/1/2, 161, 3ff.

such sin, death, and the devil in this realm is nothing else but as dark clouds under the physical heaven, which indeed hide the heaven for a time."[41] This means that viewed from Christ, death and sin must resolve into a nothing; not from within me, not from the *opera*. If I find my position in the ethical, from my *opera*, then these realities remain realities and I will never get out from a quite specific dualism and never get to the certainty of faith.

3. Christian Freedom Regarding Works

From here we can first determine that with our entire "ethic of conviction" (German: *Gesinnungsethic*) we have depended upon a Protestant type, which harks back to the Middle Ages and to a Catholic type of piety. We no longer understand what kind of person the Reformation really had in mind. And because we no longer understand it, for that reason so much for us in Germany is askew. There is much talk of faith and Christianity, but this talk no longer corresponds to reality. Perhaps orthodoxy is still there, a pure doctrine, and there are perhaps still a few practices and gestures there! Today in fact, in order to become conscious of one's Christianity, one absolutely needs Communism. Should this no longer exist, when we ask people what it means for them that they are Christians, they would no longer know. We "need" the war against Communism, otherwise our entire "Christian Republic" loses its actual self-definition. That is the real cancerous disgrace. It affects not only us: "God, I thank you, that I am not as this one there," is the primary formula.[42] Here Christian existence is always understood by specific deeds, and from that point the distinction is drawn. And it would nevertheless have to be understood from this that here a man appears who stands over against his works in the superiority of freedom. That is the Christian as he/she is born from Luther's doctrine of justification. That the works lie at one's feet is the ethical definition of freedom in Luther, not merely the theological. And, likewise, the person is free from responsibility for their works. One cannot at all be responsible for them if toward them one is not free. From that viewpoint we would have to put the question how this freedom, seeing that in Christ one is lord over death and sin, relates to the concept of freedom in Kant's "practical reason." For Luther I am in any case not free

---

41. WA 31/1, 245, 22ff. (On Psalm 117, 1530).
42. Reference to Luke 18:11.

CHRISTOLOGY

in the moment in which the works, good or evil, define my being. I am then prisoner of my own deeds, walled in the tower of my deeds like a slave: "When you see what you do, then you have already lost the name of Christian. It is certainly true that we should do good works, help others, counsel, and give, but for this reason no one is called a Christian, and for this reason also there is no Christ."[43] And further: "To make pious people does not belong to the Gospel, it only makes Christians. There is rather a being Christian distinct from being pious. One can indeed be pious, but not a Christian. A Christian knows nothing to say of his/her piety, finds in oneself nothing good or pious; if one will be pious then one must look around for another and alien piety."[44] This then is the criticism of the ideal of piety during the waning Middle Ages. Here it is clear that this theology no longer identifies being Christian and holy. In other words: if you want to know what a Christian is, then you must not investigate the area of piety.

If being a Christian no longer is thought dependent on works, but that this entire relationship is turned around, then we can no longer make being Christian dependent on being pious. Here it dawns on one why a Reformation is arrived at, for here disgraces and lacks are not healed, but here the ideal is rejected which in all the Middle Ages determined the shaping of existence: "Therefore one is not called a Christian because one does so much; there is something higher there, but because one takes, draws something from Christ, and allows only him to give. When one no longer takes from Christ, then one is no longer a Christian. So, the name of the Christian is only to be in the taking and not in the giving or doing, and that one takes nothing from no one except from Christ. If you notice what you are doing, then you have already lost the name of Christian."[45]

4. Law and Gospel

There is much dispute over the relationship of law and Gospel, but we must not overlook the fact that by faith in the gospel Luther meant I truly fulfill the law. That is God's commandment. The Gospel is not simply merely offered to me, and says to me, "when you need it, then take it," but

---

43. WA 10/1/2, 431, 6ff. (Summer Postille 1526. Gospel for the 24 Sunday after the Trinity, Matt 9:18–26).

44. WA 10/1/2, 430, 30ff.

45. WA 10/1/2, 431, 1ff.

it is also demanded of me. If you do not believe it, then you are lost. Lack of faith must have as its result that one imagines that by works one creates one's goodness. In other words, with these reflections the result is always that this division of being and doing is only the reflex, the reflection, the fruit of faith in Christ. The natural man, as he is, must judge his being on the basis of his doing. In this sense, we cannot learn Protestantism as a lifestyle because then it becomes a laxity, a libertinism, and it leads to the point that one says, "In my action I may remain back behind the law, but in my inner attitude I meant what is right." This is the Protestantism which has developed to the point where it detaches this definition of Christian existence from faith in Christ. Luther always states that faith can never live by itself, but only from the fact that it takes hold of Christ. Seen from this point of view the true Christians are a judgment on the false saints. This means that there, in the true Christians, the false saints are disarmed, shamed, disappointed, rejected, and in continual war with a contra-type, which as "saints before the world" are on the scene. It is not so that the true saints, thus his own, who live by faith, now simply enter on the scene, as if the entire world waited for them and will be happy and joyful that finally these Christians appear. Then they would neither be his own, but we would make of this an ethical, cultural value. The doctrine of justification alone in Jesus Christ will have to suffer much in the world. We could also state it in this way: The doctrine of justification alone by grace is much preached, proclaimed, believed, lived vaguely—but is valued as orthodox—for example, by the liberals. Luther does not understand it in this way. This doctrine, when rightly understood (although and precisely because it is orthodox), will be made subject to many internal conflicts and rejections. The *doctrina* shoulders the destiny of Christ himself. Whoever truly proclaims this doctrine cannot avoid the destiny Christ has and bears. It is, so to speak, not without a history in the world. We cannot put this doctrine in an abstract space of dogmatics. Paul was absolutely not able to develop the doctrine that Christ has died for us other than by dismantling Jewish theology. The result was war, and for this reason the doctrine must suffer. Perhaps this determination goes back to Jesus himself. Jesus himself must first of all have fought his way through this world to dismantle the righteous, since without the dismantling of the righteous, of the results of late Jewish piety, he could not bring the lost sheep of the house of Israel to God.

But we will never arrive at the purpose of God in Jesus Christ if we believe we gain access to it by Christians, who are humans. Whether

Christianity be described as Catholic, as Protestant, whether we do it with law and gospel as the Lutherans do, or whether we do it with gospel and law, as the Reformed—it is all in vain. All this is at bottom anthropology; namely, the attempt, the belief that one can conclude from the effects to the cause. Today we have already come so far that we say, even if there is nothing behind it (behind so-called "Christianity"), the effect is still so marked that we at least retain the illusion of "what is behind." This simply means religion must be retained by the people. Christianity may forever still be the best religion, but then our whole Church is nothing but a great mausoleum. We are not to understand Luther in this way.

5. What Does it Mean: "To Put On Christ"?

Luther has not given us a new Christian type but has wanted to make clear the righteousness of God in Jesus Christ: "As many of you are baptized into Christ have put on Christ" (Gal 3:27). Luther addresses this (in a sermon from the Kirchenpostille of 1522) in, "What does that really mean, to put on Christ?" He replies, "The unbelievers have replied very rapidly here that it means to follow Christ and be like his example. But in this way, I would like to put on Saint Peter, Paul, and all the saints, and nothing special would be said of Christ. Therefore, we let faith speak here which Saint Paul endearingly describes with this word: put on. It is evident that they are baptized there, have never yet followed Christ before, rather in baptism they have begun to follow after Christ. Therefore, Christ must be put on before ever one follows him. And it must be an entirely other thing to put Christ on—to follow the example of Christ. It is a spiritual putting on in conscience, and thus moves toward the point that the soul puts on Christ and all his righteousness as its own possession and trusts in it as though it had itself done such and deserved it . . . That is the way and the nature of the right faith."[46]

What is remarkable is now—and perhaps to be explained a bit from mysticism—that Luther always conceives this relationship of the person to Christ in total isolation. It is quite false to construe this relationship of the person to Christ as an I–Thou relationship. First of all, this person must be entirely alone. This means also, the hearing of the word in which Christ meets me occurs in a space which can no longer be made conceivable by my usual relation to existence. There is no analogy for

---

46. WA 10/1/1, 475, 3ff. (Epistle for New Year's, Gal 3:23–29).

this hearing. When I say to someone, 'You must listen to Christ as a child listen to its father,' or also as a friend listens to a friend, these are all false definitions. There is no analogy from human fellowship, from estate, society, order, which would extend to what occurs when one listens to the voice of God in Jesus Christ and is drawn to this voice. Everyone who attempts from such analogies to make clear the word of God in Jesus Christ has still never heard it. This hearing is an extraordinary existence, an original existence. We could also say: the one who hears this voice encounters one's origin, hears oneself called in one's origin, hears the one from whom I exist. That is the "desert" in the language of medieval mysticism.[47] From that perspective then results the meaning of the Word for Luther. He can often say: Our righteousness does not come from our acting, but from our hearing. But this does not, as was later thought in orthodoxy, consist in going to church.

This being exposed, being singled out for hearing the Word, this being-taken-in by Christ into the "desert" is, in turn, inner conflict. But what is decisive is that Luther does not understand this inner conflict as coming from the outside. It is not so that we have a consciousness of God in our soul, and now, by the fact that we are organized as body and soul, have inner conflict, because we as spiritual beings must live in a finite world. Inner conflict is not the result of the fact that we as spirit-gifted creatures are "thrown" into the world—that is not Luther. But rather: for Luther the person is in inner conflict because the person is conflicted by God. The inner conflict is given because we have to do with God. And precisely being conflicted by God means that works profit nothing. In other words, the fact that one is an active person profits nothing before God, by such one cannot be saved. Inner conflict, when it comes from God, means precisely that the destiny and experiences of the person are not external, but come from God, and indicates that we cannot deal with God by our works, but can deal with God only when we let all our works go. In recent Protestantism one attempted to conceive and understand the relation of person and work, thus Christian existence, from the human viewpoint. As if Christian existence could be made intelligible by itself! The Reformation is just not a new ethos. It is much more. A change in ethos is naturally connected with it, but that is secondary.

---

47. See here also Ueberweg, *Grundriss der Geschichete der Philosophie*, 566, the meaning of the expression "desert" and "desert environment" in Meister Eckehart.

6. The Concept of "Overflowing Love"

It has been said that we can distinguish a twofold evaluation of works. On the one side, we have the external work forced upon the person from the outside. The legalist, so it has been thought, is necessarily unfree and does something with which he does not inwardly agree. And the other is the original, free work, done from inmost inclination. This has also been called the "ethics of intention." It is thought that the whole difference between Catholicism and Protestantism proceeds from this contrast. And that is a basic misunderstanding of what the Reformation wanted but, of course, in Luther there are innumerable quotations which can be interpreted in this way. There is, for example, the concept of "overflowing love." On this subject Karl Thieme (1862–1932) has written an important treatise in which what is decisive for Luther is overlooked.[48] Free overflowing love is specifically not natural; it does not simply flow out in the sense of a human, moral autonomy. In an important sermon on 1 Timothy 1:5–7, Luther developed this concept: "See, that means a love flowing from the heart, not carried into it, for it finds nothing in that, so as to create it. But because he/she is a Christian and holds to the Word, which in itself is totally pure, the same makes his/heart so pure and so full of upright love that he/she lets his/her love flow out to everyone and does not allow itself to be hindered, whether the person wants it or not."[49] Luther thus distinguishes between a "ladled" love, conditioned from outside, dependent on its object, and a "flowing" love which flows out of itself and has its source in itself. This love takes its activity, its being alive, not from the object, otherwise it would have to cripple it when it meets an object unworthy of love, such as a sick person or a sunken, fallen lost one. It would sink along with wherever it burst upon the evil, the dark, the spoiled. The genuine good work would therefore then always be related to that autonomous flowing love; that is, it would have to have its origin in itself. So far, we can entirely go along with what modern Protestantism has said about the distinction between the genuine and the non-genuine work. But nevertheless, the matter lies in the reverse. The Christian is not measured by the genuineness, the originality of his/her action; the distinction does not at all proceed from the works, but the work is measured by the Christian. "Because he/she is a Christian

---

48. Thieme, *Die sittliche Triebkraft des Glaubens. Eine Untersuchung zu Luthers Theologie.*

49. WA 36, 360, 22ff. (Sermon for November 4, 1532).

and holds to the Word, which in itself is wholly pure, it also makes the heart so pure." Here, therefore, at issue is that the Word opens the heart in this sense, so that genuine love flows forth from it. There is nothing original in the person, but something original in the word. The origin of this flowing love lies in the Word and not in the originality of human existence. This originality of human existence is something by which the Word is mediated to me. And "makes his/her heart so pure . . . that he/she allows his/her love to flow out to everyone." It is thus not a purity of the heart which we encounter in the person and by which it is born, but it is that pure love which is created by God by a word. Only the heart holding to the Word, that is, faith is a pure heart. Or, as Luther says, "A servant, when he works and neither sees nor thinks further than this: My heart gives me my reward, for which reason I serve him, otherwise I do not see him, etc.—he/she has not a pure heart or opinion, for he does not serve without a bit of bread. When that ceases, then he stops. But if he/she is devout and a Christian, then he/she is thus minded: 'I will not serve so that my master gives me or does not give me, is pious or evil, etc. but for the reason that God's word stands here and says to me: You servant, be obedient to your master as Christ himself (Eph 6:5).' Then it flows of itself from the heart so that it has clung to the Word and values what I am speaking there: 'Come now, I will serve my master and take my reward.' But this shall be my highest thing, that I do it, that I serve my dear God and Lord Christ who has promised it to me and knows that it well pleases him. There you see a genuine work from a pure heart."[50] This means, if God's word were not there, then it would not meet me as a living word, inviting me, making the deed coming forth from God possible for me, then there would not at all be a love that flows. We could actually say: Here Law and Gospel coincide. Here the word of God calling me is identical with the desire for the deed. Insofar as the work is the deed which corresponds to the call of God, which is the response to God's call to me, then that by which I respond to this call, insofar as it is a work—does not justify the person—but conforms to justification and faith in the person.

From that point it is clear that faith is not an additional capacity in the person, as if I could act without faith and could act in faith, or, as if I could at all decide for faith, as though I can decide for an action or inaction. Rather, faith is identical to the new existence: "Faith is not the human illusion and dream which some regard as faith, and when they

---

50. WA 36, 360, n. 41ff.

see that no betterment of life nor good works follow, and yet can hear and speak much about faith, they fall into error and say that faith is not enough, one must do works, if we should be pious and holy."[51] So they fall, as Luther also says, out of the doctrine into life. Now they believe on the basis of ethics, of love, in order to try to aid the matter. But it does not at all lie in ethics, it does not at all life in life, but it lies in faith. Your faith is not faith—and for that reason they wait in vain for it to bring forth fruit. The tree is not good and therefore one cannot expect any good fruit from it. That the person then stumbles into ethics in order to correct what in truth would have to be settled by faith, is his/her basic error. Luther says, "But faith is a divine work in us, which changes us and births us anew from God, John 1 (vs. 13), kills the old Adam and makes us entirely different persons in heart, courage, mind, and all powers, and brings with it the Holy Spirit. Oh, it is a living, creative, active, mighty thing about faith that (it) is impossible that it should not work good without respite. It also does not ask whether good works are to be done, but before one asks, they have done them and are always doing them. But whoever does not do such works, is a faithless person, tiptoes and looks about oneself for faith and good works, and knows neither what faith or good works are, and prattles with many words about faith and good works. Faith is a living, bold confidence in God's grace, so certain, that it would die for it a thousand times. And such confidence and knowledge of divine grace makes one glad, cheeky, and merry towards God and every creature, which the Holy Spirit does by faith."[52]

That is the love which overflows, that is the faith that makes us glad, "cheeky and merry toward God." We will thus not be able to say without further ado that faith is a human attitude. For faith is also that which reshapes a person, toward which the person is passive. Faith is no act; works are an act. Luther often emphasized that faith is actually a passion, an enduring of something done to me: I cannot do otherwise. My heart gains such confidence in God that it can do nothing else—and in this confidence it is unconquerable. Thus, at issue regarding the relation of person and work is not at all the contrast between works of the law and an ethic of attitude, but that the commandment of God is the only principle of my action, the only motive for the deed. To live by faith means that God's commandment makes the person a doer of his deed; that if there

---

51. WA DB 7,8, 30ff. (The New Testament 1522. Commentary on Paul's Epistle to the Romans).

52. WA DB 10, 6ff.

were no commandment of God this person could do nothing. A person who thus does everything he/she does, does it because God demands it—that would be the person who lives wholly by faith.

Basically, we can say that whoever encounters the commandment of God by a right faith, has already done the work, before going to work. Faith fulfills the commandment of God. That is the thing. Thus, the action, the work of the Christian is already fulfilled, is already done, before the work occurs. For it is not the works that fulfill the commandment, rather faith fulfills the commandment: the works are only what comes after, what corroborates. Therefore, works always limp behind; they are never perfect. They are only a *signum* (sign) of the fact that faith is present. In the writing "the Freedom of a Christian, 1520" it is stated: "The works . . . are a dead thing . . . but here we seek something not done as works, but done on its own, is master of the work, honors God and does the work. That is none other than the faith of the heart."[53] Faith is master of the work. Luther does not move from the analogy of natural life, that the person is the actor and the work his/her work, but he asks: Who then is the doer? The work must have an independent doer, a work-master. The good work is always justified in faith, whether it succeeds or not, whether the person brings it about or shatters on it. The person never receives his/her justification from the success or the failure of a work. Then, of course, he/she would again made dependent on the work. That is, so far as I understand, the new understanding of "person and works."[54] This relationship just cannot be reduced to the relation between person and an act, as, for example, in the Catholic doctrine of sanctification.[55] Faith in this sense is not an actor as, for example, in the new Protestant conception, an ethic of intention. Naturally, it also never means: if only the intention was good, then also the failure of the work amounts to nothing. It is not a matter of intention, not a matter of good opinion, but the fact that faith fulfills the commandment before it is a matter of keeping the commandment, and since, where faith fulfills the commandment, the work cannot be absent, every work which we do—not, say, a specific work—is the fulfillment of this faith. In this way, as we will yet see, the ability to define good works is at an end. It is totally non-Lutheran to say, "When you intend to do this or that good work, then you must believe," as if faith were a kind of precondition. In the moment I believe, the good

---

53. WA 7, 26, 23ff. (On the Thirteenth) = BoA 2, 16, 26ff.
54. See also for other places the section in H. J. Iwand NW IV, p. 56–80.
55. See e.g. Möhler, *Symbolik*, 175ff.

work loses its name; loses its definition. It could then be that the not-bringing-about of this good work is precisely the good work; that I must do something quite different, be led on completely different paths than on those I had taken before. Faith leads to the deed, to doing, but this doing is no longer determinative.

7. The Self-Chosen Works

The classical document regarding the dismantling of self-selected works, thus of a basic attitude which proceeds from sketching an ideal of one's own sanctity, piety, goodness, and truth, and to live according to it, is contained in "*De votis monasticis iudicium*," 1521 (A judgment on the monks' vow),[56] one of the most significant writings composed by Luther. Luther breaks with the monk's oath not because he cannot fulfill it, but for the reason that otherwise he cannot be subject to God's commandment. God's commandment leads him out of a life beneath his own oaths; leads him out of the cloister into the world. The commandment of God leads him to the certainty of faith, to his Christian existence. The person, so Luther means, cannot at all exist under the commandment of God when he intends to live by his own "oaths" of sanctity, of godliness, and of perfection. Thus, at issue is not that he reduces piety to the commandments of God, that he dismantles a monkish, superlative superstructure over the "commandments of God," and that he retraces the way back to day-to-day, daily work. The opinion that Luther dismantles the ideal and by it makes possible a broad practical Christianity, is pure nonsense.[57] This is now what is unheard-of in Luther's theology: This life is disobedience toward God and all the works in it are lost. God's commandment, the Decalogue, wrenches the person out of their self-chosen commands, out of the sublime products of their own piety. There is thus no quantitate difference between commandment and oath, as if the oaths transcended the commandments of God, being there only for a few special

---

56. WA 8, 573–669 = BoA 2, 188–298.

57. Here we find the following remarks in the raw manuscript published by F. Wolf, that is doubtless by H. J. Iwand: "One would at least wish, that this would disappear at last from the minds of Protestant preachers. The laity are even worse. From the piety of the laity, we get all of the problems in the church. They constantly live in "natural" theology. And they see to it that the pastors lose their way and the church its teaching. The constantly strive towards works like a camel to water. The natural urge of man is to think: 'If I just do something, then everything will be different; everything will get better.'"

elect. There is rather a qualitative difference: the monk's oath leads to self-chosen sanctity. To this oath indeed also belongs the ideal of poverty. It is quite striking that among the orders in the church that were edited during the Reformation, the ideal of poverty is also combatted. "Poverty" (*paupertas*) is no ideal; it is not willed by God. From that point emerges the high evaluation of work. Poverty is not the expression of an existence that is true, or more conformable, to God. On this matter the Reformers are fully isolated between the Russian-Orthodox and Roman-Catholic Church; in both there exists the monkish ideal of the Christian existence. Luther gives up the monkish life. He recognized that when the person, according to a self-chosen lifestyle, lives an "angel-like sanctity," the call, the commandment of God dies away into nothing. The commandment of God no longer finds a "doer" since the doer has taken flight to his/her own ideals of piety, purity, and sanctity.

I believe that on the basis of the antithesis of "oath" (*votum*) and "commandment of God" (*praeceptum Dei*) the entire writing "On the Monk's Oath," and also the way in which Luther deals with it, must be understood. He intends to eliminate the "human doctrines and hypocritical, superstitious usages which God has not commanded."[58] The bulwark on which everything stands, as Luther says in that writing, is the word from Rom 4:23: "But what does not come from faith, that is sin."[59] "Oaths" cannot at all occur from faith, for they are indeed not commanded. They can only occur from human striving after piety, sanctity, after being good. This "self-chosen being good" is Luther's problem. That is the great seduction—not the fact that we cannot keep God's commands, as one later broadly described it—as if it were the essence of Christian existence that one even once was not able to fulfill God's commandment! Certainly, we will fail. But we must fail because the self-chosen piety is a false ideal and, as such, idealizes disobedience toward God. Therefore, it is no accident that Luther opens this writing with an address to his father, that is, with the fourth commandment, where he reminiscences on what his father said to him about his resolve to enter the cloister because he had an experience that called him to it: "If only that was not an illusion or a trick (*praestigium*)!"[60] Luther means this resolve to enter the cloister was rightly judged by his father. At that time God spoke to him through his father. Luther states regarding this sentence: "This word penetrated,

---

58. See WA 8, 574, 18f = BoA 2, 189, 34–35.

59. WA 8, 591, 9f = BoA 2, 209, 9–10.

60. WA 8, 574, 2 = BoA 2, 189, 14.

so to speak, as though God spoke through your mouth (in me) and sunk into my inmost."[61] Moreover, Luther means that at that time he took this step into the cloister by transgressing the fourth commandment. Looking back, it is clear to him whither the commandment of God had wanted to lead him and for this reason, God stuck him in the cloister so that what occurred there he had to experience and suffer, so that opportunity was not given unbelievers to say vaingloriously to their "future enemy" (*in futurum adversarium*): 'You damn what you don't' know."[62]

Whoever has desire for his/her own sanctity will never have desire for the Lord's commandment; for him/her the commandment will always be a burden. It all breaks apart here. At issue during this entire period from 1518–1522, in which the writing "On the Monk's Oath" appears, was involved the continual wrangling over the Decalogue alongside it its exposition. The Small and Large Catechism contain the fruit of this entire effort. In dismantling the monk's oath, the understanding of God's commandment arises in a new way. Here there would still be infinitely many questions to discuss, that is, insofar as here the claim of "natural theology" becomes visible and not as if it were the approach to the commandments of God as one later understood it, but insofar as the commandments of God no longer demand of me that which not everyone who rightly inquires of his/her own reason would have to recognize as true and good and right; namely, "Do unto others what you would have them do unto you."[63] This briefly summarizes the fact that the good work is nothing exceptional, so that the person would have to say: really all of us would have to live in this way. At the very depth what stands behind this is: The good work to which the commandment of God leads me will be something so self-evident, say, so unaccented, simple, that it speaks a language everyone understands.

Indeed, today we suffer from the fact that we make heroes of martyrs and of the people of the "Confessing Church." I have anxiety over the heroic epics of the witnesses of the "Confessing Church." That will still be more horrible than that came out of the heroic epics of the First World War; for that was only an idealizing of a military and a soldier's heroism. This would now indeed be an idealizing of Christian heroism. From this

61. WA 8, 574, 2f = BoA 2, 189, 14ff.

62. See WA 8, 574, 28–29 = BoA 2, 190, 6ff.

63. This phrase is contained in almost all world religions. It is generally known as the "Golden Rule." See, among others, in the Hebrew writing Tob 4:16; Matt 7:12; Luke 6:31.

idealizing of the martyr much has to be understood of what went wrong in the churches; namely, the idea of exceptional sanctity. That has never been the case in Protestantism. The martyr is the person who deals with reality as it is. The person in inner conflict is the martyr, not the one to be glorified; the person who is unveiled in all his/her weakness, the person by whom it is actually discovered what the person is. Luther expresses this in the writing "On the Monk's Oath" also in this way: Those who apply to themselves a self-chosen sanctity assume ownership of the name of God. "That is the blasphemy of the name of the Lord before the heathen so that the holiness and hallowing occur under another than under the name of God and is ascribed to him," as if the oaths hallowed their followers, "and as if it were holy to follow them while in fact only the name of the Lord hallows and to follow him is holy."[64] By this Luther means that self-chosen sanctity is always bound up with the fact that by it the person makes a name for him/herself, and thus the *nomen Dei* (the name of God) is stricken out." That they see your good works and praise you (oneself!)" (Matt 5:16 where it says: "praise your Father in heaven"), that the person as witness must appear in a spoiled, sunken, godless world as witness to the piety which by it makes for itself a name. So as the pious Pharisee (Luke 18:9–14) in a sunken, dissolving world displayed himself and preserved the fathers' place in hourly prayer, paying interest, holding aloof from society with sinners, and thus was really "pious."

This is what I mean when one bothers to look at the definition of what Luther understands by "his own," when he always says: "Christ and his own." So, I think that a specific concept of holiness, a portrait of *sanctitas* (holiness) residing in the human, supplied with the name *homo*, must be smashed—a portrait indwelling in us all by nature, dear, seductive, and adhering to us. Therefore, for Luther, the break with the cloister denotes nothing subjective, no existence, no path into the natural or actually into the worldly life, but it denotes the embrace of the good work. Luther sees that good works are necessary. The good works which he had sought in the cloister are possible in hearing the commandments. One of his essential writings in which he summarizes his side of the Decalogue is the writing "Of the Good Works, 1520"[65] The Reformation continually resisted the claim that it forbad good works. It rather meant that now we know for the very first time what good works are: good works are the

---

64. WA 8, 619, 19ff. = BoA 2, 241, 35ff. (i.A. trans. By H. J. Iwand)
65. WA 6, 196–276 = BoA 1, 227–98.

works which bear God's name, because he commands them, because he will have them. And in his commandments God has set his name over all these deeds. He has let a ray of his grace fall on these deeds: on obedience toward parents, toward the preserving of life, toward the hallowing of marriage, toward the preservation of property, toward the preservation of honor and a good name.

8. Hallowing and Holiness

The work that I do is not good in itself. In this connection Kant with his formalism was absolutely right and is a successor of the Reformation (cf. II (I, p. 131 *passim*). There are no works that are materially (as to content) good, and others which are materially bad, so that I could set up an entire catalogue of good works and a catalogue of bad works and could arrange my life accordingly, or could check off from my life, as on a scale, whether my life has an ascending or descending line. The work is the commandment of God. If, in what I do, I have no command of God, then I act on my own accord, then I can do what appears best, "let my body to be burned by fire, give all I have to the poor" (according to 1 Cor 13:3)—and yet it is all for nothing. And only from that perspective does Luther let Christians into the world; opens the door, as in a sea, without a beaten path and fixed ordinances, perhaps in such a way that the Christian, when God's word leads him/her, at times finds his/her way: "Your word is a lamp unto my feet, and a light unto my way" (Ps 119:105). From that point the life of Christians is now determined by nearness to God. When that collapses, then everything collapses. One will not find existence by way of the "ethics of intention." But now, since the possibility is omitted of describing the Christian life according to performances, according to particular deeds, now also the possibility is omitted of describing Christian existence in the world as something exceptional. That by which one recognizes the Christian is the Word, the sacrament—these are the signs. There is no possibility of form (German: *Gestalt*), but there is the deed. And I would even not say: the good deed. We will then best understand Luther when one says: the deed. The transition from faith to deed is by way of what he/she is able. The world is opportunity for deeds. "Doers of the Word" (according to Jas 1:22), these are the Christians. This word which they have heard, from out of which they live, in which they are hidden, raised up, protected, this word of God becomes deed. Of course—this transition from faith to deed is the most problematic point in Luther's ethics. The distinction hides in itself (probably) the origin of the" Doctrine of the Two Kingdoms." In the one kingdom I am passive, receptive, taking, believing. There I live from what God has done for me. In the other kingdom I am active, working, making. The Christian is really only in this kingdom a doer.

A few quotations by which it becomes clear that we have not wrongly understood Luther's concept of holiness are: "For no one brings it about that for him/her a grey coat washes the heart, or that a cloister made his heart pure, but God through faith and the Holy Spirit must purify the heart (Acts 15:9). When the heart is pure then for him a house is like a field, and the field like a house. And the mark of the cloister is not a work; no site or clothing any longer that I can call holy, for me the one is as the other, since sanctification is entirely drawn into the heart, so that it says to me, you are devout, I will be your father, you will be my child. We should persist in this that we are holy and without fear and are his servants. This means to praise and explain the blessing of Abraham, that God will bless the world, and from damning turn to benediction. Here a Christian has his title."[66] Thus God will not only bless me but will bless the world. The distinction between a sacred and profane district, set by the medieval concept of holiness, is at an end. The world is no longer a damned, cursed, evil, lost world. God will bless it. And for this reason, he now leads me into this world and shows me all the good works. Luther can compare that with Adam in paradise. By faith the human is placed again in the situation of Adam in paradise, who was innocent, whom God gave to work in the world, not because he was devout, for indeed he was devout, but that by it he might shape the world and work in it. "To change from damnation to benediction," from curse to blessing: "Here a Christian has his title and also shows this color that he is holy without fear and care and a servant of God."[67]

In this connection there is a further passage: "Again, what the devil does through his hypocrites and false saints, which glitter and shine, so that the whole world unlocks maul and nose, and wonders about it, as though it were a splendid, costly thing, but is just the devil's deception and lies. When one takes to reason for counsel, then the work of a servant, a maid, a master, a wife, a major and judge are common, lowly works in

---

66. WA 17/1, 310, 27ff. (Sermon on Luke 1:67ff. 1525).
67. WA 17/1, 311, 11ff.

contrast to a Carthusian's watching, fasting, praying, and eating no meat. But if one takes to God's word for counsel, then the work of all the Carthusians and monks, when one met them all together in a heap, are not a good as the work of one single, poor servant girl, who is set through baptism in God's kingdom, believes in Christ and waits in faith for the blessed hope."[68] We see quite clearly here that the servant girl's worldly activity as such is praised, but through baptism has been set in God's kingdom, "believes in Christ" and given the "faith in the blessed hope." And in the same sermon Luther says: "Even a servant girl does good works, when in faith she carries out her calling and does what the woman does, when she sweeps the house, pours, and cooks in the kitchen, etc. Though such works do not appear as the work of a Carthusian, who have a cocoon about themselves and unlock the maul for the people, they are yet much better and costlier works before God than that of a Carthusian, who has on a hair shirt, keeps his class hours, at night stays up and sings for five hours, eats no meat, etc. For though the works are glittering and shining before the world, nevertheless they have no command and order from God." (That is decisive!). How then can there be good works which please God? Just as when a citizen or farmer is helpful toward his neighbor, serves him/her, as he is able, warns him that he/she might suffer harm to his body, to wife, child, sibling, cattle, and goods, and helps him where he needs help, etc. Such works do not shine, nevertheless they are sheer good, costly works."[69] We are always involved with the question: "Christ and his own" but at issue is that we cannot understand the question of Christian existence by itself. The point at which everything coheres is the relation of "faith and works." Can I tell from my own works without looking toward Christ? Is it possible that a person—apart from the works of Christ to which he/she clings—abandon his/her own works? It is not so that Luther would have seen that my works or works of humans are worth nothing at all, and that for this reason he clings to the work of God. They are for this reason worth nothing because God wills that we cling to his work, not because the works in their substance are bad, but because they become bad because I cling to them where God is involved. Thus, I am disobedient toward the command of God when I cling to my own works. Then I do not do the good work, but the self-chosen work. That approach suggests that Luther should be understood such that he

---

68. WA 34/2, 133, 14ff. (Sermon on Titus 2:13 1531).
69. WA 34/2, 132, 23ff.

recognizes the human person is always sinful—is only half right. For this being-evil of the human must not consist in the worthlessness of his/her works, or that they are morally bad, but the being-evil can consist in the fact that the human does self-chosen/selected works. And from this point the concept of holiness breaks apart. Luther grasps the Decalogue because he finds in it the true hallowing of his life apart from a *sanctitas* (holiness) which rests on specific performances, or self-chosen works. For this reason, Luther leaves the cloister and breaks with a tradition, the unholiness of which has become evident to him. Precisely because he would like to serve God, live to God, he saw that this form of service (i.e., the cloister) to God is false.

It has been said regarding these ideas of Luther that Protestantism is the surrender of the ideal of holiness; that various sects had in a certain respect still retained it, but that Luther enters into a compromise with the world. But the matter lies elsewhere. Luther is of the opinion that there is no specific work for Christian existence. In other words, we can engage in no work which leads us beyond human possibilities. In this way we understand the passage from the writing, "Of Good Works," where at the very beginning "in the fourth paragraph" it reads: "From faith and no other work we have the name that we are called believers, as from the chief work. For all other works are what a heathen, Jew, Turk, and sinner may do. But firmly trusting that he pleases God is not possible except for a Christian who is illumined and established by God."[70] And Luther continues: "But that this talk is strange, and some accuse me as a heretic because of it, occurs for the reason that blind reason and heathenism are followed whereby they have set faith not over, but alongside the other virtues."[71] Thus, they have not regarded virtue, the *virtus* as a matter to be named from the view of faith, but rather faith as a virtue. And more yet: They have given "it a work of its own, separated from the works of all the other virtues, so that it alone makes good all the other virtues, makes them acceptable and worthy by the fact that it trusts God and does not doubt, so that before him all one does may be done well. Yes, they have not let faith be a work, but, as they say, have made of it a *habitus* (clothing, quality); but the entire scripture gives to no other the name of a divinely good work than one's own faith."[72] That is the good conscience. Faith "makes good," that is, faith qualifies the work as good. When I want to say

---

70. WA 6, 206, 14–15 (On the Fourteenth) = BoA 1, 231, 9ff.

71. WA 6, 206, 18ff. = BoA 1, 231, 14ff.

72. WA 6, 206, 14ff. = BoA 1, 231, 17ff.

what is good, I cannot proceed from the materiality of an entirely specific *opus*. For Luther the good is not a material worth, and since he smashes it, life can no longer be aligned with an accounting table of virtues and vices, and I must cease to be my own judge.

Once more: The Christian is not someone special and does nothing special. He/she does what others also do. But what is peculiar about him/her is that he/she is free over against his/her doing. Let us hear Luther again: "In this faith all works are the same, and one is as the other; the difference among works falls away, be they great, small, short, long, many or few. For the works are not for their own sake, but acceptable because of faith."[73] And from this it follows that a Christian person who lives in this faith does not need a teacher of good works, but what occurs to him he does, and everything is done well."[74] Behind these sentences stands that certainty which for Luther, especially in the years around 1520, occurs in the foreground, that is, the conviction regarding the "universal priesthood of all believers." All believers have the Spirit; they are not referred to the authority of a teacher when it is a matter of how they live, how they should behave. They are free, they will thus undertake the tasks and works which they have to do, in this confidence which gives them certainty. They will be capable of it; they will find a way. They will do what is right. Luther has thus removed the "angst" in the transition from faith to life. As if he wanted to say, now when it comes to doing, to life, to acting, have no anxiety that by it you will lose your Christianity, your being a Christian. But rather this: you must go to work in that freedom which knows that the work is dependent on the faith with which you undertake it, and your faith is not dependent on whether the work succeeds.

Here we can naturally ask: Where then do the commandments remain? When then does Luther write the Small Catechism? Why does he say that he has always been a pupil of the catechism, so that he prays the catechism every morning?[75] Why has he his whole life long bothered with the exposition of the Decalogue? Does this not contradict the entire argument? Not at all. For when Luther says that the Christian does not need a teacher of good works, then by it he means that he/she needs no human teacher of good works. When God instructs us that is something entirely different. In the Decalogue God is our teacher, and when God teaches us then he always teaches us first to believe in him and take on the

---

73. WA 6, 206, 33ff. (On the Fifteenth) = BoA 1, 231, 29ff.
74. WA 6, 206, 207, 3ff. = BoA 1, 231, 37ff.
75. See II, 84 (n. 53).

work from out of faith. For Luther this means the commandment of God: "With your command you make me wiser than my enemies" (Ps 119:98). And this becoming-wise means God's commandment protects me from falling into the hands of human teachers, which he calls "moral;" namely, what society thinks is of value as right, true, and good. That, which for example Martin Heidegger[76] wanted to express by the term "one;" one says, thinks, does, whether it involves the state or the society or any other anonymous powers, as if it were a matter of establishing an ideology. On the contrary, the Christian knows what is good. In Luther's opinion it is impossible that I am a believer in God and do not know what is good. As if I still had to have another teacher to come, perhaps a theologian or a pastor or deacon, who now must tell me how a Christian should live. In the moment where in this transition from faith to life someone else is interposed, whether the person in the guise of a church teacher, all freedom is lost. Thus, Luther never interprets the Decalogue in the sense that in it individuals are told you shall do this and leave that. The Decalogue is always interpreted in such a way that the person is addressed in his his/her decision of faith. His/her work must be his/her own—if I may put it in this way. When I teach the other, I can only teach him/her in this way, that he/she retains his/her freedom to choose the work, which conforms to his/her faith. If he or she does not believe, then he/she cannot choose. The result is that something is broken which our natural man longs for. There is no shape to hallowing. We cannot determine, "a saint lives this way or that way." Persons of faith do not live in the style of the saints: neither Abraham, nor Jacob, nor David, nor—Jesus himself. According to Luther the true saint is the person who endures inner conflict (Jas 1:12); he/she is the naked, discarded, person, who in their battles with death, arrive at the reality of real life. It is the one so conflicted by the reality of sin and death. One can almost say the conquered person who has "suffered"—he/she is a saint. But whoever by an externally produced form secures him/herself to the point that inner conflict does not at all approach him\her is not Christ's servant. And whoever goes through the sufferings of this world, through what happens to the person on the right and on the left, for whom all this does not pose a conflict, may they be so good as he/she will—is not a disciple of Christ and Christ's servant. The Christian and the true person cohere in this way. The saint is not a superman. As early as in the "Lecture on Romans," Luther says: "Therefore in

---

76. Martin Heidegger (b. 1889), famous existential philosopher whose main work is *Being and Time*, 1927.

astonishing foolishness they all lead those to an apish bit of fable who want to imitate the works of the saints and boast of their fathers and forbears as the monks do now (those of the orders). But the fools do not ask first about the spirit of the fathers and forefathers in order to be like them, but they only try to do the same as they, and in doing do not observe the spirit."[77] So here the *imitatio* (imitation) is rejected which supposes that when I imitate certain activities, I will be as those who carried out these activities. Behind this stands the rejection of the whole Aristotelian ethic; the idea that the activity, the mere exercise of it, gives to persons a particular character. This of course agrees with education, but not in the sphere of faith, of being before God. Faith always looks to Christ who died for me. This is faith: the "perspective" which I have undertaken in obedience to Christ. Now I may no longer look for these in myself, make the judgment on myself depend on how it is with good and bad deeds, but I am basically free respecting my deeds. Now, what is the deed? The deed now is everything. The deed is the preservation of freedom in the work. Now the deed becomes joy and desire. Now the person must do deeds, now he/she is—if you will—deed-desirous and deed-hungry. This is what Luther means when he says faith is a "living, creative, whetting thing."[78] For the person now goes to his/her work as he/she never clung to his/her work as a reflective person, in the freedom of one liberated by Christ, in the freedom of the children of God.

9. Faith and Works

In this connection Luther can actually speak of the "beauty" of the Christian. In the "Lecture on Romans" it is stated in one passage: "We are his kingdom, but the beauty in us is not ours, but his; with it he covers our loathsomeness."[79] It is thus Christ and his righteousness which glitters, as a coat is spread over us. So, our goodness does not come to light from a human work but rather from Christ's righteousness. The human works which he does in this faith receive their quality from faith by the fact that Christ's righteousness is spread over it like a coat. In theology, the meaning of the words is changed: in the moral meaning of *facere* are related

---

77. WA 56, 335, 26ff. (Scholien) = Fi (Scholien) 165, 14ff. (BoA vac).

78. WA DB 7, 10, 9 (The New Testament. 1522. Lecture on Paul's Epistle to the Romans.)

79. WA 56, 280, 8–9 (Scholien) = Fi (Scholien) 115, 17ff. (BoA vac.)

all the "hypocrites, who have the false opinion of God and want to be justified by the law."[80] That is, they have that *facere*, that doing in the sense which follows from the right reason and the right will. Therefore, their *opus* is a moral deed: "Therefore their work is entirely moral or reasonable, but not a believing one or a theological (God-instructed) one, which includes faith."[81] Luther means that the "good work" offered to us by the commandment of God can neither be understood from a moral or a natural theology. It is an *opus fidele se teologicum* (a believing or theological work).[82] The *ratio* must first be illumined by faith. But if one has the right opinion and knowledge of God, then occurs the *recte ratio*, which is illumined by faith, in the work as in the Incarnation. In this work the *recte ratio* becomes deed, indeed, if you will: flesh, happening, event. The work then in this sense will always have a connection with the person. All human performances will be an expression of it; they will speak as a signal.

Here grace must now be spoken of. Once more Luther: "It is truly a great, strong, mighty, and active thing about God's grace. As the Baptists *fabulate*, it does not lie in the soul and sleeps and lets itself be carried like a painted board has a color."[83] Luther says this by assuming the scholastic concept (nominalism!), as if the soul by grace receives a new *qualitas*, a new skill, as one learns to make a bed. No, not so: "It bears, it leads, it drives, it draws, it changes, it does everything in the person and can be felt and experienced. It is hidden, but its works are not. Work and word indicate where it is, just as the fruits and leaves of the tree indicate its kind and nature. For this reason, it is too little and too meanly preached, so one no longer agrees that it beautifies and helps to carry out the work, as the sophists, Thomas, Scotus, and the people err and mislead."[84]

Now I ask: With us is grace preached differently? What then does Luther mean when he says that "one no longer agrees that it beatifies and helps to carry out the works?" If we, for example say: "Yes, when I do that as a Christian, then that is something entirely different than when you do that simply by way of the *ratio*." Certainly, that is something different. But

---

80. WA 40/1, 418, 3–4. (Commentary on Galatians 1531).

81. WA 40/1, nn. 20–21 (1535, Dr.)

82. See also 417, 25 (1535, Dr.) *Theologicum opus est fidele opus* (A theological work is a work of faith).

83. WA 10/1/1, 114/ 20ff (Church Postille 1522. Sermon for early Christmas on Titus 3:4–7).

84. WA 10/1/1, 115, 3ff.

Luther goes on to say precisely this is meant by "beautify:" "It does not alone help to do the works, it does it alone, yes, not only the works, but it also changes and renews the entire person, and its work is much more (directed toward) how it alters the person (as toward a result), how it carries out the person's works. It will make a bath, a rebirth, a renewal, not only of works, but of the whole person. See, that means preached free and full of the grace of God."[85] The work of faith, though materially it looks quite similar to the works of the natural man, is as a result the incarnation of the grace of the word of God. In this work there occurs the Word—that is what is meant. Since the Word occurs through us, it however always remans sin, it always remains behind what is truly good. But it is a sign, a witness, a reference.

Consequently, two types always stand alongside each other: the type of the false saint, the type which lives by its works, and the type of faith. In other words, the decision which involves faith, will always be a decision of this sort, that it chooses the work which praises the grace of God. It means this: When in the gospel the two types are set alongside each other—the Pharisee and the Publican (Luke 18:9ff.), the son who remains in the house and the one who goes to a foreign land (Luke 15:11ff,) the Pharisee Simeon and the woman who washes Jesus' feet (Luke 7:36ff.)—then in these different attitudes we have two forms of saint before us. The true saint is the publican. But only faith is able to recognize that his work, the prayer of the publican, is the proper one. Whoever does not believe in Christ, who does not belong to Christ, cannot recognize this. Only faith is able to recognize what the woman does, whom the Pharisee Simeon deplores, of whom he says that if Jesus were God's son, then he would know what the matter with this woman is. She is the true saint. That is unheard of. Luther gains this knowledge by the view that now the work is judged and evaluated apart from the history of the person, and I must not allow myself to be blinded by the works behind which the person is hiding; where nothing is evident but where I must rightly decide. However, that is a decision made by faith.

I thus would say that the deed that decides respecting the existence of the Christian is the deed of God in Jesus Christ, and by it is taken from our deeds the character of decision. But by it we are really set free for doing. My doing may now bring to expression what I am and how weak I am in my faith. My doing no longer carries the weight of an eternal

---

85. WA 10/1/1, nn. 10ff.

decision. The decision lies with God, which I can certainly not bear. If it were to depend on my deeds, then I would burden myself with a decision which would break me apart. God has taken it from me. And thus, the person is free for a deed previously never imagined and attempted. That is the *facile facere seu theologicum*[86] that Luther has in mind. Now the point is that something is done; that the transition occurs from faith to deed. The point is not that this deed succeeds fully and completely. One can make that clearest in prayer and similarly at the Lord's Supper. When I rouse myself for prayer, when I am in the mood, when inwardly I am really so far that I think I can pray, then it is false. I cannot wait until I have come so far, for it will never be that far for me; or at any rate when I have come so far then it will certainly not be the model prayer. Luther writes in "Confetimini of 1513:" "Therefore learn here whoever can learn. If only one were a falcon that can loft itself into the heights in such distress. And first of all, know for certain, and do not doubt that God does not send one such distress for ruin . . . but that by it he will drive him to prayer, to calling and to strife, by which he exercises faith and learns to know God in another aspect than he did before. He also gets used to warring with the devil and sins, and by God's help to win. Otherwise, we would never learn what faith, word, Spirit, grace, sin, death, or the devil were, if he/she were to always go in peace and without inner conflict. In so doing we would never learn to know God himself, in short, we would no longer be true Christians, and could not remain Christians. Distress and anxiety drive us to it and preserve us intact in Christianity. For this reason, tribulations and crosses are as necessary as life itself and even more necessary and useful than all the world's goods and honor. This means I call on the Lord. You must learn to call (you easily hear this), and not sit there by yourself or lie on the bench (letting) hang your head and shake and with your ideas, bite and gobble yourself up with worry and seek how you will be rid (free) and look at nothing else than how badly it is going with you, how sorry you are, how miserable a person you are. But rather: hold on you lazy bugger, fall on your knees, hands and eyes raised to heaven, pray a Psalm or the Our Father, and in your distress with weeping complain and appeal to God as this verse (Ps 118:5) teaches, and in the 142 Psalm (vs. 3), and say: 'I pour out my prayer before him and I show before him my distress,' and Psalm 142 (vs.2), 'My prayer must be offered before you (be of value, be worth) as incense and the lifting of my

---

86. See III, 160 (n. 82).

hands as an evening sacrifice.' Here you hear that praying, indicating distress, and lifting up the hands are to God the most suitable sacrifice. He desires it, he wills to have it, that you should lay your distress on him, not let it lie on you, and by it pull, eat at, and martyr yourself, by which you make of one misfortune two, yes, ten and one hundred. He wills that you should be too weak to bear and conquer such distress, so that you learn to become strong in him, and he is given praise in you through his strength. See, there are people out there who are called Christians, and are nothing else than vain scrubbers and gossips who spit out much about faith and Spirit, but do not know what it may be or they themselves say."[87] There we see something of the transition from faith to deed. Faith must aways be *in actu* (in activity)—so also the work. Faith can never give over to reflection. I am of the opinion that the change from faith into reflection, which later enters into pietism, was the greatest misfortune for the understanding of the Reformation; for in faith I step beneath God's command, and his command leads me to the deed, not to my own work, but to the deed that God in his command promises me. Since I take hold of God's will in his command, the deed has already occurred, for I lay hold of his promise, and in faith in this promise I go to work. Luther knows right well that the work is nothing other than the manner in which God fulfills his promise to me such that the work does not stand in relation to what I promised myself it would, but the work often will appear quite differently than what I have planned. Luther calls this suffering (German: *Anfechtung*) or inner conflict. Inner conflict is the separation of the person from this work: his shattering on his own plan. Inner conflict consists in the fact that the person is now put to the test, whether he/she trusts God. Persistence under the command of God preserves a person. Only this makes him/her actually capable of a proper deed and a right performance. In this way the work is linked with the human person him/herself. It always has the color of faith. This becomes still more clear in view of other people. The freedom of the person toward the work enables him/her now for a deed toward the neighbor which is similar to the deed of God in Jesus Christ. What Christ has done for me consists in the fact that he has taken my sins on himself. Luther now concludes that once again the deed of faith consists in the fact that I cover the sins of the neighbor with my righteousness. This is not the righteousness which I have before God, but it is my earthly, my bourgeois, my civil, my moral righteousness.

---

87. WA 31/1, 95, 3–97, 2 (Lecture on Psalm 118).

Luther is of the opinion that the goodness of the person is as much worth as he helps others to become good: "These are the godly shapes that one must remove so that the shapes of the servant are in us, for in all these things we must stand before God, and must work as mediators for them, because they do not have them, since we clothe them as it were with a strange garment and before persons over against their slander, and toward those who use force on them, in that we serve them with the same love."[88] Here it becomes clear that the concept of service toward the neighbor plays so great a role and is only understood when we proceed from the manner in which God served us in Christ. It is not service in the sense of subordination, but it is the service in the sense that the one who subordinates him/herself is free. So, Luther states in the writing "The freedom of the Christian, 1520: "And whether he (the Christian) is now totally free (then he should) in turn willingly make himself a servant to help his neighbor, go with him, and act with him as God through Christ acted, and all this for nothing."[89] And: "As God through Christ freely helped us, thus we should by the body and its works no differently help the neighbor."[90] Thus what I have as "erudition," of wisdom, is not mine, but belongs to the *ineroditii*, to those who do not know it. From that perspective we understand Luther's urging that one make schools so that people do not remain uneducated, that no educational difference should exist between the aristocracy of education and the people, an idea that has its whole deep root here. Indeed, from this point one recognizes what the *communio sanctorum* (communion of saints) means practically for Luther: "As now Christ has become common to all, Jews and heathen, as from some other reason, thus we should also be common to one another, each one to accept the other, bearing his burdens and enduring frailty, without all external difference of person, name, position, and what that may be."[91] And from a sermon of Luther on the parable of the Pharisee and Publican (Luke 18:9ff.) must be cited here: "If he (the Pharisee) had thus said: Oh, God, we are forever sinners, the poor sinner here is also one just as I, as the others, and had been dragged into the congregation and said: O, God, be gracious to us, then he would have fulfilled God's

---

88. WA 2, 606, 10–15 (Kl. Commentary on Galatians 1519. Trans. H. J. Iwand).
89. WA 7, 35, 25ff. (On the Twenty Seventh) = BoA 2, 25, 4ff.
90. WA 7, 36, 6ff. = BoA 2, 25, 21ff.
91. WA 10/1/2, 89, 8ff. (Advent Postille 1522. Epistle for Second Sunday in Advent on Rom 15:4–13).

command."[92] The congregation is God together with the publican, and the pharisee stands outside. Had he been dragged into the congregation with the realization that he was a sinner, then he would have been saved.

We have asked: What kind of life or human existence corresponds to the doctrine of justification by faith? We must first of all declare that this life cannot be grasped directly by means of oneself. Christ does not give us life and then remain outside. He does not bring it about *causaliter* (from a cause) and then let it run by itself. Rather, this is what is particular, the incomparability of this life, that it can only be grasped from the inseparable connection with Christ. Faith lived from this life is non-transmissible; that is, I cannot give my faith to another. Faith itself thus cannot be treated as something alien to the soul in which I could settle in or feel my way. There is no entrance to faith by means of psychology or the understanding of existence as such. Whoever does not take his/her way by faith in Christ will never understand "his own." This was the thesis that has concerned us all this time. We were obliged to proceed from the question of who Christ is; thus, from Christology in Luther and of course from his *theologia crucis*, or the cross. Therefore, we have abstained from sketching a portrait of piety. What is unheard of, what has occurred with the proclamation of the gospel in the Reformation, is that indeed here something approximating earliest Christianity in character has begun again, that the person as believer is surrendered to reality without interpretation.[93] However, the theologian of the cross declares what is real. From this fellowship won by faith in Jesus Christ now the person is able to see and to say what the reality is.

10. Inner Conflict

The reality in which we, "his own," are surrendered is, according to Luther's conception, the devil's world. The world is now simply evil, it is

---

92. WA 10/1/2, 351, 26ff. (Summer Postille 1526. Gospel lesson for the 11th Sunday after Trinity Sunday).

93. In connection with the concept of the "incomprehensible reality" H. J. Iwand refers in this lecture to one of the most significant German philosophers of the recent past, the almost forgotten Eberhard Griesbach (1880–945), who taught first in Jena and then in Zurich. Iwand placed him, with only a few short cogent remarks, in the same camp as Gogarten and also with Heidegger. Griesbach proceeds from the idea of an "incomprehensible reality" and includes such influences in his ideas as Kierkegaard and Martin Buber (*Dialogik*). A short orientation to Griesbach can be found in the book by Michael Theunissen, *Der Andere*, 361ff.

irreparable, and here the person now simply has to be on guard regarding the danger of submitting to it. Also, the Christ to whom I am bound in faith has to do with this reality. But in him this reality is abrogated as reality. In him death, hell and sin are abrogated. And for the Christian, reality now does not mean I take the person, I take the world, I take the kingdom of the world as they are and set myself on them. But the encounter with the reality of this world has set the task for the believer to use these powers and shapes toward faith in the victory of Christ. But now, accordingly, there arises the inner conflict of the Christian. The so-called "secularization" of faith is not a genuine understanding of inner conflict; it is not a "taking into-oneself" of inner conflict. This inner conflict is not a battle; it is no longer a deed and no longer victory and its conquest does not consist in that I myself come to freedom. Rather, Luther means something very deep by inner conflict. That is, all creatures begin to set themselves against him/her and they become, as it were, symbols of the wrath of God. The whole world is changed into an accusation against the person. Thus, it is also with one's own works. The devil changes my entire human life into a worthless, vainly lived existence rioting against me. For this we have an example from Luther's writing "Von der Winkel Messe und Pfaffenweihe, 1533," where Luther speaks of inner conflicts which have come over him and still come, since was a priest and a monk for so long: "I will boast and perform a small confession before you holy fathers. Give me a good absolution, which is not harmful to you. Once I was wakened at midnight, when the devil began such a dispute with me (as he actually can make bitter and sour enough for me): 'Hear it you highly educated, do you know that for fifteen years long you have held Winkel Messe almost every day? How if with such a mass you had urged idolatry and not Christ's body and blood, but adored mere bread and wine there, and held apart from adoring other things?' I answered: 'But I am an ordained priest, have received consecrated oil and consecration from the bishop, more, and all such at the command and done obedience, how I should I not have consecrated since I spoke the words earnestly and with all possible devotion celebrated mass? You know this for sure.' 'Yes,' he said, 'it is true. But the Turks and heathen also do everything in their churches on command and in earnest obedience. The priests of Jeroboam at Dan and Beersheba did everything, perhaps with greater devotion then the proper priests in Jerusalem. What if your blessings, consecrated oil, and consecrations were unchristian and as false as (those) of the Turks and Samaritans?' Here I really broke out in a sweat, and my heart began to shake and pound. The devil knows to pitch his arguments and bring them forward and has a heavy, strong argument. And such disputes do not occur with long and many concerns: but one moment is an answer for the others. And I have well experienced how it happens that in the morning one finds people dead in bed. He can strangle the body, that is one thing. But he can also make the soul so weary with disputing that it must fade in a moment, as has almost happened to me. And now he has embroiled me in this dispute. And I would indeed not happily allow myself such an unholy heap of horror before God, but defend my innocence, and listen to him (God), what evidences he would have against my ordination and consecration."[94]

Then follows the whole dispute between Luther and the devil, and Luther's continual attempt to appeal to his ordination, his consecration, above all to his church, and how the devil denies all of it. This coheres with the fact that all creatures—and all earthly churches are also creatures, used well and badly, properly, and falsely—during inner conflict interpret everything as accusations. The idea that the "world is too narrow for me," sounds throughout in Luther's dispute with the devil. The thought that the world is too narrow for me originates in the Psalms. In the petition of the Psalmist, it is confidently stated: "You place my feet on a broad space" (Ps 31:9b) and further: "Lord, be gracious to me, for I am anxious" (vs. 10). We can interpret these ideas in view of Luther's dispute with the devil such that in the moment of inner conflict everything is in flames. Everything is threatened by fire, even my best work. I cancel myself out as nothing. And for this reason, the first side of inner conflict means that God robs me of all good works, of trust in my own works, of those of other creatures, also of my neighbors, of my volition, and finally of any other thing. But even this spells the person's rescue because it means that God draws him/her wholly to himself. It means that he will support him/her on something which does not fall. At this point it becomes totally clear again that the word of God in the proclamation is not a human word and that it cannot be the word of a creature, otherwise it will go up in flames. This is true also of Jesus Christ who in inner conflict is transformed into one who is against me. K. Holl has seen this problem. He writes in his essay, "What did Luther understand by Religion?" that "Luther was regularly overtaken by inner conflict . . . Thereby, for Luther

---

94. WA 38, 197, 17ff. ("On Winkelmesse and Pfaffenweihe," 1533) = BoA 4, 241, 22ff.

God and the devil are confused with each other."[95] From this point it becomes clear that what is also at stake is an idea of Christ that does not help us in inner conflict. A Christ-idea can only be creaturely; we may also use the term "rational." Thus, in such an idea Christ appears to me as a portrait that the creature makes of him, say, in the quest for the historical Jesus. In this inner conflict all such portraits are burned up, for they are creations of man. Add to this the portraits which the so-called faith of the elite, of the moralists, of the idealists, but also the Christian socialists[96] have made for themselves. All these portraits are in the flames in inner conflict, in the fire of our days.

Here is added a second inner conflict. It originates with the creature. In Leviticus 6:36 it is written: "To those who remain among you, I will make a craven heart in their enemies' land, so that a rustling leaf shall chase them . . ." Luther took over this image from the *sonitus folii voluntis* (rustling of a flying leaf; cf. the Vulgate on this passage). The person flees from the inner conflict as from a rustling leaf, just as Adam, after the fall into sin, was afraid when God draws near in the cool of the evening and moves like a wind through the leaves. These are observations which of course today are, on average, far from Christian consciousness. Our Christianity is so domesticated that we no longer understand it. We have demythologized the rustling of the leaf. But it has *de facto* remained: the human being has not at all been changed. He/she has not changed, even though modern man believes he can avoid the accusation by suicide. Suicide is merely a sign that the person is no longer up to the inner conflict. For the rustling of a leaf frightens him/her, and then occurs the unholy deed. This coheres with the fact that in inner conflict, which is no subjective state, but a reality that encounters me from without, the reality of the wrath which does not immediately affect me, just as it affected Christ, but mediated through the creature, the entire creation is a reflection of the *ira Dei* (wrath of God). When the inner conflict understands this, then imagination is not involved, but it is the true face of life. Thus, "superstition" is the imagination of those who maintain that "something like this cannot at all occur."

All this is highly significant for Luther's theology because it is from this point that he understands the life of the saints. In this sense they are

---

95. Holl, et al (Iwand 47, n. 32) 38. For more on this entire paragraph, see the section on "Inner Conflict" in H. J. Iwand, NW IV, 292–304.

96. H. J. Iwand ostensibly means here the religious-social movement at the turn of the century that was influenced by L. Ragaz, H. Kutter, P. Tillich and E. Heimann.

successors of Christ, for Jesus is the truly inner conflicted man, the true man. And so, Luther can say: "So we are solely by faith led through unknown ways, devoid of all human help. These are sufferings and distresses. But as there the pillar of fire (Exod 13:21–22) walked each moment before their presence (of the children of Israel), so here faith has God ever present, thus, as it were, from the presence of the ever present God proceeds the illumination of the heart (2 Cor 4:6), so that in a proper and unique way the light of the presence of God is there, which means the recognition and the loyalty of the ever present God. That is, whoever has not known the ever-present God on his/her behalf, who does not feel, does not yet believe, and has not yet the light of the presence of God."[97] This means, as well for believers, that inner conflicts are necessary, indeed, that they are indispensable in order to exercise faith. And yet—if the person sticks it out (*perseveret*) and hopes against hope (*et contra spem in spem speret*) then he/she will be found preserved (Rom 5:3ff.), and in this inner conflict will be clothed with his merit and clothed with hope and will be crowned with an indestructible crown of eternity. That is, God is not actually wrathful; he does not intend that guilt is to be unforgivable, but he tests (*tentat*) us, whether we hope more in his pure mercy than in our own merit."[98] Hope is, if you will, an "existential" thing; a definition of my existence. To be one who hopes, means to be one who waits for what God gives him/her, or better yet, who waits for God. And that is what is attractive in this passage, that Luther defines the perseverance of faith (*perseveratia fidei*) from the perspective of hope, not of *opus*. Later, one has wanted to rediscover the perseverance of hope in good works. It would have been better, if one had held firm to the fact that love is preserved in good works (cf. Rom 5:5) and more clearly had defined the fact that the perseverance of faith is the *spes* (hope). In these inner conflicts occurring in the one being stripped of all merits, there is instruction in how to be one who hopes. Only in this sense can one be empty and naked when one lets the word of God be everything; it is merely the reverse side of being bound to the Word. Regarding the relation of faith, love, and hope to each other Luther says further "What else is faith than that movement of the heart, which is called credere (believing), hope other than the movement which is called *sperare* (to hope), *caritas* other than

---

97. WA 5, 118, 10ff. (Works in the Psalms, 1519–1521).
98. WA 5, 166, 34ff.

the movement which is called "loving" (*deligere*) ?"[99] Faith, hope, love, are thus understood as action, not as condition.

In this context Luther expressly distances himself from mysticism. He says: "I regard that as human illusion to distinguish condition and act, especially regarding the godly virtues, in which there is nothing else but: suffering, being torn away, a movement by which the soul (*anima*) by the word of God is moved, formed, purified, marked, so that the task of these virtues is nothing else than the pruning of the palm tree, as Christ says (cf. John 15:2, according to the Vulgate), by which the pruned tree should bear more fruit . . . It is indeed a steeper and more narrow way to leave behind everything visible, to discard everything sensuous, to step out of all that is customary, and finally this: to die and go to hell . . . The mystical theologians call this, 'to go into the dark, to step out beyond being and not-being.' Truly, I do not know whether they themselves really understand it when they ascribe what they say to specially aroused acts (of faith). It would be more proper if they believed that the sufferings of the cross, death, and hell were described with it. The CROSS alone is our theology."[100] Here the difference between mysticism and Luther becomes clear. Luther takes up the portraits of mysticism, mystical forms of speech, but the content is no longer an internal event, but an event of the word of God.

From this point one will perhaps have to understand the famous letter that Luther wrote to Melanchthon on August 1, 1521, and in which there is the famous sentence: "If you are a preacher of the grace of God, then do not preach an imagined but the true grace."[101] By the use of the "imagined grace" (*gratia ficta*) ideas are meant which intrude between reality and me. And when I project death and sin, the inner conflict in this sense, in my idea, then I can give it a reason, understand, explain, perhaps also direct it; I have it in my power. But Luther means that the word of forgiveness does not redeem the person in view of his/her ideas, but in view of the reality, thus of the *esse in re* (actual being), and not of the *esse in conscientia* (being in conscience). Of course, it can absolutely be so that I am conscious of no guilt and yet stick deeply in sin. Once more: "If you are a preacher of grace, then don't preach an imagined grace, but the true grace." Today we would say: Do not preach a Christian

---

99. WA 5, 176, 9ff.
100. WA 5, nn. 11ff., (i.A.)
101. WA Br 2, 372, 82, Nr. 424 = BoA 6, 55, 32, Nr. 31 (Trans. H. J. Iwand)

world view. Then you are involved in fictions. At issue is the *gratia vera*, the true grace. And this should be held in such a way that the reality is borne by it: "God does not make healthy those who are sinners according to their imagination." And this appears in the letter to Melanchthon.[102] And at this place follows the famous quotation: "Be a sinner and sin boldly but believe more boldly yet and rejoice in Christ who is victor over sin, death, and the world."[103] By this word one can really sum up as example everything that was said about inner conflict. Be a sinner and sin boldly, which of course does not mean, "Now go and sin wantonly." What is involved here is not that one leads a life without self-control. Rather it is shown here is that it is unthinkable that there would be a reality of sin to which grace is not equal, and of course because Christ is the victor. In the passage of the letter cited it is further stated: "We must sin, so long as we live here; for this life is not the dwelling place of righteousness, but we wait, as Peter says, for the new heaven and new earth, in which righteousness dwells" (2 Pet 3:13). It is sufficient that we acknowledge through the riches of the glory of God the lamb who bears the sin of the world that the world is full of sin (John 1:29). And this sin is not wrenched from us, as if a thousand times in one day we had committed adultery or had murdered. So, do you think that the price of the forgiveness of our sins is so small in one so great as the lamb of God? Pray with all your might, for you are a very mighty sinner."[104] At the deepest level all that Luther writes here to Melanchthon means that the Christian cannot exist in the world like a monk.

We may not shrink in fear of what has been commanded us to do in the world, say, with the excuse that in all good conscience I would not be able to answer for this or that, for that would be sin. There are situations in which the person does not do God's command for fear that he/she can soil his/her own conscience. What is involved in "sin boldly!" never means that the person calmly transgresses God's commandments. Rather what's involved is that in the fulfilling of God's commandments he/she acts, does, speaks in decisions that encroach on the danger that in this instance he/she does not remain without sin. The *"pecca fortiter!"* should be no occasion for saying: I throw the commands of God into the wind.

---

102. WA Br 2, 372, 83–84, Nr. 424 = BoA 6, 55, 33–34, Nr 31 (Trans. H. J. Iwand)

103. WA Br 2, 372, 84–85, Nr. 424 = Bo A, 6, 56, 1–2, Nr. 31 (trans. H. J. Iwand. The citation in Latin is: *"Esto peccator et pecca fortiter, sed forties fide et gaude in Christo, qui victor est peccati, mortis et mundi."*

104. WA Br 2, 372, 85ff., Nr 424 = BoA, 6, 56, 2ff. Nr. 31 (trans. H. J. Iwand)

But it should always be interpreted that in fulfilling the commandments, you must take this or that on yourself. It would be false to think that you could fulfill God's commands as one who does not sin. That, as said, would be the false ideal of monkish existence. Then, *de facto*, sin enters by entirely different ways. Then one leaves to the politicians, to the merchants, to the laity what precisely should be just the affair of those who call themselves "his own." It is also wrong when we say: "We as church people, can of course not do something like this, but when you do it, then we give you an indulgence." That is the hypocrisy that is smashed with the right understanding of the word of God. And I fear that today, behind our "Doctrine of the Two Kingdoms" (we will still return to this) there is nothing else but the solidification of this hypocrisy. In any event, this is not what Luther means with his Two Kingdoms Doctrine. From the famous "sin boldly!" and from our interpretation a new theme is shown, to which we, if we reckon ourselves to be "hidden," must turn. It is the question of conscience.

The Matter of Conscience

1. Holl's Concept of a "Religion of Conscience"

When we encounter statements about conscience found in Luther, then the first impression is that of a scarcely measurable difference between what is meant by this word in Luther and how we understand it today. In looking at the concept of conscience, it is clear what kind of unheard-of change must have occurred since the Reformation between the person who received the Word in the Reformation and modern protestants. Here is the basis for the entire misunderstanding of the description which Karl Holl gives of Luther.[105] In essence, he develops Luther's theology from the concept of religious conscience. Holl states: "Luther's religion is a religion of conscience in the most developed sense of the term. As it originated in an experience of conscience of a particular type from the conflict experienced by Luther in a particular sharpness of a heightened feeling of responsibility with the divine will regarded as unalterably valid, so as a whole it rests on the conviction that in the conscience the obligation, the irresistibility with which the requirement is addressed to the will, seizes

---

105. See Iwand, 47–51.

hold of a person so that what is godly is most definitely revealed."[106] That sums up, as it were, the programmatic part of Holl's understanding of Luther and the entire Holl-school has followed him in this opinion. For Holl, Luther's theory is a religion of conscience in the most developed sense. If we ask what that means, we encounter the concept of the feeling of responsibility. Holl speaks of a heightened feeling of responsibility, that the feeling of responsibility encounters the divine will as absolutely irreversible. Holl then later states: "It is for Luther a foundational tenet that not what is chosen by the person him/herself, what is conceived by him/her, but what is lain upon him/her by a higher order, what is demanded, bears the mark of the divine in it."[107] Here we have the usual understanding of conscience before us. The conscience discloses to the person an order which stands over one; a "Should" beneath which he/she stands. The religious person feels this "Should" as God, as inspired by God. It is, so to speak, his/her first encounter with God. And then when in this encounter a particular feeling of guilt enters, then he/she turns to Christ who covers, or levels for me this consciousness of guilt. This is the line to which the theological generation of today—at any rate, to great extent—is bracketed. However, when we do this then we betray and surrender all we have tried to learn since the First World War. And the person who emerges with this is then nothing other than the introspective, radicalized, absolutized creature of the law. It is the man/woman of the law marked by his/her inner obligation, who incessantly adds that he/she cannot fulfill this obligation—and therefore needs Christ.

The quotation which Holl cites as evidence for his view, which actually has become the confession of faith of the entire Holl-school, stands at the beginning of the "Great Galatians Commentary" where it says, "The way into heaven is the line of an inseparable point, that is, of conscience."[108] Luther wrote down this quotation when he sketched out a series of brief preliminary remarks for his lectures on the Epistle to the Galatians. But how does this sentence appear when we look at the context? There it is stated a few lines earlier that one must take a position against the people "who break into the scripture with unwashed feet, and morally or philosophically adhere to (their) words. But philosophy knows nothing of God."[109] Luther then writes further that theology must

106. Holl, et al (Iwand, 47, n. 32), 35.
107. Holl, et al (Iwand, 47, n. 32), 35.
108. WA 40/1, 21, 12: "*Via in coelum est linea indivisibilis puncti: conscientiae.*"
109. WA 40/1, 20, 33–34.

appeal to the Word.[110] And further he says literally: "Narrow is the way to heaven."[111] And then under the following footnote-like sentences the fable is told of the knight Tondalus.[112] This knight Tondalus, as Luther relates in another passage, "had to pass over a narrow bridge . . . with a load on his back, and beneath him was a Sulphur pool full of dragons, and there one met him whom he had to avoid . . . A Christian leads such a weary life, as though he/she went on a narrow rise, in fact on a mere knife blade, thus the devil is beneath us in the world, who without letup snaps at his/her back, so that he brings us to impatience, despair and murmuring against God. Added to this, the world goes against us and will not go away from us nor leave us alone, so (heavily) does our own flesh lie on our neck."[113] And Luther continues: "We must accustom ourselves to the comfort that we can learn to make of the closed portals and the narrow way a wide space, and from the small heap a great crowd so that we do not gawk but direct them (our eyes) by faith and by the Word to the invisible; namely, to Christ himself and to all the heavenly hosts that are with me and have gone the same way, and with a beautiful long procession have gone before me into heaven, and to all Christendom that walks the same street (with me) till the last day."[114]

Here we have the portrait again: Christ and his own. The *conscientia*, the conscience, is still only the narrow gate; the bridge on which we walk is the inner conflicted self in which we are no longer the leader, but the leader is Christ. Thus, what Luther first of all wanted to say with the Word, cited by Holl: "The way to heaven is the line of an inseparable point, that is, the conscience," is best interpreted to mean that whoever goes the way of the knight Tondalus cannot be lax regarding the question of faith. The question of faith stands here at the center. And Luther probably means that with his remark, which immediately follows the quotation cited by Holl: "Against those who enviously burden us with the argument of love."[115] When I, as the night Tondalus, have to go over this narrow bridge, with the abyss beneath me, and the opponent before me

---

110. See also the following lines.

111. WA 40/1, 21, 9.

112. WA 40/1, n. 10.

113. A note in the WA in the "Commentary on Galatians" that refers to the Sermon on Matt 7:13–14 where Luther tells the fable and its meaning. See WA 32, 502, 32ff. (Weekly Sermons on Matt 5–7. 1530/2. Printed 1532.)

114. WA 40/1, (WA 32!), 503, 29ff.

115. WA 40/1, 21, 13–14.

who will allow me no space, then I do not have to think of *caritas* (love), but I have to think of the *fides* (the faith). What leads me here and makes my way a following of Christ is the *fides*. Luther says: "Works occur by love from out of faith, not the righteousness by love, as so often has been said, that when a tree is not already good, it also does not bear good fruit. But the tree brings what is good by faith, not by love, since love itself is a fruit of the good tree."[116] The line of an inseparable point of which Holl speaks is thus not the feeling of an obligation planted in a person, but the *conscientia* is marked here by faith. *Conscientia* is here identical to *fides*. Whoever binds conscience only to the least *opus*, to anything else than to faith, learns that a person tanks into the abyss, into the nothing, and into hell. So, I believe, that this Luther-quote, continually cited for the thesis of the religion of conscience, must be understood in its context, and that *conscientia* for Luther is to be understood from the concept of faith.

2. Law, Conscience, and Faith

In the magnificent exposition of the Book of Jonah, Luther describes the concept of conscience very expressly. For Luther, the fact that Jonah is in the belly of the fish means that the person who is frightened by his/her conscience, who goes under, goes to ground in his/her conscience, is distant from God: "That God has actually let himself be seen as horrifying, as though he were so wrathful that he would not have enough of death and punishment to which Jonah willingly surrenders, but cannot horribly enough take revenge on him/her. For the whale's revenge cannot indeed have been anything other than a frightful abstraction for the poor lost and dying Jonah, as the mouth of the fish opened so wide, and the sharp teeth stood about like sharp pillars or boards and thus a wider cellar in the stomach. Does this mean trusting in death? Is this the kind glance in dying? Does this mean that dying and death should not be enough? That means, I think, a faith, indeed—a battle and strife of faith. That is a victory and triumph hidden beneath the greatest weakness. How God shows us here what his word and faith can do, that all creatures can chip nothing away from him, not even God's wrath itself, though everything highest and most horrible rages. But by this Jonah had to show the whole world how his heart stood and how the heart of every believer in the same inner conflict . . . For just as the sea with all

---

116. WA 40/1, 23, 5ff.

its violence wants to drown Jonah, and the whale wants to swallow and chew him up, so the conscience feels sheer violence from God's wrath, and death and hell and damnation will painfully eat up the soul."[117] And Luther states earlier: "What a battle has been there in his heart. There he too no doubt would have for fear been able to sweat blood. There he must all at once fight against his sin, against his own conscience and feeling of his heart, against death and against God's wrath alike. There his soul will have to hang on a silk thread over hell and eternal damnation. Oh, it is a great thing done in the heart (having happened in front of one) by God's power, that he has remained and held on. For that he has remained in faith well proves his redemption—God helps no godless one out of such death and sorrow—so he confesses himself that he is God's servant and endures the punishment."[118]

Here it is quite clear that in inner conflict the conscience strikes on the side of the powers of death, of the powers that are hostile to humankind and that the conscience says something about God that is not true. That is, it becomes a revelation, an eloquent mouth of the wrath of God; that thus, in the place of his innermost, absolute certainty, he/she is headed for the greatest error of their life. That really is the erring conscience. In the Middle Ages it is understood under the viewpoint that the individual never can know what is good and evil, and thus needs an objective criterion which the church, thanks to its revelation, gives him/her. Here the error of the conscience is an uncertainty, an "incertitude," with respect to the "material" of good and evil. For Luther the erring conscience errs in this: that it says the truth. The erring conscience is, of course, right; all that it says is true, correct. It says who I am, it says what I have done; it shows me death and it shows me the wrath of God. This conscience erring in this way is indeed no longer to be instructed by any kind of objective entity, say, by the church or by the Bible; for all objective entities of this kind will not be able to withstand this conscience (because they are just creatures). It is only to be resisted by the *verbum Dei*. Consequently, Luther then can speak of a new man viewed from faith, "who lives in a new world, where there is no law, no sin, no conscience (!), no death, but unabashed joy, righteousness, grace, peace, life, salvation and honor."[119] The conscience is thus for Luther dependent on the relation in which the believer stands to Christ. The conscience is subordinate to

---

117. WA 19, 218, 28ff. (On the Prophet Jonah. 1526)
118. WA 19, nn. 12ff.
119. WA 40/1, 47, 12ff. (Gr. Commentary on Galatians, 1535. Dr.)

faith, it is ruled by faith. Luther draws boundaries between the kingdom of the law and the kingdom of the conscience. He says in a passage in the "Great Galatians Commentary," "You, law, want to rise up to the kingdom of the conscience and rule there . . . and cancel the joy of the heart which I have by faith in Christ, and grind me in despair so that I perish . . . Stay within your limits and exercise lordship over the flesh. But conscience touches me not."[120] Here faith separates the conscience and the law. Here the *conscientia*, the conscience, the consciousness of the person is defined only by the fact that Christ is my lord. Nothing else. And this kingdom of conscience is so superior to the concept of the *lex*, thus to the concept of obligation, that Luther shuts the door when the obligation would like to make itself lord over human self-consciousness. That is the task for us, to which I here can only allude, and which is of far-reaching consequences. For this of course means, after all, that faith does not find an obligation in its self-consciousness, not at its base, in its nature, but finds there a history, a report, a message of that which Jesus Christ is, what God has done for us. It finds an indicative, not an imperative. The "protestant" person, however, always finds an obligation at the base of its being. And here then Christ has still the task of healing the rupture between obligation and being that means that he is still present there, to keep us further sleeping in our incurable idealism so that we do not waken. When the conscience wants to get started, when the consciousness of guilt is announced, then a preaching of Christ steps in, which immediately puts this conscience asleep again. For this reason, the church is also for many persons irreplaceable. From that perspective it is also understandable why German people today are in such need of the church and why we allow ourselves to be used by it. In the Middle Ages the church taught how to apply a universally construed law to an individual instance and from this then resulted the "casuistry" of moral theology. Today this is no longer the function of the church but is the function of one's own autonomously construed conscience which we now call "protestant freedom."

I want to set before you a quotation from Luther in his" Lectures on Genesis from 1535–1545." There, in the section on Genesis 43:9–22, he speaks of the conscience and says: "Therefore, let us make every single effort to be freed from this evil and hellish beast . . . The conscience enflames and strengthens death and hell and arms the entire creation

---

120. WA 40/1, 50, 30–51, 13 (1535, Dr. = i.A).

against us."[121] Nietzsche has thus, in his fashion, attempted to get free of this "beast."[122] It is shocking to see how Nietzsche, who has really grasped what an internally conflicted conscience is, cannot cope with this inner conflicted conscience and finds no Christianity to help him. Nietzsche breaks out in the "Genealogy of Morals" and says the conscience is the burned-in sign of punishment that one has burned into the beast so that it is tamed. One has taught man, who is actually a predator, to lacerate himself, and brought him up with a conscience and by it made him an enemy of himself. Nietzsche hopes to get free of conscience in this way; to lead man back once again to the innocence of the impulses, of instinct, to train a new type of man who lives "beyond good and evil." But "beyond good and evil" is also at issue for Luther. However, for Luther the way that Nietzsche deals with it, based on modern biology by setting man again in relation to the animal, to understand himself from the perspective of the animal, is not the way out. Rather, Luther has seen that this "beast" has been conquered differently and must be conquered differently: that not only a psychological process occurs with it, but behind the psychological process man becomes aware of a reality; that is, the reality of death and the wrath of God which he cannot escape. If the event of conscience were only an intra-human event (Nietzsche would understand it thus as it was the result of pietism in which of course he himself was raised) then one could solve the question of conscience in a psychoanalytic way. Freud stands in the further development of this struggle with the concept of conscience.[123] Freudian psychoanalysis is nothing other than the medical technique for which Nietzsche gave the actual philosophical bases. This is the end of the "protestant" person who no longer remains, or has remained in Christ, but who in his/her "conscience" has found his/her new being, his/her new "self-understanding."

Added to this comes the death of Christ the moment when, through external events, the conscience erupts, contingent, sudden. When the disciples go across the sea with the Lord and the elements are roused (Mark 4:35-41 and parallels), when horror awakens the conscience when the cock crows (Mark 14:66-72), when Balaam's ass speaks (Num 22ff.), then conscience moves. Luther readily uses the expression of sleeping. So also, Jonah slept quite peacefully on the ship until the storm came and the

---

121. WA 44, 546, 30ff.

122. H. J. Iwand develops the following idea mainly on Nietzsche's work, *The Genealogy of Morals*, (Part II: "Guilt," and "Bad Conscience," and related).

123. Sigmund Freud (1856-1939) is the founder of psychoanalysis.

people woke him. Suddenly, the conscience is there. And when it is there, it is over with the person. Luther probably quite rightly understood the biblical person.

What is remarkable about Luther's teaching regarding conscience is that he does not proceed from a theoretical "concept" of conscience, but from specific phenomena of human life which he describes. In this respect he resembles Shakespeare who allows his Hamlet to say: "Thus, doth conscience make cowards of us all."[124] When the conscience speaks, then the person loses his\her understanding, his/her reason, and does the most irrational things. No person is without a conscience, in any case, potentially (according to possibility), he/she can any time be overcome by it, even the greatest rascal. And that is just what is remarkable, that the speaking of conscience can cohere with the tiniest events. In this regard, Luther continually cites the rustling leaf of Leviticus 26:36:[125] "Nothing is lower and more despised than a dry leaf which lies on the earth, when all the little worms run over it, and cannot defend itself against one bit of dust . . . But when the hour comes, there should fear his rustling steed, man, spear, harness, king, princes the whole force of the army and all power . . . Are we not fine fellows: we do not fear God's wrath, and stand stiff and yet fear and flee from the wrath of a helpless dry leaf. And such rustling of a leaf should make the world too narrow for us and become our wrathful God, we who earlier could pound away at heaven and earth and death!"[126] The creature can unexpectedly attack us. It can become the voice of God as we think of him; of the God who does not meet us in his word, in Jesus Christ, but of the God who meets us according to our "self-understanding," according to this final and profound concept of *conscientia*. But it does not appear to be thus, as if God had nothing to do with the world. In modern Protestantism we have also secularized the concept of conscience, to the extent that conscience has nothing more to do with the external world. That is not Luther. In so doing we would annihilate a decisive characteristic of an "erupting of conscience." Conscience is present in such a way that the person is not master of him/herself. And conscience reveals to us a "being in," the person's being in the world, such that we no longer find room. Conscience makes clear to us that we have no room in the world, it makes the person a fugitive. Goethe

---

124. Shakespeare, *Hamlet* III, 1, from the soliloquy at the beginning, "To be or not to be . . ."

125. See III, 171.

126. WA 19, 226, 16ff. (On the Prophet Jonah, 1526.)

has Faust say: "Am I not the fugitive? The homeless? The prehistoric man without purpose and rest . . . ?"[127] Remarkably, we see what is then linked to conscience it wishes that there were no God.

3. The Origins of Atheism

Here we discover the origin of atheism. It has its roots in the fact that the human is affected by his/her conscience: "When the conscience feels sin, it also feels the wrath (of God). For this reason, it desires that God might not exist. For it looks at the club and has a suspicious eye toward God. Just as a thief wishes that all hangmen were dead because he/she is struck by conscience that he/she is committing sins."[128] The denial of the existence of God is thus, so to speak, only a secondary form of atheism, a theoretical one. There is yet another form of atheism which is that one would like to set God aside. The person left to his/her conscience cannot at all desire that God is God. This is what Luther means. The person cannot give credence to the first commandment. He/she would like, on the bias of his/her own decision and knowledge, to decide what is good and evil. Then he/she will be rid of his/her conscience: "Such a downcast heart looks here and there, does not know where it should be, the world is too narrow for him, that he (the person) must say: 'See, you drive me from the earth.' (Gen 4:14). These are sheer desperate words. How should he drive him from the earth—the world is still so wide. But conscience made a thousand worlds too narrow for him."[129] The person not only loses God but also loses the world. Their conscience does not let them live in the world any longer. That is the truly godless person.[130] The fact that the creation, so to speak, assumed the *alienum opus Dei* (the alien work of God), that a rustling leaf wakens the conscience, is experienced by the person who is on a flight from God. The actual awakening of conscience, and of course of the *conscientia* toward life and faith, occurs by the *verbum Dei*. Thus,

---

127. Goethe, *Faust I*, "Forest and Hell," 3348/49.
128. WA 20, 511, 4ff. (Sermons for the Year 1526. Matt 22:34ff.)
129. WA 24, 140, 21ff. (Sermons on Genesis, 1527. Chapter 4).

130. On this point we find the following remarks by H. J. Iwand: "There was an investigation that had an excellent start in highlighting the phenomenon of the conscience in Luther. It was done with the help of Heidegger's existential philosophy, which outlined certain structures and ways of knowing, through which it is easier to interpret Luther than through the idealism of Kant and Fichte." See Jacob Gunter, *Der Gewissensbegriff in der Theologie Luthers*, Tübingen 1929, New Ed. 1966 with Kraus Reprint Ltd., Nendeln, Leichtenstein.

what the mute creation does to the person fleeting from God, that is what God does in his grace to the same person in the proclamation of his word, in his revelation. Only the one who throws God's revelation to the wind will encounter the disguised God—the Not-God—who is in the shape of the creaturely, but from the creaturely has risen to the demonic, and fills him/er with horror, wakes his/her conscience and is thus the ruler over the person; although it is a continually struggling, warring master with all sorts of forces erupting about in the conscience.

But we ought not remain there: The person who lives in faith, is, according to Luther's teaching one person with Christ: *Fides facit ex te et Christo quasi ubnam personam* (faith makes of you and Christ as it were one person).[131] The person's being captive to his/her conscience occurs in the moment in which he/she wants to be a personality for him/herself. In wanting to be-for-oneself, in the concept of personality which stands by itself and lives by itself, is the weakness of the person over against his/her conscience: the conscience convinces him/her of the fact that his/her freedom is nothing, and the conscience convinces him/her of the fact that this presumed freedom breaks apart when he/she is surrendered to the world. The person will defend him/herself against it in such fashion that he/she attempts, in particular actions, in works, to secure him/herself against the intrusion of this conscience. These are the *opera legis*; they are thus such works of the law which rescue the person from the intrusion of his/her conscience, in that he/she is of the opinion that when he/she does them, he/she is safe from the voice of conscience. For this reason, Luther opposes the *opera legis*. He is not against, say, doing good works, not against faith as an act, but that the person in misunderstanding the *lex* uses this law to save him /herself from the appeal of conscience. Therefore, because these works are not at all done so that in them the command of God is fulfilled, but because they are done by the person who is on flight from God in order to rescue him/herself from his/her conscience, for this reason Luther smashed and wrecked these works. Thus, my conscience shows me the impossibility of my existence. When conscience speaks, it shows me that the person set by him/herself leads an impossible existence. Since I in faith no longer gain and live my existence on my own but seize hold of my existence as God in Jesus Christ has presented it to me, I carry out that change which rescues me. Here results the genuinely liberated conscience; namely, the good conscience.

---

131. WA 40/1, 285, 5 (Gr. Commentary on Galatians. 1531. Hs.)

The good conscience is the result of the fact that God cannot be against himself, that here in Jesus Christ there is no one who accuses me. The person will hold back from taking on the battle themself with the powers which conscience has shown him/her, so to speak, as the horizon of his/her own existence: with death, with sin, and with the law. And it will now lead me by faith to interpret my relation to death, to sin, and to the law as being on the way to Christ, not on a detour around Christ.

The Powers

1. Overcoming Death

Whoever lives in the "world," in "flesh," in "sin," cannot be in Christ, cannot act from out of the power of the Spirit. He/she cannot put his/her members at the disposal of service to the "righteousness of God" (Rom 6:19). This is a final antithesis. One may that say the force of the powers beneath which the person stands must be broken at that point. The person cannot free him/herself from it. Precisely this situation becomes clear to the person in the conscience. In the appeal of conscience, the person discovers the reality of him/herself; that is, he/she discovers the world, the "cosmos," as it is; namely, as defined by death. Since the person recognizes this certainty of death, his/her faith is confronted by death and an entirely new problem emerges. The believing person is not only set before the question of the conquest of sin, for this has indeed no meaning if death is not overcome as the last power. For this reason, the question of the powers surrounding death is foremost. Here Luther develops the Doctrine of the Resurrection, of Christ's victory over death.

Perhaps one can say that Luther's theology is falsely understood where it is limited to the forgiveness of sins because, accordingly, it must then be subjectified and related to the conquest of the consciousness of guilt. However, everything that we have heard about conscience is only properly understood when we proceed from that point to the question of the conquest of death. I believe that the entire problem of "the last things," and perhaps also the problem of demythologization, needs to be grasped on the basis of the idea of death. It is impossible to be happy and free in conscience through Jesus Christ, to actually know what "the forgiveness of sins" means, if I cannot believe in the conquest of death. We will still have to learn in theology that the doctrine of sin is not to be developed apart from the doctrine of death. That was the failure of the

19th century; namely, to think the forgiveness of sins already guarantees eternal life. In that regard one has often referred to Luther's Small Catechism (V:2): "Where there is forgiveness of sins, there is also life and salvation."[132] And so one has left out the entire problem of death, which today is being avenged.

2. The Meaning of the Death of Christ

How Luther interprets the resurrection by way of death on the basis of scripture is best seen from a few passages in Luther himself. In connection with the two passages in Paul: 1 Thess 4:15ff. and 1 Cor 15:52, he says: "He (Paul) tells of three things Christ will have with him at his last advent: the war-cry, the voice of the archangel, and the trumpet of God. And he speaks in the manner as occurs on the field of battle; for war-cry, *keleusma*, means, when the warriors in the army admonish and move one another to fight in knightly fashion.[133] Come on, come on, come on, strike, strike, strike! Trombones are the *drometen* (trumpets) used in armed conflict. So, it is on the field in armed conflict. When one begins the battle and the enemy attacks, then one blows the trumpets or *drometen*, beats the drum, and from it sounds the *taratantara*! The war-cry is sounded: attack, attack, attack, attack! The first lieutenant or captain whom the battle leader has put in command orders the infantry to attack the enemy in knightly fashion: Hui, hui, hui, hui! And the infantry advances: step lively, step lively, step lively; kill them, kill them, kill them. So, it happens when one party has won, then one says: 'The other part has been subdued'. When the Turks go into battle, this is their watchword, and the whole army yells: Allah, Allah, Allahu, Mahomet Regil Allah (There is no God but God, Mahomet is God's servant). The Greeks also did the same in battle; they had their war cry and shout, their trumpets, and drums. In the same Greek manner St. Paul speaks here and says: On the last day, when Christ will come down from heaven, there will be a war-cry: Hui, hui, hui. The great angel will pound the drum, whether the angel Gabriel or another angel, for Gabriel is the highest power among the angels, the highest commander in heaven, who wields the sword, who is the king's marshal, who has the emperor's greatest power in the field, as the name signifies 'Gabriel:' 'God's power,' 'God's 'might.' When he wants

---

132. WA 30/1, 390, 7–8 (The Small Catechism, 1529).
133. The Greek word *keleusma* means "signal" or "command."

to use his power then he kills everything that lives on earth; such an archangel or select angel among other angels, who is God's might, will beat the army drum and let his voice be heard, and God will blow his trumpet. But it will not be such a weak war cry nor such a small voice, nor such a trumpet of metal or bronze as on earth, or of silver, as were the trumpets of Moses (Num 10). But it will be a strong, powerful, heavenly, and godlike war-cry, voice, and trumpet."[134] And the description of battle ends with the famous passage in 2 Pet 4:10: "Then heaven and earth will fall in a heap with a great crash, the elements will melt with heat, the earth and the works within it will burn up."[135]

But does this mean for the Christian that our life in this world is destined for transitoriness? On this question let us hear again a quotation from Luther: "Too much thought have I given to the temporal life and the perishable realm on earth. One always has this transitoriness in sight, thinks of it, worries about it, and rejoices over it; but to those things which are imperishable turns one's back, day and night one chases the former, throws the latter to the wind. Now it should really not be so with Christians but should be the opposite. A Christian should only see this temporal life with closed eyes and blindly, but should see the future, eternal, entirely opened eyes and with a clear, bright light, and only with the left hand should be in this life on earth, but with the right hand and with the soul and whole heart should be in that life in heaven, and always happily wait for it in certain hope."[136]

Thus, the Christian must look to the death of Christ. In a funeral address for the elector Duke Johann of Saxony Luther says, "So, as truly difficult it is, one should get used to learning to see to the death of Christ, by which our death is strangled. And though it appears much differently for our eyes, yet the Holy Spirit mingles this sour vinegar with honey and sugar, so that our faith arises in God and learns to see the dead not in the grave and tomb, but in Christ." There you see the concept: *en Christo*, in Christ. "When we see him resolved in this, then the dead corpse is no longer in the tomb ... as St. Paul in the first (epistle) to the Corinthians, in the fifteenth chapter it says: We bury the body in all dishonor, that is true, but do not look there; for he will rise again in all glory (1 Cor 15:43ff.) ... So he always leads our heart—because he cannot lead the eyes in this way—from what the eyes see, to that which God says, and in Christ, that

---

134. WA 49, 735, 22ff. (Sermon for May 10, 1545. 1 Cor 15:51ff. Dr.)
135. WA 49, 738, 14ff. (Dr.)
136. WA 34/2, 110, 29ff. (Sermon for August 19, 1531 on Titus 2:13, Dr.)

we should have no doubt that he will lead us with Christ. So, whoever could only believe that, would have good comfort in his own dying and others' dying."[137] And further; 'Therefore it is a comforting death, which so gently only his five senses dies away, where a man only rightly sees that one so leads us to being wound up in our Lord Christ's sufferings, that our Lord God says: 'For you I alone will let the devil be bodily choked, so do not look so hard on your death. Look at this, that my Son has died for you and where you also are spiritually choked. So, I will now send you death so that you die only with your five senses, as in a sleep.'"[138] Luther was of the opinion that the person really dies the death, a spiritual death by faith, in that he surrenders himself, and no longer thinks of what is his. This occurs in baptism. Baptism is the conquest of death in a manner similar to the way in which Christ overcame death. For Christ conquers death. It was not, say, a natural law of his life; he chooses death. So, the person chooses death in their baptism. Baptized persons no longer flee from death, but they die the death "in Christ." Therefore the bodily death which they die is still only something which happens to the five senses, and is deceptive; in reality death means only a sleep.[139] On this subject let us hear another word from Luther: "So, if we want to be concerned, we should indeed be concerned with Christ's death which is called a real death, not only in itself, that it was so bitter, shameful and great, but also for the reason that it is so powerful, has baptized all the other dead, so that they should not be called dead, but sleepers."[140] Luther always described the death of Christ very precisely, similar to the way the passion story does, that it was a human suffering and journey into death. Luther writes: "For this is certainly true, as we see in the passion, that Christ died as none ever dies nor will die."[141]

Here the question arises, which also today we consciously or unconsciously see before us: By what right do we personify death? We could answer: Death was not yet in the world, because Adam had not yet sinned. In this way, for example, Paul speaks of "personifying" death (cf. Rom 5:14 and 18; 1 Cor 15:21). In his exposition of Psalm 90 Luther spoke to this question and meant that Moses speaks here in his peculiar fashion,

---

137. WA 36, 243, 32ff. (Sermon for August 18, 1532 on 1 Thess 4:13-14. Dr.)

138. WA 36, 248, 24ff. (Dr.)

139. In the hymn, "In Peace and Joy I Go" the last stanza of the first verse says: "Death has become my sleep." See WA 35, 439, 2, Nr. 13 (EKG 310, 1).

140. WA 36, 241, 14ff. (Dr.)

141. WA 36, nn. 18ff. (Dr.)

and Moses is really the first to discover death for us. The Greek philosophers did not see death in this way; basically, they continually struck the portrait of death from their sight. But Moses discovered that death is the *ira Dei* (wrath of God).[142] This whole question which we can just as well put in regard to sin and probably also the law, reads: How are these entities as such to be seen? We must keep this before our eyes when speaking of the powers according to Luther. Now I think that only in regard to God do the views of death and the vices of sin appear. That death is an entity in and of itself is possible only in a world that is no longer God's world; is possible only apart from the *basileia tou theou*, the kingdom of God. It is thus a possibility which actually is an impossibility. In the world that is no longer God's, death is an entity by itself; there sin is an entity by itself, and rules in the conscience; then also the law is an entity by itself, and an ideology. Where a Doctrine of the Powers is concerned, we would probably have to conceive the order of rank by proceeding from death, and from there come to sin and the law, because by death this being-for-oneself of the cosmos is not only clearly evident, but also has its reality. In the moment in which we skip over death and ignore the horrors of death, and overlook its enmity toward God, then we have misconstrued the reality of the world.

3. The Reality of Death and the Resurrection

At this point I would like to briefly refer to Heidegger's above-mentioned book, "Being and Time."[143] Here we see death as a constitutive of our existence in the cosmos. This modern view of death, which is precisely a myth of death, stems from the first encounter of the young generation with death in the First World War which did not bring along faith in the resurrection, was surrendered to death and the phenomenon of death as such and had to face death in the bravery of heroic existence. This is the context for what Heidegger developed in a genial conception in his book "Being and Time." Accordingly, there is no longer an understanding of human existence in modernity because death has been degraded to an accident. So, we eliminate death. Our modern society lives as if there were no death at all. For the first time again, Heidegger has made clear what all

---

142. H. J. Iwand refers here to Luther's interpretation of Psalm 90. See WA 40/3, 484–594, esp. pp. 493–94 and 536–51 on verse 7 (*Enarratio Psalmi* XC. 1534/35.)

143. See III, 158 (n. 76).

of idealism could not: that death is an ultimately valid phenomenon, an eschatological phenomenon, and a constitutive component of cosmic existence. But he has made it so clear that death was an ultimate event, and therefore Heidegger is also, if you will, the end of a philosophical epoch. Every genuine philosophy would have to go further where Heidegger has stood still. So, these two factors stand over against each other: On the one side a new opening for understanding the problem of earth in theology with the discovery that Golgotha is not the last word, but Easter; and on the other that German philosophy is bracketed by a fact that was not there for Idealism, nor for Marxism, that is—by death.

What is remarkable about Luther is that he never exemplifies faith in the resurrection based only on the fact of the resurrection report. The entire resurrection is for Luther primarily a Gospel, a "good news." And when we inquire of Luther whether he thinks that if an angel had really appeared, then we would soon be corrected. Luther not only based faith in the resurrection on the resurrection reports, but on the fact that God speaks with us; thus, on the first commandment. He continually arrives at this point: When God says, "I am the Lord, thy God," then with that the resurrection is already given. In other words: In the covenant (of the law) which God makes with humankind, certainty of the resurrection is given. What is witnessed to in the resurrection of Jesus is nothing else than that God is God. And what will be attested to in the return of Christ is also nothing else than that God is God. This means that the being which death has assumed to be, will, in the final perspective, be shown to be a non-being; and the being which Jesus describes, will be revealed to us as the fitting being. The "being in Christ" is thus an expression of the unique reality that exists. On the other hand, death's presumed reality, which is a reality because the wrath of God stands behind it, is shown to be a fraud. Luther says: "These are our *principia*, reasons, and chief articles on which all of Christian teaching stands. For all of scripture speaks only of God and his Son and the apostles, that their preaching is the proper word of God, and whoever believes in it, is blest. Now, if you will deny all that, then I have nothing to do with you, for whoever denies God and his word, his baptism and gospel, easily has to deny the resurrection of the dead. If you dare to say that God is not God, and neither teach or believe the apostles and Christianity then you have done well, and no better than completely knocking the bottom out of the barrel and saying, there is no resurrection, no heaven nor hell, no devil nor death nor sin, etc. For what will you believe when you do not believe that God is anything?"[144] In other words, faith in the resurrection of the dead is faith that God *is* something, that God is not merely an idea. If God were merely a picture, a sketch one makes for oneself because one needs a partner beyond the stars, then God would not be anything. Luther saw precisely that the denial of the resurrection of the dead is ultimately the spiritualizing of God. If God does not have his kingdom, his power, his revelation, his word for and through himself, if he has it only in the sphere of Christian consciousness, then there is no resurrection of the dead.

Thus, by way of death it is clear that the world in which we live is not God's world—that creation is lost. We must live from the perspective of the resurrection to gain a proper relation to earthly creatures; we must live "beyond death." Luther says: "Come now, that is a good interpreter and a strong confutation (refutation), which can make from the word of death a healing switch. The Holy Spirit and the right hand of God must teach the art."[145] And Luther explains further: "Here then it truly depends on a good expositor who would out-shout and overcome the devil with this verse and say, 'Nevertheless it is not death nor wrath; nor is it gracious correction and fatherly punishment. I still know that he does not hand me over to death, and I will still not believe it is wrath if all the devils in hell in a heap said it.' Yes, even if an angel from heaven said it, then let it be cursed (cf. Gal 1:8), and if God himself said it, I would still believe that he tempted me like Abraham and appeared so wrathful and still were not in earnest, for he does not retract his word."[146] Death cannot have the last word. If it were only this finite world of death, if this were the only world, then the *verbum dei* (word of God) could not be sounded in this world. Where the word of God comes, there the doors of death spring open. Where the Word is become flesh (John 1:14), there must be the resurrection. The resurrection of Jesus is no accident, for then the victory of God would also be an accident. The resurrection is given by the fact that God has spoken to us. Very often Luther appealed to the fact that God is a God of the living (cf. Matt 22:32) wherever we hear God's word and wherever we encounter God's word.

In the moment that modern theology, as early as in the Enlightenment, dismissed the "resurrection," there one knows nothing more of God's word, but one knows only something about pious self-consciousness. We

---

144. WA 36, 527, 17ff. (Sermon for September 22, 1532. 1 Cor 15:12–15, Dr.)
145. WA 31/1, 158, 27ff. (Interpretation of Psalm 118. *Das Confitemini* 1530, Dr.)
146. WA 31/1, 159, 26ff. (Dr.)

have tried to make clear that the view of the hostile powers which play a role in Luther's theology, coheres with the conscience, and that the conscience disclosed to humankind an understanding of existence which no longer sets one within the sphere of one's own possibilities, but discloses that one is captive to specific powers of life in this world. Luther simply speaks of the presence of these powers with the concept "world," in the distinction between world and the kingdom of God. World for him is not simply a given in the sense as we conceive it today. Luther would never have been able to express the understanding of the world, say, as idealism did, as if the presence of the world were the material or the matter of our duty, before which we had to exercise ourselves, freely, as determined by the spirit. The worldview of German idealism cannot be reconciled with how Luther understood the world. One might even go so far as to say that (for Luther) the world is a great historical variable, even a variable of fate. Human existence in the world means, in effect, that one is always subject to powers which define and rule against one's will. What is decisive and great about Luther's theology becomes precisely clear in Luther's concept of death. Luther distinguishes between the two kinds of death: the one death is the dying of the old man, the death of death, life from the Word, the great act of liberation and the other is the "little death," the small death, the dying, the rest allowed the dead; the flesh, which must be changed just as I myself by faith in the Word have been changed from someone captive to death, into life. Luther says of these two deaths, "The first death from Adam will be cast off and changed into a spiritual death, by which we die to sin, so that the soul wills no sin, and the body no longer does it. And so, already before death which sin had brought on us, eternal life is begun in you. Because now you are free from the horrible, damnable death, accept this sweet, holy, blessed death; so, die to sin that you protect yourself from sin and do not serve it. For this the death of Christ shall work in you, in which you are baptized, that such baptism also brings a death with it because Christ himself died for it and for this reason also commanded you to be baptized that the sin be drowned in you. The other little death is now the external dying (which scripture calls a sleep) laid on this flesh, so that it does not cease (because we live on earth) to resist the spirit and his life. For the spirit or the soul says: I am the death of sins, I must use my life as long as I live. The spirit says: I believe that God has forgiven and taken from me my sins through Christ. On the other hand, the body: What do I know of God and his will? The soul says: I must be mild, sweet, chaste, humble, patient, etc., and strive for the future life. The flesh howls against it: So! what in heaven's name? Did I not have enough milk and bread, money, and goods here? etc."[147] "The flesh always does this as long as it lives here, stretches, and draws sin after it, defends itself and will not die, therefore God must finally execute this too, that it also has its death from sin. And yet this is also a finer, calmer death and really nothing else than a sleep, for it shall not remain in death (because the soul and Spirit is no longer in death), but come forth again, purified and cleansed on the last day as spirit. Then it will be a finer, purer, more obedient body, without all sin and evil desire."[148]

Luther goes on to say, "What we lack of it is only that now the ignorant flesh cannot conceive it; it is still horrified by the larva of death." For the Christian, death has lost its substantiality, it is still only a larva, a mask. The flesh "thinks the old death still suffers for it does not understand the spiritual death of sin, cannot judge otherwise than as it feels and sees, that the human dies and wastes away under the earth and is consumed. Such horrible and hateful larvae before his eyes make it so that it will not down, and is still only his guilt of ignorance, otherwise it would eagerly allow nothing to be feared or horrified by it."[149]

In the funeral hymns of the protestant churches there is this widely extended alteration of death, this saying "Yes" to death. And yet no one, not even our church community, can live in this certainty come from death, as if it were too powerful for us, as if we no longer had the power as has been shown us in Luther's teaching. That, naturally, is present in our theology. Indeed, for Luther death is not optimistically shoved aside, but is seen realistically. And those "in Christ" are those who take into themselves ownership of death, dying to it: "And here is raised the narrow gate, the narrow way to life (Matt 7:14), which everyone must gladly consider, for it is really almost narrow, but it is not long. And what happens here is that as a child is born with danger and anxiety from the tiny dwelling of a mother's womb into this wide heaven and earth, which is on this world. Thus, one goes from this life through the narrow gate of death. And even though the heaven and the world in which we live is seen to be great and wide, so everything compared with the future heaven is much narrower and smaller, as the mother's womb compared with this heaven. Therefore,

---

147. WA 22, 110, 3ff. (Cruciger's Summer Postille. Epistle for 6th Sunday after the Trinity. Rom 6:3–11). The last sentence possibly contains a play on words by Luther (the "heaven" is juxtaposed with "enough milk"), which doesn't appear in Nhd. (D.H.)

148. WA 22, 110, n. 27ff.

149. WA 22, 101, 22ff.

the deary only dying is called a new birth, and its festal days are called in Latin *natale*, a day of one's birth. But the narrow way of death makes us think that this life is wide and that life narrow. Therefore, one must believe and learn from the bodily birth of a child, as Christ says: A woman when giving birth, suffers anxiety, but when she recovers never thinks of the anxiety since she has born a man into the world (cf. John 16:21). So, one must also in dying consider the anxiety, and know that afterwards will be a great space and joy."[150]

Thus, for Luther death is integrated into life; it has become a function of life. In this way God makes his own alive; without death we could not live. Death is thus willed by God, the answer to life. And in this respect Christ is the model for us, that he took death upon himself; he did not pass by it. There is scarcely a writing in which the problem of death is so clearly seen as in Plato's' "*Phaedon*."[151] Here the problem of death is overcome by the doctrine of the immortality of the soul. But this means death is not set in reaction to the nature of the whole person, thus of the "I" itself. But Jesus goes directly towards death. He takes death directly on himself. Luther very clearly describes this immediacy of death and resurrection of Jesus Christ for the individual, the Christian, and for his own, precisely in view of the destiny of the soul, when in a sermon on 1 Cor 15:25 he writes, "But a Christian, by the very fact that he has become a Christian, is thrust into death, and every hour carries it with him wherever he goes and stays, must wait every moment because he lived here, since the devil, the world, and his own flesh give him no rest. Yet, on the other hand, he has the advantage that he is already out of the grave with his right leg, and has a mighty helper, who reaches a hand to him, that is, his Lord Christ, who is already long since out of it, and seizes him with his fist and is wrenched more than half, so that nothing more than the left foot is left behind, for his sin is already forgiven (blotted out), God's wrath and hell extinguished, and already lives in and with Christ as to the best piece (which is the soul), sharing eternal life. Therefore, death can no longer hold him nor do anything to him, without the other piece, the old skin, flesh, and blood having to waste away, so that it also becomes new and can follow the soul. In any case we have already come into life, because Christ and my soul are no longer in death."[152]

150. WA 2, 685, 22ff. ("A Sermon on Preparing for Death," 1519, On the Third) = BoA 1, 162, 5ff.

151. Plato (427–347 BC), Greek Philosopher, ("Theory of Forms" in *The Republic*).

152. WA 36, 581, 18ff. (Sermon for November 3, 1532).

For the well-known view that all that has occurred to Christ has occurred for us, and is related to dying, there is a really brilliant expression of Luther on Rom 4:25 where it reads Christ was delivered up for our sins and raised for our justification: "Here the fame and comfort is taken from those who through their merit want to make themselves holy before God. Because such a death had to occur for our sins, which there is called the death of Jesus Christ, and such a resurrection had to happen which is also called the resurrection of Jesus Christ, it is good to reckon that either our merit is nothing and lost, or Christ's death and resurrection is of no use and in vain. God forbid, Amen."[153] And equally brilliant is the following brief exposition of Rom 8:31: Si *Due pro nobis, quis contra nos?* (If God is for us, who can be against us?) If we could decline the pronoun *nos* and *nobis* and understand them, then we would also conjugate the noun *Deus* and make a verb from the noun which would read: *Deux dixit, et dictus est* (God has spoken, and it is spoken of him). Then the preposition *contra* would apply to all crimes, and finally there would be from it an *infra nos* (among us), as it will and must happen. Amen."[154]

To decline means to inflect, to relate to us—then we would conjugate the word *Deus*, which means to join, *conjungere*, and make a verb from the noun, which means: *Deus dixit*. In other words, if we, in face of the power of death, could properly apply this to ourselves that God is for us and could see that herein is God's promise, then the *contra* would be an *infra*, when we now would say, to wit: these powers are all liquidated, death is no more.

Death does not simply cease to be against humans when one explains it, when one makes excuses for it and takes the fear of death from it, but it is actually against us; and it is only not against us when God speaks, and the word of God overcomes death. Without God himself taking on death and thus cancelling it, it is not cancelled, otherwise there can be no *infra* from the *contra*. Luther says on John 8:51 ("Whoever keeps my word will never see death"): "All the world fears death and yet despises this medication against it, that is, God's word. How does that happen? The world will and cannot believe that God's word is God's power. For it sees the letters with cows' eyes or the oral space, does not think that there is something more behind it, especially such a great power of God. But whoever believes it, as St. Paul in Rom 1 says, that God's word is God's

---

153. WA 48, 203, Nr. 272 (Sayings from the New Testament).
154. WA 48, 203, Nr. 273.

power (Rom 1:16) will hold it dear and of worth. For death, which he otherwise cannot avoid except by God's word, will certainly teach him."[155]

The *dynamis* (strength, force) of the word of God is a power that annuls the world of death. If God is for us, that is, if he implants his word in me, then the power of death is overcome by it. The *verbum Dei* is always spoken toward the world of the resurrection—and it is impossible that the *verbum Dei* could be in the world of death without bursting the rule of the world of death: "And here we should learn the rule, that where in the Psalter and in the scripture the saints thus deal with God about comfort and help in their distress, that there very certainly eternal life and resurrection of the dead are dealt with, and that such texts always belong to the article of the resurrection and eternal life, indeed, to the whole third section of the creed, thus of the Holy Spirit, of sacred Christianity, of the forgiveness of sins, of the resurrection, of eternal life and everything flows from the first commandment, where God says: I am thy God..."[156]

The resurrection is thus not simply an isolated event in which we have to believe—whoever will actually force us to believe in such a fact—but that God is something for which the resurrection is a sign. We could say: If there were no resurrection, then God would be an idea, then we will have to fight with the atheists of today as to whether we will live in the modern world with such an idea of God or without it. And one does, indeed, often have the impression that the battle today is really a battle over a phantom. Some say, "Behind your idea there is nothing," and the others say, "There is something behind our idea," and the others say, "Certainly, there is something behind our idea." These, then are two world views and for these world views living persons are sacrificed. However, for the living God only one person was sacrificed: He, himself. The resurrection is thus as certain as God is God. If God is only an idea one forms for oneself, in order, by way of it, to have a concept of order for the existence of the world, or a guarantee for the moral law, or a judge over good and evil, or to have comfort for one's inner conflict—if God is merely that, then in fact we need no resurrection.

---

155. WA 48, 156, on Nr. 204.
156. WA 31/1, 154, 27ff. (Interpretation of Psalm 118. *Das Confitemini* 1530, Dr.).

The Word of God

1. Beyond Law and Gospel

The doctrine of the word of God in Luther should be as closely as possible moved up next to the doctrine of the "powers" and death because it is so very clear that with the word of God a new world is present. The word of God is there in the antithesis—as Luther happily states in the "reflection"—of the powers. Precisely by this the presence of these powers and the determination of our life by them is put into question. The Doctrine of the Word of God according to Luther has been thus far scarcely developed, and it is ruined by the fact that it is immediately split into the Doctrine of Law and Gospel. The one word of God is beyond law and gospel. This one word of God, which is not yet separated in the dialectic of law and gospel, that is the antithesis to the powers.[157] Now we inquire of Luther as to whether with him there is this concept of the *verbum Dei*, which is beyond law and gospel, and what it means, and how this word of God suits his theology. We will understand the concept most clearly when we see it in the antithesis to the "powers." In a sermon on the Canaanite woman (Matt 15:21–28) Luther says: "All the ideas, what you feel, see, and hear, you should strike from your heart and not decide whether it is temporal or eternal, whether you feel shame or honor, have poverty or riches, death or life, heaven or hell, God's wrath, or grace. But keep clinging to the Word: do not let it be taken from you, judge yourself by it, then there is no distress. For God only thrusts before your eyes sin, death, devil, hell, God's wrath, and God's judgment, so that he drives you to cling alone to the Word with the heart. He intends that you should not set foot on anything else than alone on the Word you have heard. Thus, naked, he will have undressed you. Come into heaven or to hell, you shall remain with this Word. Where that remains, you remain and say: There

---

157. On this topic we find in the afterward to H. J. Iwand's lectures the very clear statement identified in quotation marks: "In the Lutheran Confessions, the concept of the word of God per se is difficult to find, because the concept of the word of God is not there. The Confessions begin immediately with the contrast between law and gospel whenever they talk of the word of God. We encounter this issue anew in K. Barth's truly inspired discovery of this problem as he perceives it within Protestant theology. Lutheran orthodoxy had lost track of it. It had immediately identified the word of God with the "Scriptures" so that there are plenty of references to teachings on the scriptures, but not on the word of God."

I have the Word, I will make my way in it; feel as I will; I will not be wrenched away from this Word."[158]

The entire scope of what Luther happily describes by the concept *sentire*, sensing and feeling, of *experientia* (experience), is transcended by the *verbum*.[159] The Word is never an expression of feeling. Luther states this emphatically in the address to the provost of Leizkau, in which he speaks of the *nativitas ex verbo Dei* (birth by the word of God).[160] In this sermon it is stated that all her sins are forgiven by the church and do not so heavily take on weight as sin when it does not offer the Word. For when the Word is not there, then the new man cannot be born. As the Word, so also the birth; if the Word is false, then also those coming from it will be false saints. If a pastor can build churches and do great things, it is all for nothing if the Word is not on the scene.[161]

2. The Eschatological Character of the Word

Here we see that from the beginning (1512) for Luther the category of the *verbum Dei* has played a decisive role. Indeed, we can actually say: Luther established anew the eschatological character of the *verbum Dei*. For with the existence of the word of God the new world is present; it is present beyond sin, death, and hell, and it is present in our Aeon. When we naturally, as has occurred in Protestantism, derive the word from experience, when, for example, the word of Paul or the word of the prophets is interpreted from the personal experience of those who are speaking here, then all is lost, then the *verbum Dei* has been transposed and sunk in *sentire*, in the *experientia*, briefly, in everything only thinkable and possible within the powers of death. And this in fact has occurred in Protestant theology, probably not without being caused by one's having shattered the unity of the word of God into the distinction between law and gospel. Now there is no longer an overarching concept, now the entire relation between law

---

158. WA 21, 113, 16ff. (Winter Postille 1528).

159. The word of God is a generally valid and strongly necessary concept. (D.H.)

160. This possibly has to do with one of the earliest sermons by Luther, which he wrote "for the Propst von Leitzkau Georg Masco" in in 1512 (!). See WA 1, 8-17.

161. See also p. 13 of the often-cited phrase: "It is clear: the church is not born and does not come from nature, but only through the word of God." (Jas 1:18). The concept of the "*verbum Veritatis*" can be found in this small, seven-page sermon in the WA not fewer than 23 times. Additionally, the astute reader will notice the juxtaposition of "iustus et peccator" (also 11, 6-7)

and gospel is interpreted from the varying different situation in which the word of God affects me—whether it frightens, judges, damns, or whether it comforts, supports, builds me up. So, the entire problem of the word of God is inveigled in the psychic situation; in one's varying understanding, whether of the natural or the reborn person. But it can be made clear that for Luther there is another concept of the word of God: "This is certainly true: if it were a matter of feeling, I would be lost, but the Word should be valued above my and the whole world's feeling and remain true, however slight it appears, and also however weakly we believe it is. For we all see and experience the work, that sin absolute (absolutely) damns and judges us to hell, death devours us and the whole world, which no one can avoid. And you speak to me of life and righteousness of which I do not see the slightest spark, and indeed it must be a frail life. Yes, truly, a frail life respecting our faith, but as frail as it is, when only the Word and a little spark of faith remains in the heart, then such a fire erupts from it that fills all life, heaven, and earth, devours both death and all misfortune, and like a little drop of water penetrates the frail faith, so that one should neither see nor feel sin and death any longer. But there is a mighty battle that goes with it, so we should hold to the Word against our feeling and seeing."[162] Thus, the Word enables me *extra me stare,* to stand outside myself: "Therefore our theology is certain, because it places us outside ourselves (*quia point nos extra nos*). I need not support myself on my conscience, feeling, person, work, but on the divine promise and truth, which cannot deceive."[163] That is the reason why our theology is certain. It wrenches us from ourselves; it frees us from our feeling and begins first where psychology ends. As much as psychology appears in Luther's theology, it is aways governed by one point: *extra nos.*

What this means for us and our relation to the word of God, Luther states (again in the sermon on 1 Cor 15): "What should I do? If I should shut the door on such feeling and my ability, then I and all men would have to despair and be ruined. But if I want to be helped then I must truly turn myself around and look to the Word and repeat 'I indeed feel God's wrath, devil, death, and hell, but the Word says otherwise, that I have a gracious God through Christ, who is my Lord over the devil and all creatures. I feel and see indeed, that I and all men must rot in the grave, but the Word says otherwise, that I shall rise with great glory, and live

---

162. WA 36, 497, 19ff. (Sermon for August 11, 1532, 1 Cor 15 Dr.)
163. WA 40/1, 589, 8ff. (Gr. Commentary on Galatians, 1531. Hs.)

eternally'"[164] This also means, if I want to be certain of the Word, then I must change, says Luther, or turnabout. The concept of *mutatio* (change, alteration) is already found early in Luther, when he speaks of the *verbum Dei*. A pregnant passage from the "Lecture on Romans" (Rom 3:4) reads: "So he changes us into his Word, but not his Word into us."[165] With all this change something must be constant, otherwise we could not speak of change. Either the "I" is constant and changes the "Word," that is, changes the understanding of the Word, but then I must have a certain constant in the "I." Or, the Word is the constant, and one is newly born. The person is the variable of the constant *verbum Dei*. Then we could naturally say of *verbum Dei* God's faithfulness, God's identity with himself. If it were merely a matter of understanding the word of God, then man would be the constant. Thus, for Luther it is not a matter of understanding but of something entirely different. Let us hear Luther once more in connection with the quotation from the sermon on 1 Cor 15: "I must surely turn around and look to the Word and repeat it . . ."[166] and, "I indeed feel and see that I and all men must rot in the grave, but the Word says otherwise, that I shall arise with great gory and live eternally[167] And a bit later it says, "So the two must remain here, that we are lords of the devil and death and yet at the same time lie under his feet. One thing is to be believed, the other to be felt. For the world and what belongs to its nature must have the devil for its lord, who hangs on us with all his might and is far superior to us, for we are his guests as in a foreign hostel.[168] But since I seize hold of the Word, I share in the victory of Christ over the powers, over death. Then I can also feel, experience, this faith as a feeling as a result. It determines my entire "I." Christ must go on before, he must go on before in such a way that nothing is there but the Word, on which I support myself. I must dare to cling to the Word in nothingness, for it has no other way of existing than through itself. It is what it is, not through something, but through itself. I must risk allowing nothing other than the Word. The last verse of Luther's hymn, "A Mighty Fortress" expresses this:

A mighty fortress is our God:

164. WA 36, 495, 3ff.

165. WA 56, 227, 4-5 (Scholien) = BoA 5, 234, 29-30 = Fi (Scholien) 65, 17-18. The Latin in this sentence reads: "*Et ita nos in verbum suum, non autem verbum suum in nos mutat.*"

166. WA 36, 495, 6-7.

167. WA 36, 495, nn. 9ff.

168. WA 36, 495, nn. 18ff.

> And should they in the strife
> Take kindred, goods and life;
> We freely let them go . . .[169]

Thus, everything else is so appointed that it counts as nothing; that it is taken from me. According to Luther, the Word is only properly understood in that it is present by itself. Only in this way does the Word interpret itself which is nothing else than the result of the fact that I read the scripture with reference to the word of God. For this reason, Luther's thesis is that the "Scripture interprets itself."[170] It does so not merely by itself, but for the reason that and insofar as it is the word of God. There is no analogy, no point of beginning, there is no norm, by which I could say: That is God's word. However, we have set up such norms and have said: What speaks to you in the conscience, what rescues you from the law, that is the *verbum Dei*. We have cited *experienti* (experience), *conscientia* (conscience), and *persona,* in order to establish by means of them what is God's word and what is not God's word. But that is impossible. For then we have already, once again, employed worldly categories by which to measure God's word, and in so doing we do not let God himself be judge. In the exposition of Psalm 110 from 1518, Luther says: "A rod of righteousness is the rod of your kingdom, and that is the rod one draws going from the mouth of Christ flowing to the rainbow, and the word of God is both sword and rod, the royal scepter, and the royal sword. And that it is painted from the mouth and not from the hand means that it is nothing else than the just and sharp word of God which cuts away all that is evil and unjust, and judges everything crooked."[171]

3. Word and Sacrament

God's word is for those who cling to it, who entrust him with the victory over all their struggles. Where "I" entrusts it to him, there the victor is won; for the Word in itself is the victory. For: "As much as you believe, so much you have."[172] Whoever can let everything else go and take hold of the Word, has it. Whoever does not let everything else go will never

---

169. WA 35, 457, 8ff. Nr. 26 (EKG 201, 4).

170. Foundational sentence of old Lutheran theology, in this form (Latin: "*Scriptura seipsam explicat*") in Hollatz, *Examen theologicaum*, 160.

171. WA 1, 694, 21ff.

172. WA 2, 719, 8 (A sermon on the sacrament of confession. 1519)

have it. Whoever holds to the Word with only the one hand and with the other to creation, to his life, wife and child, house, and court, never has it, and that is then the condition of our general "piety." We will not be totally moralistic, not merely live from the goods of this world, but we will also not live totally from God's word. And that is called living in both worlds; "walking between both worlds."[173] So it is with us by far. For Luther, both God and his word are identical. The Word does it. The existence of the word of God among us is the existence of God in our midst. And there is no other existence of God. In Luther's conflict with D. Karlstadt,[174] the issue was that the salvation of humankind does not result from practicing Christianity. All knowledge in this sense, according to Luther, can be one's imagination, that is, the forming-in-oneself the portrait of Christ. Luther will have none of it, all that is "Frau Hulda," or clever reason.[175] Luther defends the Word against such forming-in-oneself. At issue is the concluding formula of the Lord's Supper: "Do this in remembrance of me." This remembrance of Christ should be an external remembrance, where one says of someone: "Thus with the word 'do this do in remembrance of me' Christ intends the same as Paul with the "You shall proclaim the LORD'S death," etc. Christ will have it that one preaches about him, that we enjoy the sacrament, and speak the gospel to strengthen faith; not sit and play with ideas in the heart and make a good work out of such remembrance, as Dr. Karlstadt dreams."[176] Everything depends on the proclamation of the Word.

In another passage of his debate with Karlstadt's view of the Lord's Supper, Luther says, God's word is not identical with our "hissing and blowing." It has nothing to do with that fact that a mortal man speaks God's word: "Also, where have we ever taught that by our hissing and blowing the bread becomes better? But hey, when then? (Note in the WA: Why not? thus, from here on). Come now, I will also swear an oath. If Dr. Karlstadt believes that any kind of God is in heaven and on earth,

---

173. Title of a book by Walter Flex (1887–1917) which was well-known during WWI and received enthusiastically among the youth movement.

174. Karlstadt (aka Andreas Bodenstein), was born in 1480 in Karlstadt am Main and taught at the University of Wittenberg beginning in 1505. He belonged to the early supporters of Luther but broke away later due to a disagreement over the sacrament of communion and died in Basel in 1541 (See also IV, p. 290ff.)

175. The subtitle of one of Luther's writings against Karlstadt is: "Von Frau Hulda, der klugen Vernunft" ("On the shrewd Mrs. Hulda", Trans. R. Lundell). See WA 18, 182, 11–12. (Against the spiritual prophets . . . Part 2, 1525.)

176. WA 18, 197, 26ff.

then Christ my Lord should nevermore be sweet and gracious to me. That is what is truly sworn. Then reason is this: Dr. Karlstadt knows that we neither blow nor hiss over the bread and wine, but speak the divine, almighty, heavenly, holy word, which Christ himself with his holy mouth spoke at the Lord's Supper and commanded to speak ... Indeed, if a devil spoke them, they are still God's word, and for that reason to be held in all honor, as it deserves."[177] Luther meant at bottom that Karlstadt is atheistic in his entire view, because he really acknowledged nothing other than the human act in speaking the word of God. Luther thinks that for Karlstadt there is no word of God at all. And where there is no word of God for anyone, there, in Luther's opinion, there is no God. Where the word of God can be annulled in our "hissing and blowing," where it is only a function stemming from our dead world, there also God does not exist. Luther is of the opinion that whoever does not allow the Word to stand does not allow God to stand. The test case involved is always whether we allow God to stand in his word. Luther never reckoned with a given fact to which the Word is added in order then to interpret the fact. He never reckoned with the "fact of Christ;" there is no such thing for Luther, and the miracle of the sacrament, the mere presence of bread and wine in the sacrament means nothing at all to him. He is never concerned with the fact, but always with the Word. In the Word is set the facticity of all facts. The facts with which faith deals never have their facticity in themselves, but through the Word, in which everything that is God is what it is, in the freedom of God himself.

Luther further states: "This, however, is our teaching, that the bread and wine are of no help, indeed even the body and blood in the bread and wine are of no help. I will say yet further: Christ on the cross with all his suffering and death are of no help even when most ardently, most heatedly, most heartily is known and recognized, as you (Karlstadt) teach. Another thing must still be there. What then? The Word, the Word, the Word. Listen, you lying spirit: The Word does it. For whether Christ was given and crucified for us a thousand times it would all be in vain if the word of God did not come and share it and give it to me and say: 'This shall be yours, take and you have it.'"[178] Christ by virtue of the Word reaches into my heart. Without the Word he will never come into my

---

177. WA 18, 202, 2ff. Compare for clarification ibid. 136, 33ff. "Should one eat the bread of Christ in the house as a sacrament? No, no. One must eat Christ's body in a spiritual setting."

178. WA 18, 202, n. 32ff.

heart. Without the Word a Christ-piety will at best arise, a heart-of Jesus-love, but never the conquest of the Crucified over sin and death.

In the conflict with Karlstadt at issue is that the word of God, and the action of God in Christ, has sovereignty over me. The Word is the reason that God's action occurs in me. The Word is the basis of the fact that God's action occurs in me at all. Here free will has no place. The appropriation is not a matter of free will. Not my "I," or an I-relation which first qualifies the revelation of God as real, but the revelation of God is in itself real through the Word, and in that I am drawn to it, I receive my reality. This actually goes so far that Luther can even let go of the "real presence" (the actual presence of Christ) in the Lord's supper. "Oh, you false prophets, you have no word in the sacrament which grants or gives you forgiveness of sins. I say once again: he (Karlstadt) wants to make the Word on which we stand in the sacrament conflicted, disputing and poking, and would like to have proved that it wasn't in it. So, he would have been a faithful knight anyway, for even if mere bread and wine were there, as they say, then the words "take and eat, this is my body given for you," etc., would still mean the forgiveness of sins in the sacrament on account of this word, just as we confess mere water in baptism. But because the word of God is in it, which forgives sins, we freely say with Saint Paul that baptism is a bath of rebirth and renewal. Everything depends on the Word."[179]

4. The Word as the Authority of God

This Word is an external word, that is, it is what it is through itself. It is *extra me*. It is present, and the form of its existence in the world is its form, and that is the scripture. On this Luther indeed states that the spirits of the rotten ones (the fanatics) "do not point you to the external gospel, but to la-la land, and say: Stand in the tedium (the meaning is the inward sinking as mysticism practiced it) as I have stood, so you also will experience it: Then the heavenly voice will come and God himself will speak with you. If you ask further regarding the tedium, they know as much about it as D. Karlstadt does from the Greek and Hebrew language. Do you see the devil there, the enemy of divine order? How he opens his mouth to you with the words Spirit, Spirit, Spirit, and meanwhile defines both bridges, step and path, ladder and everything by which the Spirit should come to you, that is: the external ordinances of God in the bodily

---

179. WA 18, 204, 11ff.

baptism, a sign, and in the oral word of God, and will teach you, not how the Spirit comes to you, but how you should come to the Spirit, that you should learn to go on the clouds and ride on the wind, and yet not say how or when, where or what, but yourself should experience how it is."[180]

The Word is always an entity *sui generis* (unique, of a special kind). The Word must be there, so that I can believe. It is present, there by itself; it moves, it speaks, it preaches; no one signals, feels it, and no one hears it approaching. One hears only the Word. All glittering things are put away, all appearance, every external thing; this it is which makes one truly devout."[181] And further: "All appearance passes away; we can take none of the glittering words with us after death, everything goes away under the hands. So, we must have something eternal to which we cling, that justifies us and by which the soul is nourished, which is not transitory, God alone. I get this when I hear the Word from him, to which I cling, whether I see it or not. Where that remains, there also I remain. Now this foundation remains standing eternally, and so I am held along there, for only that is the eternal good."[182]

The Word is thus the guarantee, the certainty of eternal life, and thus the certainty of the truth, the certainty of God. Luther occasionally spoke against those who wanted to make the Word a positivistic entity, for example in the writing "Instruction, how Christians should bother with Moses, 1525" he says, "One must deal and proceed crisply with the scripture. From the beginning, the Word has occurred in many ways (Heb 1:1). One must not only view whether it is God's word, whether God has spoken, but rather to whom it is spoken, whether it concerns you or another. It is divided there like summer and winter. God spoke much to David, told him to do this and that. But it does not apply to me, it is also not spoken to me. He can indeed speak to me when he will. You must look to the Word which concerns you, is spoken to you and not what concerns another. There is a dual word in scripture: One does not apply to me, does not concern me; the other concerns me and that which concerns me (on this) I may fervently wager it and rely on it as on a strong rock."[183] Luther means: It is all God's word, but I must know and pay attention to whom the word of God is spoken. Here then the

---

180. WA 18, 137, 6ff.

181. WA 9, 618, 8ff, (Luther's sermons collected by John Poliander, 1519 until 1921. John 8:46ff.).

182. WA 9, 618, 8ff. nn. 36ff.

183. WA 16, 384, 33ff.

whole question of the historical situation plays into the exegesis of the word of God. Of course, Luther drew the distinction between law and gospel in the word of God. But we will not understand the distinction if we overlook the fact that it is the *one* word of God that is present in both. It is the Word in which God carries out his epiphany (appearance). So, the Reformation is founded on the word of God, because here God carries out his epiphany, no longer on the sacrament. The word of God is a category not to be derived from anything else, for which reason it is the authority. It is authority in so far as we, when we stand over against it, stand over against our origin, against that which has created and creates us. We area *creaturae verbi Dei* (creatures of the word of God). This means through the word of God he sets us in relationship to himself. If you want to encounter your relation to God, then cling to his word. And this way of encountering the relation to me established by God—namely, to live under God—is called faith. As isolated as the *verbum* stands in the world, just as isolated is faith as part of my existence. It is instituted by the Word; it is not grown from my nature, thus at issue is the rejection of free will with all its contingencies for faith. Faith is not simply obedience, not simply trust, but is the new birth of my life by the Word (Jas 1:18). It is the sign that the word of God to me does not occur in vain. It is the way of living from God, which pleases God, which he will have from his creature, human being. It is the way of living which the word of God, this gracious form of his revelation, is offered and makes possible for us.

5. Christ and the Word

Since Luther discovers the word of God in this axiomatic,[184] since he conceives of it and emphasizes that it stands in the world as strange—as strange as Christ himself was—as an absolute, he accordingly makes the revelation of God independent of creation, history, and of everything that exists. God did not have to reveal himself in his word, he was evident in his creation (Rom 1:19ff.), which Luther states in many passages. Of itself the *theologia naturalis* (natural religion) was correct—Why not?—but the revelation of God in the Word is, so to speak, his grace itself. That we do not only have the stars, not only conscience, history, not only our way of life, not only, say, the documents of a high standing, pre-Asiatic

---

184. The term "axiomatic" is understood in the area of epistemology as the teaching on axioms. An axiom is not provable and as such does not serve as a necessary presupposition for a series of conclusions. (J. Haar)

religion, but that we have the Word is the miracle of the revelation. That behind all the voices where God is only anticipated, suddenly there is his voice; a call, which is his call. Let us hear Luther: "For this he uses a beautiful parable of the hen who gathers her chicks under her wings, and so protects them (Matt 23:37; Luke 13:34). In the creation God has taken into account his divine will, which surely will help everyone."[185] So that means, when Jesus speaks the parable of the hen, God has considered the parable of his will. That is theologically very profoundly said: "The wings denote the holy word of God. When he lets his word go out, then it is nothing else than that he will cover and protect everyone with it . . . Thus God spreads his wings, that is his holy word, offers us his grace, and so we are protected under the shadow of his wings. For the shadow of his wings means faith."[186] That is a passage of which I would say in a certain respect is perfect for what Luther means. It is not yet troubled by theological reflection. Today we are always used to interpret faith by what is actually only the fruit of faith (i.e., such concepts as obedience, deciding, trusting). In so doing we will not understand Luther's concept of faith. But just as the word of God is a matter *sui generis*, underivable, without any analogy, underivable from nature, history, so is also faith underivable, as Luther says: It alone justifies.

That the word of God stands over me and I let it stand over me, that is faith for Luther. Only from there results obedience, deciding, trusting etc. Luther says of God, "He will thus require nothing from us if we only set such confidence in him. If we have faith, then we are already devout, have kept all the commandments, need nothing more, by which we should become devout, already have everything. No one can see this faith when he has it, for it is inward in the heart. You will not come to this freedom if you do from the outside (externally) what you will, for in doing so the heart is not pure, devout, free, by it gets no joyful, uncaptured conscience; you must lift up to one higher. Freedom comes from within, that we are one with God and know how we stand with him."[187]

Why then are we one with God, when we live under his word? But this only because God's word is identical to his covenant. His covenant is not something else besides his word, but his word is his covenant. That God is with us, "Immanuel," that means his word. His word is not

---

185. WA 9, 529, 15ff. (Sermons by Luther collected by Joh. Poliander 1519–1521. Matt 23:34ff.)

186. WA 9, 529, 15ff., n. 18ff.

187. WA 9, 567, 16ff. (Luke 2:22ff.)

a formal concept—with God there are no formal concepts that are not also content at the same time. Accordingly, certainty corresponds to the revelation. There must be a certainty there, which is distinct from all other certainty. We can never gain it from our notions of the existence of God. It must be superior to all other certainties. It must be free of all uncertainty, that uncertainty immanent in the form of doubt. The faith that lives under the Word, or better said, the faith which God's word allows my life to be, which awaits every answer from there, that is, from God: this faith is certain. In it there is no doubt. I mean this: The faith which lives from the word of God has in itself no longer a trace of doubt. Every other faith—in the tradition, in the scripture, the faith founded on the confessional writings, on experiences—has doubt immanent in itself. But that is not to be confused with what Luther here calls faith: The faith which lives under the Word is pure from doubt. On this let us hear Luther again: "First of all we should give thanks for God's mercy (also: think of) that he has thrown this child into the bosom of the woman, the sinful nature which is in us all, thus honored, yet on which there is no good at all. He has sin, shame, and all our sorrow covered and adorned, so that it could not have been more highly adorned. So, he has told us that he has covered our shame with such costly clothing, takes it away and makes it pure."[188] The unsinkability of our faith depends on the fact that God in Jesus Christ has done all his work, that sin is forever covered, that the clothing laid around us here is totally pure. For this reason, this faith has no doubt in it. For this reason, it can also be stated in scripture that God tempts no one (Jas 1:13). The Word would be empty without content, without substance, without its "that there,"[189] to which it points, what it means, if there were no Christ.

When Luther interprets what the Word is, when he states the "there it is" of the Word, then he says: Christ. The relation between Word and Christ has in fact also been felt by Luther to be a problem. In his German exposition of the Our Father for the simple laity of 1519 he says: "Christ is given you from God, in whom you believe and thus should be enjoyed, that his righteousness alone upholds you so that you appeal to it and rely on it, and faith is nothing else than eating this bread (John 6:32)"[190] . . ."Now you see how it is related to this daily bread, that Christ

188. WA 9, 566, 21ff.

189. Reference to the first category of "being" (*ousia*) in terms of the Aristotelian "Table of Categories." (J.H.)

190. WA 2, 113, 14ff.

is truly this bread. But he is of no use to you, you cannot also enjoy him, unless God makes words of him, that you can hear and so can know him. Because he sits in heaven or under the shape of bread, how does this help you? It must be distributed, fished up and become words by the inner and outer word. See, that is then truly God's word. Christ is the bread, God's word is the bread and yet a thing, a bread. For he is in the Word and the Word in him, and to believe the same word, that means to eat the bread, and to whom God gives it, lives eternally."[191] Here something very important becomes clear: that by the Word one, as someone who knows and recognizes it, can take and value the Word, can reflect on it, and receive a share in Christ. God makes words of Christ. I mean, without over interpreting, that Luther in thus stating it conceives the entire concept of revelation in trinitarian fashion. That God makes words of him, that is the action of the Spirit, the witness of the Holy Spirit (*testimonium spiritus sancti*), that we encounter again and again in Luther's Doctrine of the Word. The words in which the scripture speaks to me is the way by which God makes Christ for me, so that I can hold him. It is, so to speak, the "apperception" of God himself in Jesus Christ. If there were no word, then we could not apperceive him. And that means that Christ dwells in pure hearts thanks to the word of God. He does not enter me except that the word of God prepares the dwelling for him in me. He does not simply dwell in a dark, fleshly, natural heart. It is not simply so that the desires, the cares and the despair and death and the devil withdraw from the heart and then Christ enters as in the empty house. One has widely understood it in this way, especially the mystics. But he dwells in us in the Word. That is the form in which he would be mine. He has his form in which he dwells in me: that is God's word. He has his bed in which he is laid, when he becomes mine: that is God's word. If I do not allow God's word to be in me, then also Christ cannot be mine. When Luther continually says, "He dwells in my heart by faith," then we must take that in—otherwise we immediately come to the *unio mystica* (mystical union). The manner in which he dwells in me is the word of God. In this way God himself has prepared the manner in which he becomes my God.

---

191. WA 2, 113, 14ff., nn. 35ff.

6. The Word and Preaching

For Luther the presence of God himself is given with the *verbum Dei*. *Verbum Dei* does not mean that human words are made about God, but *verbum Dei* means that in this word God attests to his presence. The question of what was really at issue in the Reformation can be answered thus: At issue was plainly the rediscovery of the foundation of the Church. So, the issue was to understand the Church from the word of the Lord. Indeed, the word of God is never absolute; that is, the Word must always be related to the one who speaks it. In Luther's theology there is not what could be called *kerygma* (proclamation) because the *kerygma* is no *neutrum*, it is *kerygma* of the *kyrios* Jesus. When one thinks in the beginning was the *kerygma*, one has falsely read John 1:1: "In the beginning was the word, and the word was with God, and the word was God." In the beginning is the relation of God and his word. It is impossible to reduce the Word to God or God to the Word. Luther thinks we must always go from the Word to God and from God to the Word: "Now the prophet intends that Christ exercise no other power toward the world than the word of God alone; as we then daily see that he deals against sin, sinners, and the devil in no other way than with words, and yet with the same word has converted and brought the whole world under himself."[192] The Word is thus the form of the world-rule of Christ, to be supported by nothing else. At issue is really the rule of the world, which is expressed and announced in this word. One can never otherwise proclaim the Word to the despairing person, or it would not comfort him; otherwise, one cannot oppose the dark powers and forces of the world and will never repulse them.

The Word is the form in which God's kingdom happens to me and the world. So, it also stands in the New Testament. With what does Jesus go through the world, meeting the sick, the possessed, the dying, those in despair over their sin? He goes with the word of power by which he shows himself to be Lord over sin and death. The Word is thus always the Word coming to us. It does not have its home here. If the word of God were the enemy of history, as we sometimes think, then it would never come to us, then it would somehow already be with us. In this sense the Word has no "being" at all except in itself. It is what it is "through itself." It works what it works by itself. For this reason the Word also remains a strange word, as Luther calls it, a word coming to me from the outside, a word for which we can only pray: "If you had all the wisdom of the entire

---

192. WA I, 695, 1ff. (Interpretation of Psalm 110. 1518).

scripture and all reason, but it does not come from and is not sent from God, it is all nothing."[193] I can know the entire scripture by heart and yet I can pass by the word of God—God is and remains subject of the Word. I hear him through Paul, through Jeremiah, through Isaiah. If I do not hear him, I do not have the Word: "For God will not allow that another should teach or master others, for he will himself be master."[194] The preacher is thus not the virtuoso on the chancel who inspires his hearers, who makes the dead word alive, but the preacher is merely the bearer of the Word that does it. For this reason, Luther can also say in the writing "Against Hans Wurst" (a writing that is much attacked), that the preacher, when he comes from the chancel, does not need the forgiveness of sins.[195] Luther, of course, never meant he did not need forgiveness of sins for his person and his preaching, but that there is an ultimate certainty of proclamation that no longer needs the forgiveness of sins, because it is itself the forgiveness of sins. That is what is meant. The preaching which itself brings the word of God and has it for its foundation, for this reason needs no forgiveness of sins, because the word of God itself needs no forgiveness.

The Word in its coming is entirely free. It is not bound, and not bound to the scripture in the sense that one could say: "When I have the scripture, then I have God's word." Never is the Word in this sense bound to scripture. Luther says: "The Gospel is and should be nothing else than a speaking or *historia* of Christ, just as occurs among men, that one writes in a book about a king or prince, what he has done, and spoken, and endured in his days."[196] In saying this he is thinking of the freedom of the Word over against the Scripture. The Word is always free. Therefore, it has many relations in the scripture to which Luther points in his exposition on the Lord's Prayer: "The holy word of God has many names in the scripture for the sake of its innumerable virtue and works. For it is forsooth everything and almighty. It is called a spiritual sword (Heb 1:3; 4:12; Eph 6:17), that by it one resists the devil and all spiritual enemies. It is called a light (Ps 119:105), a morning rain, an evening rain (Jas 5:7; Hos 6:3–4), a dew from heaven, gold, silver (Ps 119:72), money,

---

193. WA I, 695, 1ff., nn. 14–15.

194. WA I, 695, 1ff., n. 16–17.

195. What is meant here is clearly the place in WA 51, 517, 22ff. (Against Hans Worst. 1541) = BoA 4, 347, 13ff.: "A preacher does not have to pray the Lord's Prayer or seek to forgive sins when he has preached (when he is a good preacher), but must say with Jeremiah and declare: LORD, you know, that what proceeds from my mouth is right and pleasing to you" (Jer 17:16).

196. WA 10/1/1, 9, 11ff. (Church Postille 1522).

clothing, ornament, and much like it. So, it is also called a bread, because the soul is fed by it, strengthened, great and fat."[197] Equally numerous are the designations for the Word precisely then when it deals with its judicial activity. An example: It is the way of God's word that one does not regard (that one does not think of it), as if it is a still and restful thing, as highest reason proposes, because it disputes so harshly, makes such protest, would so happily give aid to matters, so there would be unity. I can allow that one deals with it, but when it comes to it, Ishmael will aways lay his hand against us, when we beautifully offer ourselves, in most friendly fashion. So, one must allow them to be mingled, some Ishmael, some Isaac, and always let them go hand against hand."[198] And yet he speaks more concretely in the same sermon: "It is not at all possible there is a council that unanimously decided without flesh and yeast. I have never yet seen one council among them all, where the Holy Spirit is reigning. There is, of course, in one a portion or two that is Christian, but that it would be entirely pure, I have not read."[199] And: "God lets that happen because he himself will be judge, and not allow that humans judge. Therefore, he commands everyone that he knows what he believes."[200] And in the conclusion Luther states: "Now then because God will have it how we see that his Word should endure no other judge than he, so no one should separate (differentiate) here; there can also be no rest. And God help us when it would be still and restful, then it would be all over with the Gospel; it must protest wherever it comes. If it does not do it, then it is not right."[201]

7. The Word as "Inner Word"

It is the root and origin of inner conflict when the *ratio* attempts to judge over the word of God, and, of course, without the word of God. "Should God have said?" is the word of the serpent to Eve (Gen 3:1), which means this: If you want to have a measuring stick over what is God's word, then you really should be able to find the measuring stick within yourself to know good from evil. In the moment when the *ratio* attempts to find the

---

197. WA 2, 111, 9ff. (Interpretation in German of the Lord's Prayer . . . 1519).
198. WA 24, 313, 34ff. (Sermons on Genesis Chapter 16, 1527).
199. WA 24, 312, 30ff.
200. WA 24, 313, 19ff.
201. WA 24, 313,19ff., nn. 25ff.

measuring stick in itself, from which it could say, "That is God's word," then it is all over. And we stand here again in the center of what Luther calls the Doctrine of Justification. When, for example, there are works by which I could judge whether I am justified before God, then I have already again used a measuring stick. For Luther there is no measuring stick. And only there where there is no measuring stick to measure God's word, precisely there it encounters me.

Of course, there must still be pointed out that very early Luther finds a passage in a sermon on Jonah 1, in which it is said the Word is what is most internal in humans. Luther speaks there of the fact that the Word is the "inner" word (*verbum Internum*) which he at the same time calls "counsel, thought, wisdom, judgment, truth and intellect of man himself."[202] Perhaps Luther means (I am interpreting him here) that the person in Being-for-oneself speaks with oneself in that I say "I" to myself.[203] Idealism had thought it is the miracle of the human being that one can think of oneself: *Cogito ergo sum* (I think, therefore I am).[204] For idealism, this reflection is the miracle of self-consciousness. The Reformers do not think in this way, as far as I can see. This reflection is not the concept, but is the Word, and of course the *verbum internum*. The human being is, at its core, capable of words. Later Luther exchanged this word with Christ. Christ lives in him, just as the word of God lives in him. When Paul says: "I live, yet not I but Christ lives in me" (Gal 2:20) then Christ lives in him, "because Christ speaks in him, works and makes use of all dealing."[205] That is not Pauline, that is Christian life.[206] Or, Luther says: "As the glory of the sun is reflected in water or in a mirror, so Christ is reflected and gives glory from himself to the heart. Thus, we are transfigured from one glory to another (2 Cor 3:18), that we daily increase and the more clearly know the Lord, then we are changed and transfigured into the same image, thus that we all are one cake with Christ. So, it does not happen that we do it ourselves from our own powers, but God must

---

202. WA 1, 23, 33 (Sermon on John 1. 1515, given on December 25, 1514, in the Augustinian church.)

203. WA 1, 23, 33, nn. 38ff.

204. See Rene Descartes, the great French philosopher (1596–1650), *The Meditations*, (1641) v.a. Med, II, 6ff. (Two language edition by E. Chr. Schröder, in *Philsophische Bibliothek*, Vol. 250, Hamburg 1956).

205. WA 40,1, 287, 33 (Gr. Commentary on Galatians, 1535. Dr.)

206. WA 40,1, 287, n. 34.

do it, who is the Spirit there."²⁰⁷ The word of God dwelling in a person makes the whole wide world like a heaven for him. When the Word is taken from the heart then the world is too narrow, then the powers of death rule. Where the Word penetrates one as *verbum internum*, then the basis is formed for the final and deepest foundation of everything that one feels, thinks, plans, and knows, and any other spiritual actions it imbues in me. What the philosophers call self-consciousness, is in theology here faith; that is, the faith which sees the word of God as the ultimate foundation of all that transpires in one, so that also the movement of one's feeling, one's sinner conflicts, one's ideas, all are movements on the basis of the unmoved word of God that is in one. The word of God is never definable, but it is the presence of God, the *praesentia Dei*. It is the rescue, it is the salvation, it is the life and forgiveness. And these are the questions which have concerned us in the entire third part of the basic idea of "Christ and His Own." From that point everything is to be understood and is finally all that we have to say about the word of God.

---

207. WA 10/3, 425, 17ff. (Sermon on John 4:47ff., 1522).

4

Church, State, and Society

Introductory Remarks

1. The Church

THERE IS A LOT of stumbling about in the Luther research regarding the doctrines of church, state, and society, and we might also say regarding the doctrines of the institutions within which Christianity resides. It is a very large question as to what extent a definition of the church was settled in Luther's theology and in "Lutheranism," either by the historical context or through mistakes made involving the historical context. We will always run up against the question of whether the church has to do with something essential and enduring, or if it was born out of the naturally evolving life and course of the world. We must also keep an eye on the differences in doctrines evident through transmission. It appears to me that the actual task here is not simply to learn what Luther taught about these things, but also to recognize that all of the doctrines that appear here were the result of a response to actual pressing questions that one cannot solve without further solving the others. For example, the Doctrine of the Church according to Luther cannot be expounded upon without including the doctrine of the Anti-Christ who, for Luther, was the Pope. It is only because he uncovered the condition of the Papal church in which he lived that his teaching developed from within the church. Thus, the Reformation created a division in western Christendom which the Common Confession (i.e., Augsburg Confession) necessarily preserved in its true form. If one looks at both sides of what led to a blood bath (i.e., The Thirty Years' War), a period during which the Apostle's Creed was also being said and the Lord's Prayer was also being prayed, then the confessions are accordingly invalidated. However, it was not only the natural theology of the Enlightenment, nor the historicizing of the history of dogmatics by Semler[1] and Lessing,[2] but the non-binding nature of the Common Confession during the faith struggles of the 16 century that prepared the ground for criticism of the dogma. And alongside them the question arose: What is the Church? And subsequently the question of the connection between the "new" and "old" church; of continuity and tradition also arose. However, these questions arose relatively late in Luther's theology, and it is astonishing that Luther realized that when left to itself the church fell away from its fundamentals. Whether it was the Anabaptists, or the peasants, or Karlstadt,[3] or the Pope (Luther continually mentioned the names of multi-person, demonic powers) Luther's saying is famous: "Wherever a church is built, the devil builds a pub next door."[4] In the same vein, we have a statement from the later Luther "Against Hans Wurst, 1541," where he says: "Every time I ask a drunkard, someone half asleep, or a fool: 'Friends, tell me who or where is the church?' he responds ten times over with nothing other than: 'One should obey the church . . .'"[5]

Similarly, we may observe what had been pressing questions for Luther concerning the essence of authority. Here Luther says, "The sayings about mercy belong to God's kingdom, not in the world's realm, for a Christian should not just show mercy, but suffer all kinds of things: theft, burning, murder, the devil, and hell."[6] Luther stands for a strong division between both kingdoms (i.e., Doctrine of the Two Kingdoms): "Whoever

1. Johann Salomo Semler (1725-1791) was a professor in Halle and considered one of the founders of the modern history of dogmatics (see H. Hohlwein in *RGG* V, 1696-97)

2. Gotthold Ephraim Lessing (1729-1781) took part in current debates regarding doctrines of the Christian religion, especially concerning the Bible and revelation, including them in his literary writings (See O. Mann in *RGG* IV, 327ff.)

3. See Chapter III, 210 (n. 174).

4. WA 52, 828, 14-15. It literally says in this sermon from Rörer's Hauspostille 1545: "It is a common saying: wherever God builds a church, the devil builds a tavern next door." "Kretzmar" is related to the Czech word "krema" and means "tavern or inn." See Kluge and Götze, *Etymologisches Wörterbuch*, 1957, 403, under "Kretscham."

5. WA 51, 478, 10ff. (Hs.) = BoA 4, 330, 10ff.

6. WA 18, 389, 27ff. (An open letter from the stern book against the farmers, 1525) = BoA3, 81, 16ff.

would combine these kingdoms, like our false spirits of the Rhone valley (German: *Rotten*), will invite wrath into God's kingdom and mercy into the realm of the world, which would be to put the devil in heaven and place God in hell."[7] Luther also means that here a comingling of both "functions" would occur, amounting to something diabolical. He also sees certain distortions in the principles of both kingdoms at work and with them diabolical, subversive, and revolutionary movements—all of which he was against. It was in this context that his concept of bureaucracy and the state, if you will, was fixed and solidified and helped form his idea of state power.

But was it correct to interpret this movement of the peasants, which was clearly an evangelical movement, in such an ultimately theological sense? One could also believe it possible to understand the peasant's rebellion as something other than a diabolical confusion of God and the devil, and to view the matter very empirically and from a non-theological viewpoint. Every matter takes on the viewpoint of its beholder. The view of the Peasants' Rebellion in Germany is defined through the concept of the Two Kingdoms and through the construction of the concept of the state during the period of the early reformation territories. Since that time, we can see how it has been adopted in this form and in this fixed point in history.

2. The Doctrine of the Two Kingdoms

The attempt by Kant to posit the "thing in itself" (German: *Ding-an-sich*) as a generally valid and very necessary premise by which to introduce the historical perspective arose from factual ignorance of the middle class about the actual roots of its existence. As a result, people never encountered historical reality but were thrust into the world of abstractions, always looking through a telescope. This type of thinking belongs to a particular method that attempts to keep things at arm's length. The Peasants' Rebellion and the Doctrine of the Two Kingdoms are related to each other to the degree that each formed the other, resulting in the notion of autonomous power. To this day, the idea prevails that all revolutionary actions are excessive, especially when they erupt from the lower classes, as well as the obverse: that it is fine to turn a blind eye toward any revolution or lawlessness that comes from above, namely from the state.

---

7. WA 18, 390, 6ff. = BoA 3, 81, 35ff.

The famous verse, "Everyone is subject to the authority over him . . ." (Rom 13:1) became the formula by which those in authority secured the right to wield authority over others. At the same time the idea developed that the state should have a monopoly on legitimate authority. This development extended as far as Hegel and Max Weber. In Max Weber we find the statement, "The appeal to the naked power of coercion not only externally, but also internally, is essential for any political party."[8] The "digressions" from it constitute, in my opinion, the "polishing" of what in the ensuing 19th and 20th centuries has been said about the question of Christianity, faith, and the actual world in which we live. They are the expression of the end of the Western World for whom Christ is a mere "holy roller," and for whom the Sermon on the Mount is a road to political anarchy. And it is terrifying, that within the Protestant church, these opinions have, for the most part, been accepted: namely, the idea that the Gospel has meaning only internally for the private life of the person in their individual existence and that any application of the basic principles (of the Gospel) in the state and public power are nothing more than overstepping one's appropriate office and releasing the Gospel to the provenance of religious fanatics. If one reassesses all of this, then one has no doubt in concluding that we should be able to use the Doctrine of the Two Kingdoms in the sense of the commandments of God (as Luther actually intended), to solve today's political problems. There was time in the past when it seemed that a cloud started to lift over the Doctrine of the Two Kingdoms, as if we might have begun to doubt this conception of the state. But very quickly lazy thinking took hold and sank again on the part of church leaders and theologians in their interpretation of Rom 13 and similar passages, so that what was needed was again forgotten and what had been gained in the hour of internal struggle regarding the question was lost once more. In short, Luther's conception does not mean to parrot his doctrine literally, but rather to follow its intention—to separate from the factual developments those things which are appropriate to the formula.

---

8. Max Weber (1864–1920) was one of the most significant German sociologists. See regarding this quote by H. J. Iwand's: Weber, M. *Gesammelte Aufsätze zur Religionssoziologie*, Vol. I, 547.

3. Society and the Ten Commandments

The third problem area has to do with Luther's teachings on society. According to Luther's theology, there are "estates" that are sinful in and of themselves. For Luther, there are indeed sinful estates—and these estates must be done away with so that the person can find a way to live a good life as a pious Christian. We misunderstand the Reformation if we think that Luther should have stayed in the cloister and reformed it to his way of thinking; or if we think (if it were even possible) that the moral errors of the cloister could have been removed as a way of fulfilling the demands of the Reformation. This notion of the principle of "morality" does not do justice to the Reformation because in that case the Reformation would simply have been an occasion for a different kind of society where certain regulations could be overturned, including regulations that pertain to various sins. "Sinful estates," says Luther, "include robbery, usury, prostitution, and as we now have, the pope, cardinals, bishops, priests, and nuns who either don't preach or listen to preaching. These estates go against God because they deal only with the mass and singing, and do not include God's Word, so that a simple woman is able to get to heaven easier than the (clergy)."[9] And previously: "Therefore it is not in doubt that the devil's primary task is to relegate the worship of God to only the church, altar, mass, singing, reading, sacraments, and the like, as if all other works were in vain or of no use. How could the devil choose a better way to lead us astray than to limit the worship of God to such a small arena within the church and the work that it does."[10] In effect, everything is turned around. Through the false church we have completely obscured good works, and the liberation of these works as they are truly commanded and intended by God, and which make up the real reform of society. In Luther's view, I must break from whatever life brings to me through the award of certain Christian religious good works to create space for what is truly God's will and work. Thus, the cloister, the hierarchy, the regulations of a holy life are broken, because all these works are evil—not because the person who does them is evil, but because the intentions from which these works spring are against God. Only when the bowl is broken is society free to do God's will.

---

9. WA 10/1/1, 317, 21ff. (Kirchenpostille 1522. Gospel for St. John's Day, John 21:19–24).

10. WA 10/1/1, 311, 21ff.

All of Luther's writings on public life—teachings about the state, service in war, trade, marriage, education, etc., hark back to his studies of the Ten Commandments. Luther is of the opinion that the Ten Commandments must be made current for every age. That is especially apparent in his "Large Catechism of 1529,"[11] in which he addresses every aspect of daily life. It was only during the 17th and 18th centuries, and under the influence of pietism, that the question of the "internalization"—the question of one's personal mindset—came into play. The period of the Reformation, by contrast, concentrated on works and on *doing*. But *now* something must happen; something huge and decisive. The first, as we have already heard, is the building up of the spiritual life. The façade that covered all of the life of global society is removed and smashed. This is something very different than correcting a personal position; it has to do with an estate or condition, with an entire stance or an entire form of external life that is designated as unholy. Luther broke apart the lifestyle of the cloister, for example, and exposed it as sacrilegious because of its idolatry. He married, therefore, because the life of celibacy ("unmarried") is against God's command. In so doing, Luther attacked a certain ideal of holiness. This kind of structure of a spiritual life is only a representation of a type of holiness that is sacrilegious. It must be dismantled and disappear so that it is possible to do actual good works.

The current Protestantism speaks easily of a new kind of morality for people that Luther stood for and fought for. However, Luther's writings on social reform show that Luther hears the command of God anew as one who has gone astray in his thinking on morality. In this sense, God's commands are also Gospel for him. Luther's "Lectures on the Ten Commandments"[12] appearing in 1516 and 1517, which he wrote hastily for a number of people, is an indication of what we should hear again in God's commandments because in them we can find the true way to live. As a result, it means that through reflection on the law of God we are brought into the word of God by the word of God which gives us a new view of everything. This can be seen very clearly in Luther's writings on marriage. He wrote his early works on marriage after he learned how to rethink the relationship between men and women in the Old Testament. He, a monk, a celibate and unmarried, learned to rethink this issue from the word of God. His writings on marriage are a document that supports

---

11. WA 30/1, 123–238 = BoA 4, 1–99.
12. WA 1, 394–521 (*Decem praecepta Wittenbergensi praedicata populo*, 1518).

his unequivocal *metanoia* (change of heart) on this matter.[13] The entire circle, revealing Luther's efforts to come to a new understanding of the Ten Commandments, is closed here: I must step out of myself to act, a deed must not reflect on me, I do not make or determine that the deed is good or bad, and there is no connection to me that is in itself the fulfillment of what God wants in his law. Therefore, Luther concludes that any deed is thus so hidden that the doer himself does not really know if it is a good work or not (!). Only the Lord, who sees everything while hidden from view, knows. And only because the person lives from God's mercy can the work have any effect. The most important thing is to understand that when we say people live from the righteousness of God, it is not only their limbs that are "weapons of God's justice," (Rom 6:13), not only their hands and feet, but also their spirit, mind, and everything that they have and everything that they can be, that are part of God's work (1 Cor 3:9). People often feel overwhelmed by this, because in the hour of reflection and quiet they sense how much God expects of them and how little they are able to fulfill it. In his "Lectures on the Ten Commandments," Luther writes: "To venerate peace and quiet and give to God, as a person at rest, so that here God alone is at work. Here patience and hope are necessary, for here the person steps into the darkness where he is helpless and is transported on the way of suffering in a wonderful way. Whenever you rest, you are not working. Rather, you are resting, and God works in you. But you don't know the outcome, because you are at rest and a mere stuff of matter (*nuda materia*)."[14] The person should also come to realize in such moments that the law promises to encounter him also in negation, because what he can be or will be is through God's grace. In the negation of "you shall not steal" it means, for example, a community of people who are ready to care for each other. Or it is promised to me in the commandment "you shall not commit adultery," because the pure of heart love so that the person under it, in all the inner struggles of their life, never ceases to strive for purity and actually more and more come close to being pure. So, behind each of these commands there is a "Yes," and behind each "Yes" there is a person; clearly a person that we are not, but that we are as followers of Christ. And we are only thus because through Christ we have given ourselves up to him. That we are already able do His works, is the most important thing. The works and the actions that

---

13. See e.g., WA 10/2, 263–304 ("Which persons are forbidden from marrying or from married life." 1522) = BoA 2, 335–59.

14. WA 1, 471, 4ff.

the Ten Commandments addresses are works that show the dawning of a new day, of the morning glory, the *crepusculum matutinum*,[15] that has begun, as Luther calls it. Here we no longer have the ethic or the question of good works on the basis of virtue or vice in the sense of the Stoics,[16] but rather it centers on the expression of the struggle between two persons in one: the emergence of a new person from the death of the old. At this point it is clear how closely connected Luther's interpretation of works is with what he understands about Baptism, of which he writes in the "Small Catechism:" "What does Baptism with water mean? It signifies that the old person (Adam) in us with all sins and evil desires is to be drowned through daily sorrow for sin and repentance, and that daily a new person is to come forth and rise up to live before God in righteousness and purity forever."[17] Baptism is binding just as God's Commandments are binding. Luther places the Commandments and Baptism together in one book to show that Baptism is binding. Baptism is God's binding covenant of grace for us through the covenant of the grace of Christ. It entails and means, "God with us." It means a tremendous simplification of life; for it is no longer necessary to represent God's covenant through certain observances, rules, monastic regulations, and the like—all of that is a substitute, which is all drowned in Baptism. Baptism is therefore the foundation of Christian existence with which Christ has his way in the world and which also can go on in the form of life. From this vantage point we have an entirely new view of society.

The Formation of Luther's Concept of the Church

1. The Church of the Gospel

Luther's concept of the church comes with problems concerning the question of its origin. Did Luther's concept of the church originate from his conflict with the Roman Catholic church, making it, as it were, antithetical to Roman Catholicism? Or was it already found *in nuce* in Luther's theology and conceived of as a necessary concept, since he was being thrown out of his old church, making it necessary for him to construct a

---

15. WA 2, 586, 10 (Kl. Commentary on Galatians 1519).

16. The Stoics are a Greek philosophical school whose teaching on ethics extended since 300 years before Christ to today. Its main representatives: Seneca (d. 65 A.D.); Epictetus (d. 138 A.D.); Marcus Aurelius (d. 180 A.D.).

17. WA 30/1, 257, 16ff. (*The Small Catechism*, 37).

new concept of the church? Or did he already have in mind this concept of the church, and how far did this concept then claim to be the correct understanding of the church? This issue centers on the incredible problem that, resultingly, there arose a concept of the church that claimed to be the true idea of the church, the church of the Gospel, and thus the visible church of the time was seen as false and should be rejected. Thus, there were two churches side-by-side and two different concepts of the church. The church by itself cannot determine if it is the true church but must depend on a higher authority to determine its viability.

In his book, "The Origins of Luther's Concept of the Church," K. Holl tried to answer this question.[18] He came to the conclusion that in, "*Dictata super Psalterium*, 1513–16"[19] Luther's concept of the church was complete and comprehensive from the start and was "the concept of the church that Luther held his entire life."[20] It was the concept of the hidden church, which is real but not visible in the same way that the Lord of the church is not visible but yet the church lives because of Him. Holl goes on to say that Luther's concept of the church thereby seeks to differentiate itself from the scholastic understanding of the church; that the Scholastics attributed everything to the potential (possibility, investment) of the outward, visible, public church. The Holy Roman Empire provided the context for the church during that time. Everything that existed within the empire, including the receiving of the sacraments, "potentially" belonged to the church. Those who understandably believed that they were "true Christians" belonged in the top ranks of those who belong to a spiritual community or to the *religiosi*, namely to a religious order. That is not to say that others are precluded, but that among these religious groups the external representation of the church is visible. Holl says that from the very beginning Luther considered this to be a mistake. Those who truly believe, the *vere credentes*, form the church. Luther does not speak of a "potential" membership in the church, or of those living in the realm of spiritual institutions. Holl also says that looking at it from the other side, Luther's view of the church departs from tradition in that it accomplishes the decision of faith knowingly and clearly, according to the individual members of the church who see themselves in community with others and live in this *communio* together. That is Holl's basic idea.

18. Holl, et al, (I, 47. n. 32) 288–325.
19. WA 3 (entire) and WA 4, 1–462.
20. Holl, et al. 299 (D.H.)

Very early on, Luther's idea of the essence of the church is connected to his concept of the incarnation of Jesus Christ. In other words, he proceeds from the *humanitas Christi*. In fact, one could proceed in a number of different ways from this starting point. Accordingly, it says in Luther's *"Prologue to the sentences of Peter Lombard:"* "We are transferred into the realm of Christ, where he reigns through faith in his humanity and in the taking on of flesh (*ubi ipse regnat in fide humanitatis suae et in velamento carnis*), which realm he himself was given by the Father (1 Cor 15:24)."[21] Thus, it is the visibility of the church, that is this "Reign of Christ," which has been consigned the humanity of Christ and the taking on of flesh. We live in the *regnum humanitatis*, that is in the *regnum carnis Christi* (in the realm of Christ's flesh). Further, this realm means that in the meantime we live in weakness and disgrace until Christ's kingdom is realized by the Father and thus everything will become clear from out of the suffering of the church. However, it is not the case that we can find in Luther a concept of the church that stayed with him until the end of his life. A. W. Hunzinger says in his "Luther Studien,"[22] that in the young Luther we find an interesting idea of "invisibility" (*invisibilitas*) which, in rough terms, is a neo-Platonic idea.[23] Here, the invisible world is the true world. This concept of the church comes very close to an idealistic concept of the world, except that the idealist concept of the world does not concern itself only with the spiritual condition of people. Idealism as such does not gain God's world; for to place the achievements of man in some invisible world is impaired thinking by way of a reasonable idea that has gone in a false direction and which, in turn, can only be established again through the church and the revelation and the means of grace. When we live in the church, we live in a kind of hospital in which, through the means of grace, the church gives us the ability to remain in the actual world while at the same time living in the spiritual world of God's grace, which we have now only in hope, and which we only experience incompletely because we have not lost our heart to the passing things of this world. That is, I think, the concept of the church that Luther proposed and is the

---

21. WA 9, 39, 31ff. (Luther's marginal notes on the sentences of Peter Lombard. 1510/11). On Lombard see III, 121 (n. 21). See also K. Holl, et al., n. 3.

22. Hunzinger, *Lutherstudien*. I." Luther's Neuplatonismus in der Psalmenvorlesung von 1513–1516."

23. The new Platonism is based in the teachings of the philosopher Plato (203–69). It had its high point in the movement of the soul from the sensory world to the world of the gods.

church that he sought in the cloister. Moreover, that is the concept of the church that broke him. The concept of the church of the early Luther is essentially defined through the opposition between the material and the ideal world—and from this dualism he lived and thought.

2. The Conferring of the Spirit on the Believer

With this dualism we must pursue a concept that can already be found in the early writings of Luther. It is the concept of the *intellectificatio* (conferring of the spirit). In a gloss on Psalm 32 (31)[24] Luther uses the term in connection with forgiveness of sins. He understands the term *intellectificatio* as a gift to man with the ability of *intelligere*, of insight, of intellect, but he also emphasizes that this *intellectificatio* "is not accomplished in terms of human intelligence, but according to the spirit and mind of Christ."[25] He developed the expression further in the sense of 1 Cor 2, or that of a *pneumatologie*, which Paul mentions in v. 16; namely, only believers have this intelligence. Only so is it possible to know the heavenly, the spiritual, eternal, and unseen, which is only given to us through the spirit. The *carnales*, the "fleshly," are so called because they only consider the sensible world—the world they can sense as real—but do not consider the invisible world or the spiritual one.[26] However, one should be careful that this "intellect" is not speculative, but rather contemplative since it does not have anything to do with philosophy, but with a theology that goes far beyond philosophy. Accordingly, this has very little to do with a philosophical understanding. This *intellekt* is not a natural concept but is a theological one and effected by grace. That is the concept of faith in Heb 11:1: "Now faith is the substance of things hoped for, the evidence of things not seen."

The place of this intellectual understanding is God's gift of the spirit. To enter into the temple of God means to enter on one's own. In a gloss on Psalm 73 (72), Luther says (v. 16): "It is to distinguish between "before me" and "before God;" not in terms of special difference, but that we exist everywhere (*ubique*) before God, and everything is before him and before

---

24. The differences in the numbering of the Psalms have to do with the various editions, especially that of the Latin (Vulgate). Deviations in the numbering of the German Luther Bible are, where necessary, indicated in parentheses. Details in Sellin-Rost, *Einleitung in das Alte Testament*, 141.

25. WA 3, 171, 33–34 (*Dictata super Psalterium*. 1513–16).

26. WA 3, 173, 35ff.

us. It is to differentiate between the knowledge of that and its effect."[27] A few lines later Luther writes: "It is an orientation toward spiritual and divine things (*conversion ad spiritualia et divina*). Until a person thus turns, he lives in profanity before the world and himself because he only sees himself and the world. Here he is outside of the temple of God and is cast out, for the temple of God is nothing other than the soul, which turns toward God . . . Therefore one should not probe the temple and what is profane for long: they are both within us (*intra nos einim sunt*)."[28] And with a note on, among others, Isaiah 46:8 ("Take it to heart, you rebels"), this insightful section in Luther ends with the sentence: "Therefore it is the same thing: search your heart and step into the temple of God, for the heart is the temple of God."[29]

To commune with oneself, or, what we today call self-reflection, means turning to the *spiritualia* and *divina*, to the spiritual and divine things of life. The person must dismiss the world and go completely inward. To the extent he finds himself, he also finds God. That occurs because then both God and my heart are in correlation to each other: in that I discover God, I also discover my true self, and in that I discover my true self, I turn to God as both are irretrievably interconnected. But this also means that one must basically divest oneself of the world and take oneself out of the world.

One might ask, what kind of piety is behind Luther's thinking here? It is the piety of the other-worldly, of the transcendence of God in the immanence (internal world) of the person who is inwardly reflective, who knows what it means to be spiritual and close to God: "The heart is God's temple," says Luther. Only where this occurs in the act of internal reflection, where the person in this sense accomplishes a complete turn-about, where he is able to come away in his inner-most being from the pull of the world and things, then he will be given this kind of *intelligere* (insight). Any authentic "insight" involves a change in a person. One could also say it is similar to an existentially understood concept of faith that we are dealing with here in Luther, and one that is stated completely in an idealistic sense. This concept of faith applies to the church also, for the church is a world to which believers come; it is the world of spiritual order and a divine reality which they have in common with all those who are embraced by the spirit of God. Thus, Luther coined a phrase that the

27. WA 3, 479, 1ff.
28. WA 3, 479. nn. 18ff.
29. WA 3, 479. nn. 30–31.–Here Luther refers specifically to Luke 17:21.

spirit of God is always one, that therefore the world receives its unity from the church even though it may appear from the outside to be falling apart. For it is one bread that we eat and one wine that we drink (1 Cor 10:16–17), and one Christ in whom we believe and there is no other way to go. But the external things of the world are divided into bread, family, possessions, honor, riches, and all the other things that Luther mentions. Here is where people are torn apart, while we in the church, since the Spirit is one, are in *communio* with each other, where we mutually enjoy the fruits of the spirit without becoming enemies. In fact, quite the opposite: where each is brother to each. That is the starting point for Luther's conception of the church and where the dualism of external, sensory, visible world on the one hand and the spiritual world, on the other, falls apart.

However, from this perspective, it is very troubling if one looks at the question of what actually happened afterwards. How did Luther come to break with the Roman church, which he first considered a sad thing and, as he often personally attested to later on, believed was something on which he could not compromise? How did he come to the point where he saw it as a false, apostatized, or "counter church?" The Catholic perspective may help here to provide clues as to Luther's mindset. It claims that the separation from the Roman church was caused by Luther's individualistic mindset which was unable to tolerate Catholic authority due to his strong and deep convictions. Liberal Protestantism, on the other hand, sees Luther's position here as the rebellion of a liberated spirit against the church. They therefore see it similarly to the Catholics, but the liberal Protestants feel that Luther did not go far enough because he continually held to the dogma. According to the sources, neither of these answers are sufficient. It is rather a more accurate statement to say that Luther, with his teachings, simply could not continue to remain in this Roman church. Indeed, Luther often referred to his teaching and research later on. We will discuss these next.

3. The Church as the Creation of the Gospel

This doctrine is not an expression of some new kind of life or being. Luther did not come up with a new concept of the church out of his own life experience. Rather, his life experiences can be explained by his teachings, since that is what he was called to do: he was compelled to convey this teaching. Luther was of the opinion that the entity, that is, the entity of the church, is something that was independent from his person and, as such, stands or falls. This is what is meant by it. And one could also say that Luther was stigmatized for what he thought and taught. His teachings drew him onward: they formed him, he did not form them. And this is where the freedom lies in his teachings—but not for him personally. So those who see in him the collapse of an autonomous person, are wrong. Rather, the course of his entire existence was defined by his calling to teach this doctrine. And here we have the decisive point. The church is powerless against the doctrine; it can only witness to it. It cannot formulate it. The church has no power to formulate an article of faith. It has neither the power nor the authority for how we are to engage with God, nor can it command what we are to believe about God. If that were the case, we would confuse what was commanded with the symbol of the command. That is the *ductus* which is detectable in the development of Luther's concept of the church. He says about the relationship between the Gospel and the church: "Although the Gospel can exist without the church . . . the church cannot exist without the Gospel. Therefore, the Gospel is greater than the church."[30] And from this Luther concludes: "The church is under the Word and not over it" (*sub verbo et non supra*).[31] Clearly there is a hierarchy in this over-and-under. For "The Gospel establishes the church by its supremacy over the church (*more majoris*) . . . The church however acknowledges the Gospel in the manner of an underling (*more minoris*)."[32] From the mutual position of obedience between the church and the Gospel, which is brought into existence by the Word and lives from the Word, and from this relationship of obedience we have the term *approbatio* (approbation), by which the church is able to perform the task of proclaiming the Word. The church does not engender the truth, it rather recognizes what the truth is: namely, the truth that has established it and by which it continues to exist. To the extent that the church recognizes this truth, it confesses the Word of God through

---

30. WA 30/2, 682, 10ff. (*De potestate leges ferendi in ecclesia*. 1530).

31. WA 30/2, 682, 10ff. nn. 18–19. See on the relationship between the church and the word from H. J. Iwand's *Gedächtnis* the important work by K.G. Steck: *Lehre und Kirche bei Luther* (FGLP, ed. E Wolf, 10. Row, Vol. XXVII).

32. WA 30/2, 687, 10–11. In this regard, H. J. Iwand refers to the citation from the major work "*De potestate leges ferendi*." and the preceding outline: "The church appropriates the gospel the way a servant does the seal of his master." (IBID 680, Nr. 19).

which it has been created. Accordingly, Luther continually quoted the verse from Jas 1:18: "He chose to give us birth through the word of truth."

The infallibility of the word of God is also connected to the idea that no one can alter this Word except God himself who must change himself if he is to change His Word. If the church can alter the Word of God, then who knows what else it might alter and then we have only the church to believe in. And the moment we do that we are cut off from any church that Luther belonged to or to any church that claims him. The church should not require people to believe in it as an entity. The church's job is to awaken faith by proclaiming the Word of God; for we are not to believe in the church itself, but we can believe its proclamation if it proclaims the word of God. That is thus a very simple formula which—as far as I can see—is what is at work in the development of the question on the doctrine of the church found in Luther. This contrast between of church and the word of God was not familiar in the Middle Ages. Many representations of Luther's concept of the church assume that one day he simply showed up and pronounced that they must base the church on God's Word. But that is not the truth of the historical process. And we find ourselves in the throes of history if we want to account for what actually happened. We participate in a process in which one man was deemed worthy to point out the mistakes of an epoch that was ending anyway, and to completely dismantle it as he anticipated its ending.

4. The Church as the "New Creature" of God

Luther did not arrive at new insights about the relationship between the Word and the church without a struggle. We have already heard in other places (Chapter III) that, in his lectures on Romans, Luther carefully distinguished between God's Word and man's word. He said, "So, His Word changes us, we do not change it."[33] This also means that any encounter with the Word of God contains two possibilities: we can change it to suit our ends, or God can change us through it. This is the axis from which everything else proceeds. Luther means that in the encounter with His Word, God will have His justice and righteousness over man; over man's *justitia* (justice) and *sapientia* (wisdom), over his *virtus* (virtue), and over all that is. To the extent that man gives God his due, he relinquishes his own wisdom and justice to God and thus is changed through God's word.

---

33. See Ch. III, 207 (n. 165).

In other words, the person is conformed to God's word. We might also say that a person becomes in tune with the Word. The encounter with God's word no longer comes under the aspect of understanding or reason, but under the aspect of judgement. God and His Word judge the person; the person does not judge God's word. To give God's word its due means, "To change the person through the word of God." It has to do with a judgement, not with an understanding, feeling, or experience. That is the essential question and that is why Luther's teaching on the word of God is closely connected to his teaching on justification in the Doctrine of Justification. Both are one and the same: when we encounter God's word it has to do with His judgement. Indeed, the Doctrine of Justification is about God's Word receiving its due. The word of God is not just a formal concept, but it is filled with profound content.

The content of Luther's doctrine is essentially about the person becoming a new creature through God's word. In the words of Jas 1:18, Luther describes the subjection of the church to the Word as the order of creation. Here we might think that Luther did not understand this order of creation as referring to the world, but rather to the church (i.e., hierarchy). Here we have creation in motion; here is where it happens. Man is not by nature God's creation since that was played out long ago, rather, he is God's creation *que fideles*, through faith. To the extent that God's word is proclaimed, and faith is created then the church is truly the *nova creatura Dei*—the new creation of God. It is, so to speak, a retreat from man's desire to create himself to a situation where he lives from God's word. Creation then means simply to live because the Word lives. When Luther based the church on the Word, he did not mean merely the literal words written in the Bible. He said very clearly, "I am not speaking about the written letter, but about the proclaimed word of the Gospel."[34] The essence of the Word is such that the person is born again. The Word does not exist alone but exists for "His own."[35] Luther distinguished the Word that comes from man and the Word that comes from God. He means: if we do not hear God's Word in preaching, then it does not represent

---

34. WA 7, 721, 15 (*Ad librum. . . Magistri Amrosii Catharini . . .1521*)" "*Non de Evangelio scripto sed vocalit loguor.*"

35. In Luther's sermon for the Propst von Leitzkau (WA 1, 10ff.) he further developed for the first time, as far as I can tell, the idea that the word of the sermon has something to do with being born and becoming, using Jas 1:18 (H. J. Iwand).

anything of God. Only the person who is reborn through the Word of God is without sin, since whoever is born from God, is without sin.[36]

When the word of God is preached as it should be ("according to plan," EKG 201,4) those who receive it are free and justified. Luther is convinced of this. His interest is not in how people are able to understand God's word. For him that is not the problem, since God's word takes care of that when it is preached "according to plan." The main problem for him was: How can we be sure that God's word is preached instead of man's word? Luther demonstrates the unseen workings of God in man in his famous lecture on the "Magnificat."[37] Here Mary, who receives God's word, is the model for Luther for a church that lives from the word of God and exhibits its faith in the words: "May it be for me as you have said." (Luke 1:38). In another place (lecture on the seven Penitential Psalms) Luther says: "The works of the hand of God are the pious whom he creates and gives birth to out of grace. This happens without any effort on their part, for thus they are and become new creations in Christ."[38] And again Luther: "Wherever the word of God is preached and believed, that is true faith. That is an impregnable rock (Matt 16:18). Wherever faith can be found, there is the church. Wherever the church is found, there is the bride of Christ. Wherever the bride of Christ is found, there is everything that belongs to her. In this way, faith contains everything that follows from it: the keys, the sacraments, the power (*potestas*), and everything else."[39] For Luther, the Word is not only a sign by which he recognized the church, but it is also a sign for the creative power of the word, because where the word is, there must necessarily also be people who believe it. Luther assumes that the word of God does not remain empty (Is 55:10–11); that whenever God truly speaks there must also needs be the community of Christ, (i.e., people). The question of how one brings the Word to people is not a theological question for Luther. It may be a psychological question, but not a substantive theological one. The question of, "How do I find a connecting point for people with the Gospel?" is something that Luther leaves to the word of God itself. That is the magnificent part of his theology and that is why he bases the church

---

36. On this point, Luther cites 1 John 5:4–5 right at the beginning of this sermon. It is then followed by further thoughts on rebirth, according to Jas 1:18 (also 20, 26ff.)

37. WA 7, 538–604 (Das Magnificat interpreted and in German. 1521) = BoA 2, 133–87.

38. WA 1, 215, 26ff. (The Seven Penitential Psalms.)

39. WA 2, 208, 25ff. (*Resolutio Lutheriana. . .de potestate papae.* 1519).

on the sermon only, because he means that wherever the Word is, there we will find a flock of believers assembled around it.

Here we see something very remarkable. Luther is of the mind that it does not only have to do with the "true" church, but also the manifestation of the church, which results in a great paradox: the church can only appear as the invisible church. As long as the church seeks to manifest itself as visible, the true church cannot be there. That is why the true church is invisible, because it is not visible and only exists as such. The invisible church is not remote but is the immediately present church. The church that is present among us is in our midst; it is true, yet invisible. It is the only church in which one can live; where one is only saved, where one has all one needs, where the Word is near and nourishes, and where we have eternal life. All previous things that have been said in faith about the church are only true precisely because it is not seen and is present only in its invisibility. Luther says, "This is how one can recognize the true Christian community: wherever the Gospel is preached. For just as one recognizes the banner of an army as a sign that stands for a Lord and his army on the field, so also one can certainly recognize in the Gospel where Christ and his army are located."[40] The faithful know the voice of their Lord whom they follow. But what about the unbelievers? They do not recognize this voice. They try to elevate the visible form of the church instead; to make it larger, to make it more obvious, and to magnify it: "They (unbelievers) do not reject the Gospel, but to the extent that they add things to the Gospel with their own glosses they lead us away from the royal highway of faith, gradually, and without our noticing."[41] And if one asks about the body of Christ, one can also find a clue to the congregation in Luther. Luther says that the body of Christ is not made visible in the church, but Christ is made visible in the Scriptures: "Touch Christ's hands, feet, and side, like the disciples did. Why should we then not touch and read the Scriptures, which are the true body of Christ in which we believe (or don't!); for all other writing is dangerous, like flying ghosts that have no flesh or bone such as Christ has."[42] Here it is obvious that Christ must be sought in the Scriptures. If we do not find Him in the scriptures, then we are dealing with ghosts and demons. There is an

---

40. WA 11i, 408, 8 (That a Christian assembly or congregation has right and power... 1523). = BoA 2, 395/396, 1ff. See additional to IV, 242, n. 32.

41. WA 7, 725, 25ff. (*Ad librum...Magistri Ambrosii Catharini...*1521).

42. WA 7, 315, 22ff. (Grund und Ursach aller Artikel D. Martin Luthers... 1521) = BoA 2, 64, 4ff.

important place in Luther's writings on this point. In his, "To the Pope in Rome and the Illustrious Romanists in Leipzig 1520" Luther says, "A congregation or community is comprised of all those who live in true faith, hope, and love, so that the body, life, and the nature of Christianity is not a physical gathering, but rather a gathering of hearts in faith, as Paul says in Eph 4 (v. 5): one Baptism, one faith, one Lord. Although its physical manifestation may be separated by thousands of miles, it is still a community of faith, as long as someone preaches, believes, hopes, loves, and lives alike, as we sing of the Holy Spirit: 'You have gathered us all together in the language of faith,' that is now actually a spiritual unity, by which people form a common sainthood, whose unity is sufficient enough to make a Christendom, without which such a unity—be it city, time, person, works or whatever else—makes a Christendom."[43] This is an important sentence: the essence of Christianity is its unity. Furthermore, it is invisible and its reality on earth has no analogous counterpart in human society. That thought is also contained in this sentence: "The essence of Christianity, the Christian life and the nature of Christianity is not that of a loving community but is the communion of hearts in one faith." It is not about Sunday worship. It is a community of hearts that does not come together only today or tomorrow but is always at work. It is a work of the Holy Spirit from which no one is excluded.

The fact that I fulfill my church duties, go to Sunday worship, take Communion, and learn and read the Bible is not a sign that I belong to the church. That can always change and falls under the concept of human "sociology." This is why Luther concludes: "There is no unity, be it of the city, generation, personality, etc., that makes for Christianity." So, can't a Christian city be unified? Can't the West be unified as Christian? Can't we be unified by our knowledge of Christian virtues? Luther praises these things but rejects them as fundamental for the church. Here he means that as long as we seek the foundation and essence—or nature—of the church in these outward forms, in these palpable things, we will never be sure whether we have before us the true church or the false church. Luther emphasizes that the true church is there where we have no doubt and where we can say: "I believe in one holy, apostolic church." However, by this Luther does not mean that since we don't know exactly what the church is, that we should therefore place it solely in the invisible world. For him it is not a step backwards into uncertainty, but a step forward to

---

43. WA 6, 293, 1ff. = BoA 1, 331, 14ff. On Luther's hymn verses see EKG 98, 1 (=WA 35, 449, 1ff. Nr. 20).

certainty. When Luther speaks of faith that lives in the certainty of salvation, we cannot expect from him a concept of the church that is cloaked in uncertainty. The church that lives is palpable in the visible world; yet it is one that never allows us to rest because we are always doubtfully chasing after the true church. The invisible church is the church because in it the invisible Lord, Jesus Christ, is at work in all of its members. This Lord is near; He is in our midst. This he has promised. With the concept of the present Christ (*des Christus Praesens*) in His Word (!) Luther answered the question of the church's reality. The key concept in the sense of a *signum* should not be relegated to the visual but must be understood as the banner of the Lord around which his people rally so that they are sure that this is their Lord. That is the true church—not in heaven, but on earth—manifested as the invisible church in which Christ is present.

The Invisible and Visible Church

1. The Relationship between the Two Concepts

In the last paragraph of the chapter concerning the question of "The Origins of Luther's Concept of the Church," it must have occurred to the reader that the pairing of "invisible and visible church" obviously plays an important role in Luther's theology. With this pairing, Luther gave the church something that it has not been able to break free from: the question of the true church. But it is a mistake to assume, as Protestant researchers often repeat, that invisibility is of itself a sign of the church for Luther. It is not. Rather, the visible church also has its characteristics and has its definition by virtue of the invisible one. I could also express this in the formula: the concept of the invisible church in Luther is so formulated that he could not, and dared not, try to make it visible. However, one should not interpret the relationship between the visible and invisible church in the same way as Christ's incarnation. In that case, the visibility of the church would be an integral moment of its invisibility and we would be coming close to Catholic interpretation. In his famous Reformation writing, "On the Babylonian Captivity of the Church," Luther distinguishes between "Law of the Church" and the law from which the invisible church lives, between the *ius divinium* as it is related in the Scriptures, and all other types of earthly church laws that men devise.[44] The fact that this is the

44. WA 6, 484—573 (*De captivitate Babylonica ecclesiae praeludium*. 1520). = BoA 1, 426–512.

basic foundation of his writings can be seen in many places, of which I cite only two: "The Word of God is above all; from it follows faith, and from faith love . . . All things hang upon, proceed from, and are preserved by its powerful Word, through which we have been created, 'so that we are the first fruits of all he created.' (Jas 1:18),"[45] and, "Through the Word of promise the person, if he is baptized and believes, should have the certainty of salvation. Here nothing can be attributed to power, but only established by the service of those who are baptized."[46]

Luther destroyed the temple. Everything that is now a part of any church hierarchy resembles a tabernacle. The regulations and orders under which the community of God comes together in the Word cannot be permanent. They must be the expression of the wandering people of God. Therefore, any kind of false idea must be destroyed so that the gates of hell (Matt 16:18) may not overtake this church which has its place in the temple. In the moment where the promise of God is referenced by the visible church, whether it is in Bet-El, in Jerusalem, or in Rome, in that moment the promises of God are falsely communicated. Luther emphasizes this in his Disputation on Matt 16:16ff., with Eck in Leipzig, where he says that the promise of the impregnability of the church was never made to an individual nor did it pertain to the function that Simon, the son of Jonas, had among the disciples, nor did it pertain to the seat of Rome, and that it is idolatry to substitute a visible church that is fragile, sinful, and erring, with the church for which the promise is valid, so that the gates of hell may not overcome it.[47] Thus, the concept of the *ecclesia invisibilis* is a concept that Luther used in his fight against the Papacy. This also has to do with the moment in which the visible church places the true, invisible church in danger of putting man's word above God's. As long as the church cannot be physically identified in human form, then God's Word and man's word cannot be co-mingled. That is the essential problem that Luther identifies when he says, "Such ideas arise when God's word is not viewed as God's word, but because it is spoken by men, people hear it as if it were man's word and stare up at the sky and create other keys to heaven. And Christ speaks here very clearly when he wants to give Peter the keys (to the church) and doesn't say that there are two keys to heaven, but only one key which he gives to Peter." The point here

---

45. WA 6, 514, 29ff. = BoA 1, 445, 30ff.
46. WA 6, 543, 32ff. = BoA 1, 479, 15ff.
47. WA 2, 272, (*Disputatio I. Eccii et M. Lutheri Lipsiae habita.* 1519). Passim.

is that God's Word is at work on earth and God's Word is to remain God's Word, even if a human being speaks it: "Why do you look to heaven for my key? Don't you know that I left it on earth and gave it to Peter? You won't find it in heaven, but in Peter's mouth. That is where I left it. Peter's mouth is my mouth, his commission is my commission for him, his key is my key. I have no other and know of no other. What he binds is bound; what he loosens, is loosened. If there are other keys in heaven or on earth, they have nothing to do with me and I do not care what function they serve to bind or to loosen. Therefore, do not turn to them and go astray. Hold to Peter, for those are my keys. They bind and loosen in heaven and nowhere else. See, that is the correct way to think and talk about the key to heaven. Any other opinion is horribly wrong and has weakened and clouded this meaning."[48] The visible church here is Peter, but the task that he performs, the true subject of the office of the keys, is an invisible one: it is Christ. He locks and unlocks with this key. And that happens in every church where believers are assembled, and where His word of the gospel is preached, in places and spaces unbound by time and place, by the educated and the uneducated.

Thus, the invisible church is here and present among us. My thesis was and is that Luther begins with a philosophical concept of the invisible church and ends with a Biblical one. The fight against the thesis of a visible church in Rome could only be led by Luther after he came to realize the true nature of the invisible church.

2. The Congregation and the Spiritual Commission

What about the "unity" or *unitas* of the church these days? One must conclude that from faith a new people is born through faith. This people are one folk, one body, and have faith and hope in the sense of Eph 4:3ff. If the church is comprised of Germans, French, Russians, etc., then one could not speak of unity. But we are talking here of people who are born of the Spirit, as is the Son of God. It is a unity that is born of the unity created by faith in God's Word. It is the only truth. In it alone is the forgiveness of sins. In it alone we have life. So, there remains only one open question: Is there not also an opposite movement? Is there not also that

---

48. WA 30/2, 455, 10–27 (On the Keys 1530?). On the "Office of the Keys" (*potestas clavium*) the ancient church understood its power to bind and to loose sin (*potestas ligandi et solvendi*) based on Matt 16:19; 18:18; and John 20:23. (See *RGG* V, 1451ff.) and its ability to forgive sins.

the invisible church can become visible? There is of course a *signum* and there is also the *verbum* in human form. And there is also Luther's phrase about the Word, where he says we cannot "draw Christianity deeply enough into our flesh."[49] Rather, there is the *signa Dei*, upon which faith is founded. But only the *signa Dei* that God himself designates. That is how the church is able to be visible at all *in carne* (in the flesh), but not completely. There is no representation of this *ecclesia universalis*, except for the Word and the sacraments. It is impossible that this church, the true church, can be represented by one particular church. And because there is no such representation, people cling to the office of the church. Their doubt unites them around what is at hand and so the visible church is the magnet that draws them on. As a result, they are pulled away from God's word and His power. Only in the moment in which God's word is certainly and securely preached here on earth through the mouths of his messengers, so that (just as we heard about Luther's Doctrine of the Keys) what we bind on earth is also bound in heaven, and what is loosed on earth is loosed in heaven, because God cannot lie, and His Word cannot be overturned—only in that moment are they the redeemed people of God. That is the church of the saints.

From this there is a further corollary: The saints of this church are free. The freedom of the church consists in its ability to pass judgement on what is taught. In this church there is no hierarchy or "over and under;" no distinction between man and woman, old and young, but in this church are only shepherds and sheep who hear His voice (John 10:14ff). That is why a teacher should be subject to the judgment of his hearers in the *ministerium verbi* (the Office of the Word). Indeed, a teacher or preacher of the Word should never be doctrinaire. The authority is always the authority of the Word. The Word makes the congregation the authority over the teacher, and the preacher, in his/her preaching is subject to and servant of the congregation. "Everything is yours, but you belong to Christ" (1 Cor. 3:22ff). That is the concept of the congregation in Luther. It is a very unusual thing in the history of the church that a doctrine resulted based on the service of the teacher to a free congregation giving the congregation the right to decide what is true teaching and what is false. Luther judges (again in reference to John 10): "Here you see, I think, clearly enough what is involved when the word of men deals with souls. Who cannot see that all the bishops, seminaries, cloisters, and

---

49. See Ch. III, 118 (n. 16).

schools with all their enrolled, rage against the bright Word of Christ, so that, on the basis of their own rules and wickedness, they take away from the sheep their ability to judge and justify themselves. Therefore, they are certainly shown to be murderers and thieves, wolves and rebellious Christians when they are publicly overruled as those who not only deny God's word, but who also set themselves against it and act accordingly, as those who are born of the anti-Christ and his realm, as is described in the prophecy of St. Paul in 2 Thess 2 (v. 3f)."[50] Luther goes on to emphasize: "Among Christians everyone is a judge of the other and everyone is subordinate to the other, despite the fact that religious tyrants have constructed a worldly hierarchy out of Christianity."[51] And furthermore: "No one can deny that any Christian has God's word and is taught by God and is sanctified as a priest, as Christ says in John 6 (v. 45, from Is 54:13): 'They will all be taught by God.' And Psalm 44 (Ps 45:8): 'God has set you above your companions by anointing you with the oil of joy.' These companions are the Christians, Christian brothers, who like you are elevated to priesthood, as Peter also says in, 1 Peter 2 (v. 9): 'You are a royal priesthood ... that you may declare the praises of him who called you out of darkness into his wonderful light.'"[52]

Luther intends that the entire Christian community should have the right to judge teaching and preaching. Only the congregation can judge. The preacher cannot judge but must be judged. The preacher and his preaching are subject to the judgement of the congregation. Preaching is a creative act. In the sermon, the sheep hear the voice of their shepherd. When they do not hear his voice, then they do not hear anything. Thus, they have given their judgement already. However, when they receive the word of God, they are the *creatura verbi divini* (Jas 1:18) and as such they judge their preacher with thanks and praise and accept him as a messenger who has brought them the word of God in its binding and loosing, so that they are certain that it is God's word. In this way the congregation is the model for freedom in this world and those who bring to it their highest and best are its servants. In this congregation we have a sample of the lifting of all earthly hierarchy; here is truly no division of over or under, no lord or serf, no man or woman (see Gal 3:28). This congregation is truly the invisible church, the *ecclesia invisibilis* as the

50. WA 11, 410, 3ff. (Dass ein christliche Versammlung oder Gemeine Recht und Macht habe...1523) = BoA 2, 397, 24ff.

51. WA 11, 410, 29ff. = BoA 2, 398, 13ff.

52. WA 11, 411, 31ff. = BoA 2, 399, 12ff.

reality of the people of God's kingdom, as those who are called by God; they are brothers in Christ, the priesthood of believers. In this way Luther fashions a reality out of the teaching on the priesthood of believers. It is the basis for everything that he wants to say about church authority: the *ministerium verbi divini* can only be exercised under the assumption that everyone is a priest. Therefore, we can teach God's truth in colleges with the assumption that we are all brothers and that we, along with what we teach, are under their judgment, because they as Christians have the power to judge what we teach.

The Mass and Holy Communion

1. The Origins of Luther's Teaching on Holy Communion

In the early days, Luther's teaching on the sacraments was especially clear and lucid. His shorter writings on it are classic and stem from the year 1519. However, Luther had no idea what a maelstrom these writings, and their definitions, would cause him later on. He also had no idea of the horrible fight that he would have to wage with the Enthusiasts/Fanatics (German: *Schwärmer*) on the issues created by his writings.

It goes without saying that for Luther the Sacraments have their place in the *communio* (congregation). Luther says: "I believe that no one can be holy who is not part of this community and is at peace with it in one faith, word, sacrament, hope and love, and no Jew, heretic, heathen, or sinner is at peace with it, even if he/she has reconciliation with it, unification, and similarity in all things."[53] (See short form of The 10 Commandments). And prior to that he says of the Third Article of the Creed: "I believe that there is nowhere on this wide earth any longer a holy, common Christian church; that there is nothing other than the community or gathering of the saved, the pious, believing people on earth, who are called, gathered, and ruled through the same Holy Spirit and who increase daily in the sacraments and God's Word."[54] This church already exists but we can perhaps also see that in Luther it is impossible to correctly understand his teaching on the church without the Doctrine of Election; namely, that of predetermination or predestination. If one understands predestination correctly, then the church is already present in the assembly of the saved

---

53. WA 7, 219, 6 ff (A short form of the Ten Commandments...1520) = BoA 2, 51, 14ff.

54. WA 7, 291, 1ff. = BoA 2, 51, 8ff.

that encompasses the entire world, and therefore cannot be limited to or believed to be one particular existing church. I believe in the church in the sense that I, in the particular church to which I belong, can only participate in the faith of the universal church; even the sacraments draw me from a particular church into the general one. The sacraments let me take part in the invisible church; in this sense, at any time, they go beyond the particular church to the invisible church. They do not constitute the church, according to Luther, but they incorporate the person into the congregation that is without sin, which is pure and imparts the promise of eternal life. Preaching on sinlessness therefore belongs to the concept of *ecclesia univeralis*, in which the sacraments stand (sic!). This is also connected to the idea that only those who belong to the church are the hearers and believers in forgiveness of sins. To believe in the forgiveness of sins means to believe God that my sins are not retained by Him and have disappeared. From this point Luther moves to his new concept of salvation. Accordingly, whoever does not believe does not belong to this church, even if they were to take the sacraments ten times over, are baptized, and eat the communion bread. Faith constitutes the community of the saved and it is this faith in which and through which we participate in Christ's life. Since He is free from sin and death, then we are also since we participate in His life. This "being in Christ" exists in the community of the saints, and the sacraments belong in its midst to the extent that they are the means of participation in eternal life. This also means that basically, the sacraments—if I may be so blunt—have nothing to do with the church. The sacraments, in their deepest sense, have to do with Christ himself. So, Luther can say in his early thesis on the "*Disputatio de fide infusa et acquisita*" of 1520 (Disputation on Infused and Acquired faith) in a famous line: "Only one Sacrament contain the Holy Scriptures, that is, Christ Jesus himself."[55] This is the core of Luther's early teaching on the Sacraments. In other words, for Luther, if the sacraments are a "sign," a *signum*, then one must really say that they are the outstretched hand that takes me out of the visible church into the invisible one. There are also other very precise explanations of this in Luther, for example: "The Sacraments are a ford, a bridge, a door, a ship, and a barge in which and through which we travel from this world into eternal life. Therefore, it is about faith: for whoever does not believe is the person who would like to traverse the ford and is so unsuccessful that he doesn't trust the ship

---

55. WA 6, 86, 7–8, Thesis 18: "*Unum solum habent sacrae literae sacramentum, quod est ipse Christus Dominus.*" See the explanations in the "*Resolutio*" to the theses, 97. 5ff.

and therefore has to remain and will never be saved as long as he doesn't take his place in the boat to cross. That is what makes for carnality and unexercised faith, for whom the journey over the Jordan goes wrong and the devil has a hand in it."[56] It helps here to note that here that there is no reference to carnality in the revelation that the trip might be going in the wrong direction (!). There is a ford, a door, a bridge, a ship, "which is useful and necessary so that love and the community of Christ and all the saints are hidden, invisible, and spiritual, and only a physical, visual, external sign is given to us. For if this love, community, and support were made public and visible, as in the person's contemporary community, we would not be strengthened by it or trained to trust in the invisible and eternal goods or to desire them, but rather would only be trained to trust in palpable, visible goods and get used to them only, so that we would not willingly leave them and follow God. For to the extent that we rely on visible and conceptual things, we are prevented from coming to God. All temporal and sensible things must fall away, and we must be weaned off them in order to come to God. That is why the Mass, and the sacraments are signs that we should practice and get used to living without any visible love, help, or comfort and rely solely on Christ and His holy, invisible love and support."[57] Thus says the early Luther on the Sacrament of Holy Communion.

2. The Sacrament as the "Sign" of the Invisible Church

These passages are an argument for the sacraments as a sign of an invisible church to which we hold and by which, through its inner tendency and according to its own inclination, it draws us to the invisible church. The signs are proof of the priority of the invisible church within the visible one. To that extent, they are signs. In them we are met by the symbolic, invisible church that we don't see—that no one can see—and in which we live in faith and in which there is wonderful community where, "there is no man or woman, no lord or servant," (Gal 3:28), which encompasses everyone. The sacraments are therefore—if we may say—a revolutionary sign in the midst of the visible church, with which the visible church is always and again guided by the invisible one, the church of faith: "Christ

---

56. WA 2, 753, 17ff. (Ein Sermon von dem hochwurdigen Sakrament des heiligen wahren Leichnams Christi . . . 1519, "On the Twentieth") = BoA 1, 207, 26ff.

57. WA 2, 752, 36ff. = BoA 1, 207, 6ff.

with all the saints through his love takes on our form, fights with us against sin, death and all evil, so that we, inflamed by love, take on His form, and abandon ourselves to His righteousness, life and holiness and are thus through communion with his gifts and our sins baked together in one cake ("bun"), one bread, one body, one drink where everything is held together in common. O, that is a great Sacrament, says St. Paul (Eph 5:32) in which Christ and the church are one flesh and one body."[58]

According to Luther, this *communio* is always present. No one dies alone. In a letter of comfort written to the seriously ill Duke Friedrich of Saxony,[59] Luther writes: "Because we are members each of the church of Christ, therefore Christ does not leave us alone in death (references to Phlm 1:21 and Rom 14:8).[60] But in the church of the saints, which here is also called the new creation of God,[61] where everyone has everything in common, just as the sacrament of the altar represents in the bread and wine, where we are one body, one bread, one chalice as the Apostle says (1 Cor 10:17).[62] So we point to this unity of the sacraments: "We are one body."[63] And Luther observes: "Thus the *communio sanctorum* and the church of Christ are so magnificent."[64]

3. Word and Sign, Promise and Faith

Luther was clear about the theological interpretation of the "signa" (signs) of the sacrament in his treatise on "*De captivitate Babylonica ecclesiae praeludium*" (On the Babylonian Captivity of the Church) of 1520.[65] This treatise is perhaps his most in-depth look at the Catholic concept of the sacraments. (If you work through the Latin text of the "*De captivitate*" and then read Luther's shorter writings on the sacrament in German, then you also will notice the Latin concepts that are used and will see how very precisely theologically the German texts correspond to the Latin concepts. However, if you start with the German writings first, you will

---

58. WA 2, 748, 14ff. (On the Fourteenth) = BoA 1, 202, 27ff.

59. WA 6, 99-134 (*Tessaradecas consolatoria prolaborantibus et oneratis*. 1520-14 Comforts for the sick of heart and encumbered."

60. WA 6. See also 123, 3ff.

61. WA 6. See also 130, 26.

62. WA 6. See also 132, 1ff.

63. WA 6, 132, 1ff. n. 6.

64. WA 6, 131, 29.

65. See IV, 250 (n. 44).

not notice it.) In the Catholic doctrine of the sacraments, we find striking emphasis on the *signum*, which is characteristic of the Lombardian definition that was typical of the Medieval Ages: *Sacramentum est sacrae rei signum* (a sacrament is a sign of a holy thing).[66] Much is contained in these few words. It has to do with the medieval theological notion of the sacrament as a "holy" thing. The concept of holiness is fundamental to the teaching of the sacraments. Luther's interpretation is one that I will try to make clear using a sentence from the "*De captivitate*" in his arguments against the Lombards: "So it cannot be true that in the sacrament an actual power of justification can be found, or that it is an active sign of grace."[67] The sacrament is not a *signa* that justifies us. It is also not a *signa* of effective grace. The *signa* themselves are completely earthly things and nothing else: bread, wine, and water. Why does Luther say this? He says this because he means that faith justifies and not the sacraments. Where there is no faith, no sacrament can help. Therefore he warns: "Therefore let us open our eyes and learn more about the Word than about signs, to pay more attention to faith than to works or the use of (*usus*) signs, since we know that where God's promise is there faith is at work, and that both are so necessary that neither can be effective without the other."[68] Faith is always the result of a *promissio*, a promise: "The efficacy (*efficatia*) of the sacraments apart from the promise and faith means to seek their support in vain and to end up in damnation."[69] If I therefore seek the efficacy of signs in and of themselves, then I am seeking to have the full effect of the sacraments in the here and now, whereupon I grasp at nothingness. Luther says the sacraments do nothing more for you than what you already believe. If you do not believe in the forgiveness of sins, then you will not receive it through the sacraments. Therefore, according to Luther, since the Lombards placed the effect of the sacraments per se as the *signum* of a *sacra res*, the concept of the *sacra res* disappears completely and, in its place, we have the *promissio*.

What kind of turn-about is this? What changed? Is there a sign, a *signum*, for the promissio; a sign by which I can grasp the *promissio*? What is the difference if a *signum* signifies a *res*, a thing, or if a *signum* signifies a *promissio*? If, for example, a *signum* is given as a sign of trust and I safeguard the *sign* of another as a gift or reminder as a sign of your

---

66. Petrus Lombardus, *Sententiarum* IV in: MPL Vol. 192, Sp. 839 (=IV, Dist. I, 2).
67. WA 6, 533, 14-15 = BoA, 467, 13-14.
68. WA 6, 533, 29ff. = BoA 1, 467, 32ff.
69. WA 6, 533, 35ff. = BoA 1, 467, 39-40.

loyalty, then this *sign* only has meaning for me to the degree that I believe in the loyalty of the other person. The *sign* itself would never bring about my faith. Only that in which I believe lends meaning to the sign. The sign in itself represents nothing; it only has meaning for me. This means that the sign enters the realm of the Word, where word and faith—*verbum*, and *fides*—are one and the same. The unbeliever does not understand the sign. The sign is God's sign, and Luther goes so far as to say that when Baptism is performed we must view it as if God himself has laid hands on the baptized; and the priests who perform the baptism are only an instrument holding the child in the water.[70] In this sense the sign is thus no longer seen as part of the invisible world, but as a sign of my friend, of my God, who holds and keeps me, as in the case of Jacob and his staff when he went through the Jordan river (Gen 32:11). The sacrament must always be interpreted from within the *promissio*. It is not the realization of invisible faith but is a sign that is attached to the *promissio*. First you must believe the *promissio*, then you can understand the sign for it. You can never arrive at the thing itself (*res*) by way of the sign, but always must proceed from the thing to the sign. Luther says: "There is therefore an insurmountable truth: wherever there is divine promise, there every person is on their own; they are claimed by faith (*exigitur*) and their attempts at self-justification are annulled and their burdens are lifted, as Mark says: 'Whoever believes and is baptized will be saved; but whoever does not believe will be condemned.'" (Mark 16:16). Therefore, each individual must make the mass beneficial for themselves, for their own faith, and cannot take communion on behalf of anyone else."[71] In his *Sermon on the New Testament*, Luther writes of four sections that belong to the Testament: 1) the *testator*, or will, for whom the testament is intended; 2) the inheritance given to the heirs; 3) the Word, or the message that is announced; 4) and the seal, which are the bread and wine, "under which true body and blood, for everything contained in this testament is alive. Therefore, it is not conveyed by dead writing or seals, but by the living word and signs thereof."[72] The phrase "living word and signs," also means that the bread and wine are not offered as things in themselves, for that

---

70. See on these generally held remarks such places as WA 41, 162, 10ff. (Third Sermon on Psalm 110, May 29, 1535): "No one can see that a person who is baptized is free from sin; he is holy and reborn by way of the hand of the priest."

71. WA 6, 521, 20ff. (*De captivitate...*) = BoA 1, 453, 30ff.

72. WA 6, 359, 19ff. (A Sermon from the New Testament, that is on the Holy Mass. 1520. On the Twelfth.) = BoA 1, 305, 18ff.

would mean they would be inert and dead signs. But Christ's body and blood are alive and accordingly, Christ's Testament belongs to the world of the resurrected Christ, the world of His life, where there is no more death; to the *communio sanctorum*, which the gates of hell cannot and will not overcome (Matt 16:18).

4. Luther's Position on the Doctrine of "Trans-substantiation"

Luther's teaching on transubstantiation during Holy Communion is not to be underestimated.[73] He writes in the "*De captivitate*:" "The church was right for over twelve hundred years and never and nowhere had the holy fathers thought anything about transubstantiation (a monstrous confusion of language and illusion) until the pseudo-philosophy of Aristotle began to swarm around in the church during the last three hundred years, whereby many other things were distorted (*perperam*) as, for example, that the divine being was neither caused nor able to cause, and that the soul takes on the basic form of the human body and similar ideas, which cannot be defended on the basis of any rational or other kind of examination."[74] Luther knew that an attack on transubstantiation was an attack on the church. And, while in the course of attacking this dogma, he also placed the validity of the Council in question. The idea that, during transubstantiation, an action or work (*opus*) occurs through which the church has a hand in its own power and authority is a theme of the "*Captivates Ecclesiae*" or the (Babylonian) captivity of the church. Luther took apart the idea of transubstantiation on the basis of two things: that it is not a viable philosophical position, and that in it the *verbum Dei* completely loses its rightful place. "If we do not hold to the position that the mass of Christ is a testament and promise, as the words say loud and clear, then we lose the entire Gospel and all its consolations."[75]

---

73. In the 12th century the laity were not allowed to drink from the chalice during the celebration of the Eucharist (the Great Thanksgiving and Lord's Supper) on the basis of the teachings of Alexander Halesius (1170–245) who argued according to the doctrine of concomitance that the body and blood of Christ are each present in both the bread and the wine. During the fourth ecumenical Lateran Synod of 1215, the already much taught doctrine of the transformation of the elements of bread and wine into the body and blood of Christ (transubstantiation) became church dogma under Pope Innocent III. Both events took place against the historical background of particular waves of lay piety within the church.

74. WA 6, 509, 27ff. = BoA 1, 440, 11ff.

75. WA 6, 523, 17ff. = BoA, 1, 455, 33ff. Here H. J. Iwand refers to a place in the

The fact that Luther's position on Holy Communion represents a departure from the Catholic notion of transubstantiation is something that I would like to summarize as follows:

a) The promissio. Luther places the *promissio* before the fact. It doesn't matter to him that we receive (Christ's) body and blood, but that we take the promise in the Word of promise seriously while receiving the signs of the body and blood of Christ. In the Kingdom of God there is only one thing needed and it is only there for me in faith; otherwise, there is only death, sin, and the world. That is the problem, says Luther, when he gives the *promissio* priority place, as he gives a new interpretation to the essence of the mass as proceeding from the Word of promise: "Therefore I fear that now in Christianity there is more idolatry in the mass as ever there was in Judaism, for we never hear that the mass is for the broadening and deepening of faith, that it proceeds from Christ himself, but only enacted as a sacrament without testament . . . that God has prepared for our faith a pasture, a table, and a meal in which our faith can expand but not without the Word of God. Therefore, we must accept and believe the Word of God above all things."[76] And further: "So He (Christ) in the mass, has given the first of all promises, a sign of remembrance (*signum memoriale*) of the great promise; namely, of his own body and his own blood, in bread and wine, as he says: 'Do this in remembrance of me' (1 Cor 11:24–25)."[77] The closer we are to the concept of promise, the more clearly the concept of *memoria* (remembrance) appears. However, Christ means by the words, "Do this in remembrance of me" not some kind of memorializing of death, but rather the way in which we remember the living. "Memoria" in this way means: The Gospel is proclaimed to us, just as Christ died for us. In strict theological terms, the *signum memoriale* means that the Word goes before the fact. Here we are not dealing with an action by the church, but we are dealing with—as strange as it sounds—a

---

"*Catechismus. . .illustrates*" of the Lutheran theologian Johannes Brenz (1499–1570). See *RGG* I, 1400–401. where he says: "The Lord's Supper is the sacrament or divine sign whereby Christ is truly present for us under bread and wine and gives his body and blood to us and makes us know that our sins are forgiven." H. J. Iwand means here: "In the moment in which the Lord's Supper is thus understood, that Christ gives to us His body and blood, the ideas of the Scholastics erupt." See here the dogma on transubstantiation in: H. Gollwitzer, "*Coena Domini*" München 1937, to which H. J. Iwand refers, among others. 279.

76. WA 6, 363, 20ff. (A Sermon from the New Testament on the Holy Mass. 1520, On the Eighteenth.) = BoA 1, 309, 1ff.

77. WA 6, 518, 10ff. (*De captivitate. . .*) = BoA 1, 449, 36ff.

"*promissio.*" We have the forgiveness of sins—not as a fact or an experience—but as a promise. God creates a new creature with his *verbum*. It is not the substance of the bread that is changed, but rather the person who believes is changed: "Therefore the mass is at is essence (substance) nothing other than the spoken words of Christ: Take and eat, etc., as if He were to say, 'See, oh, you sinners and damned, from sheer unearned love, with which I love you, because the Father is merciful, I promise you these words above any deserving or vows, the forgiveness of all your sins and eternal life, and with it you are now certain of my irrevocable promise, and will offer up my body and pour out my blood and with my death seal this promise, and I will leave both for you a signs and a memorial (*memoriale*) of this promise."[78] And still more: God creates with his *verbum* a new creature. Whosoever believes in this promise of the forgiveness of sins has been moved to heaven and placed in the fellowship of God.

b) Die communio. In Holy Communion, there is a "*communio*," a fellowship that is created which does not actively administer the sacraments, but in which God does the administering. The *communio* is completely and utterly passive. And we are, through this *communio*, through the sufferings of Christ, placed in a relationship in which we suffer each other's sins and burdens (Gal 6:2): "Carry each other's burdens." Through the Lord's Supper a community is established in which Christ is present. The formation of this community is a unique kind of activity because, since we receive the forgiveness of sins through Christ, so we should also forgive the sins of others. Christ gave himself up to death. Just as He and the resurrected church carry our cares and guilt, we should also have the confidence of being free from guilt in order to serve our neighbor. In the Christian fellowship on earth, sins are forgiven and obliterated. Just as Christ annihilates sin, so it is also the task of the *communio* of love to annul sins. This community is the place where sins are obliterated. The Christian community should be the wonderful place where guilt and sin are vanquished. Here we should reach out our hands to one another in service like Christ has done for us. This is what the kingdom of God is about—the actual annihilation of sin, not just the knowledge of it. But the reality of sin must also be acknowledged. Christianity should be the first place in which the all-consuming nature of evil deeds and guilt come to an end: "That is why in the sacraments we are given the immeasurable grace and mercy of God, so that we can lay any misery, any struggle at the

---

78. WA 6, 515, 17ff. = BoA 1, 446, 31ff.

feet of the congregation and especially at Christ's, and make the person joyful, strong, trusting, and say: 'Though I am a sinner, though I have fallen, though this bad thing has happened to me, never mind, I will take the sacrament anyhow and take God's sign that Christ's righteousness, his life and suffering was for me with all the holy angels and saints in heaven and pious people on earth. And should I die, I am not alone in death, and should I suffer, they suffer along with me. All of my misfortune belongs to Christ and the community of saints so that I have their love for me as a sure sign.' See, that is the proper fruit and use of the sacraments, to make the heart strong and glad.'"[79] And a bit later on Luther says: "Now your heart must yield itself to love and learn how this sacrament is a sacrament of love and how love and help are given to you, and how love and help are demonstrated to your brothers and sisters in Christ in need."[80] Accordingly, we can say that in the Lord's Supper, in the *communio*, we have the first instance in which reconciliation becomes a reality in a very specific form of community. It is not the case that the person comes on their own to a correct attitude toward the sacrament or to internal reassurance and peace. This kind of position could never support the unique ethic of the Last Supper. The ethic that grounds the Lord's Supper—which is very similar to the sacrament of Baptism—has to do with the way in which we cease to be an individual as we journey through life. Just as Christ gives himself up in the sacrament in order to carry our sins, so also those who are bound to him, his own, are given up to all the saints in heaven. The ability to give up one's life is something that only faith can enable, which is offered in the Last Supper. Here is the decisive point in Luther's teaching on the Lord's Supper: where God appears as judge of all, and we are all alike in His presence, means to give up ourselves and to cease to have any right to judge another or to claim judgment over others. And here is where the ethical root of the *communio sanctorum* lies in that I suffer on account of another: just as Christ lost his life for me in which he took on human flesh, so must we also lose our own lives and assume the life of a lost and alien brother or sister, so that we can do what the Son, who is always with the Father, could not do, which is to be lost among the lost and victim among the victimized (cf. Luke 15:11–32).[81]

79. WA 2, 745, 7ff. (A Sermon on the Most Worthy Sacrament of the Holy Body of Christ...1519 On the Eighth) = BoA 1, 199, 18ff.

80. WA 2, 745, 24ff. (On the Ninth) = BoA 1, 199, 35ff.

81. On the entire section "*communio sanctorum*" see also H. J. Iwand, NW IV, 193–216, especially Thesis 2, 205ff.

c) *On Faith.* Finally, Luther emphasizes that everything turns on faith. In his "Sermon on the holy and worthy sacrament of Baptism. 1519" he pens the famous sentence ("On the 15th"): "If you have faith, you have everything. If you doubt, you are lost."[82] And in the sermon titled "Sermon in preparation for death 1519" ("On the 15th") Luther says: "God has promised to me and given to me a sure sign of His grace in the sacraments that Christ's life has overcome my death in his death, his obedience has destroyed my sin through his suffering, and his love has destroyed the hell of my loneliness and desolation. The sign, the promise of my salvation, cannot be undone or taken from me. God has spoken. God does not lie either with words or actions."[83] Here and in many other places we hear how important faith is for Luther.

5. The Doctrine of Ubiquity

A final short treatment should include the later fight over the Lord's Supper, dealing primarily with Luther's argument with the Swiss reformer Zwingli (1484-1531) in his work of 1527 that appeared under the title: "That this Word of Christ 'That is my body' should remain steadfast, against the Enthusiasts."[84] This work is written with much pain and sharpness, but also with a great deal of freedom and openness. In it we can learn about the depth of Luther's understanding: "Otherwise we will tolerate if someone says HE is in the bread, HE is the bread, HE is, where the bread is, or whatever. We should not quibble over language, only that the sense and meaning remains that it is not merely bread that we eat during Holy Communion, but the body of Christ."[85] Here is it clear that the question remains open as to "how" the body is present. All attempts that Luther makes later on to explain the "how" are only dialectical attempts to solve the problem in the face of opposition that says that the body of Christ cannot be there (i.e., in the bread). Therefore, what is most

---

82. WA 2, 733, 35-36 = BoA 1, 192, 1-2. On the formula itself, H. J. Iwand writes in his Festschrift for Rudolf Hermann: "Solange es heute heisst," 145, n. 21: "This formula contains the abbreviated version of the problem of certainty and is understandably very subjective and misunderstood. It is meant in the sense of "extra nos." (Trans. R. Lundell).

83. WA 2, 693, 8ff. = BoA 1, 169, 18ff.

84. See WA 23, 38-320. On the Disagreement with Karlstadt regarding the Question of the Lord's Supper see III, 210ff.

85. WA 23, also 145, 29ff. (Dr.)

important is not the "how" but the "that." For Luther, the main thing is that the body is there (in the bread). That is what the fight is about. The presence of the body of Christ must be such that it cannot be incorporated into the internal workings of people, their memory, their experience, their thoughts, etc. It is decisive that the presence of the body is such that we grab hold of it since it has to do with the question of the *ecclesia invisibilis* and the church as such. Luther maintained the theme of presence, or contemporality, throughout his writings: "Then He is there, because He says so and binds His Word to it and says: 'You will find me here.' Because you have His Word, you also can grab hold of Him with certainty and say: 'Here I have you, just as you say.' In the same way I could say about the judgement seat of God: it is the case that before God we cannot lie. And because nothing is as you say it was (which is something you can only understand with difficulty) so also God's judgment seat binds you to it and defines you on the spot. It does this so that you might live in Christ and abide in Him. There you will find Him for sure. Otherwise, you can walk the earth among all creatures and look here and there and never find it, although it is surely there: it is just not there for you."[86] This also means that God's presence is everywhere at all times.[87] Since God is everywhere and encompasses everything, Luther's descriptions are often similar to what we might call pantheism, where everything that is and has its being is from God. But he also says this: if you try to find God in nature you will come up emptyhanded. A particular act by God has to occur so that we can find Him. The presence of God and Christ in the Sacrament always refers to God's commitment: in order for me to find God, He must first find me. He binds himself to His Word and He binds himself for me, but not to me. The basic Zwinglian idea is that Christ is there for me. Luther says "No" to Zwingli; the first sentence must read, "God is." This describes the presence of God. This presence of God is therefore not to be signified by a particular act of worship or by a mystery. The presence of God is hidden, just as He is hidden in the incarnation of Christ. Luther also says: God's honor consists in offering Himself up in all humility. He will not take away honor from us (Cf. John 5:41): "There is a difference between His presence and the physical reality of it. He is free and unencumbered wherever He is and doesn't have to be locked in one place like a boy in some pillory or cast-iron neck collar. See how the sunshine is so close to

---

86. WA 23, also 145, 14ff. (Dr.)

87. The teaching on the ubiquity of God (*Ubiquitat*) is developed in the writings of Luther that are used here (H. J. Iwand).

you that it shines in your eyes, or on your skin, so that you can feel it. But if you try to contain it and put it in a box you will be trying forever. You can prevent it from shining on you by shuttering a window, but you cannot grab it or touch it. This is also like Christ: though He is everywhere, you cannot grasp or touch Him."[88]

The presence of God is such that He is free to go where He will. If we would know the presence of God only from the relationship between God and the world, then we would have an entry way to God from out of our own existence. But Luther denies this possibility because God does not commit himself in order for us to claim him, but rather He alone is free. Wherever He commits himself, there is grace: "Here you may find me." That is also why His presence is not an internal one, but our internal natures are bound to His external presence and thus we are pulled out of ourselves: "He becomes incomprehensible and though you cannot touch him, though He is in the bread, it is the case that he commits Himself to you and humbly invites you to a particular table through His Word and points to the bread through His Word, that you should eat it. This He does in the Lord's Supper and says: 'This is my body.'"[89] We are not dealing with a tradition here. It is not a tradition of the congregation, but a call to come near to God who is everywhere present. From this presence He commits and binds Himself to us. Here he chooses His place and says, "Here, here is where you have me." If God didn't commit Himself to us (first), how could we ever take hold of Him? From the connections that we have on earth (death, life, status, neighbor) we cannot grasp Him; we always end up with an idol. However, because God in His almighty power binds himself to us, that is why we are able to find Him. This is how Luther understands the Lord's Supper (Holy Communion). Christ is at the right hand of God and is spirit like God; that is, he is everywhere though we cannot find Him except that He reveals Himself to us: "We know that it's the LORD's Supper and not Christ's Supper. For the Lord does not work alone, but is active and working as cook, waiter, arranging the food and the drink, as we in our faith have seen proof of this above. So, Christ does not speak when He commands and appoints: He does this for your salvation, so that you will recognize and love each other, and also so that you, 'Do this in remembrance of me.'"[90]

---

88. WA 23, 151, 3ff. (Dr.)
89. WA 23, 151, 3ff., nn. 28ff. (Dr.)
90. WA 23, 271. n. 8ff. (Dr.)

6. The Presence of God in Word and Sacrament

After this short representation of Luther's teaching on ubiquity, I would like to briefly summarize what we have learned about the Mass and Holy Communion. Just as the church is invisible, because it is the presence of God in Word and Sacrament, just as the *communio sanctorum* is invisible, whereby, though we cannot observe it, people live for one another, because their salvation, which alone earns this title, is necessarily present, so that they no longer cling to objective acts and facts of their own observations, so we again run into this theme of the presence of God at the Lord's Supper. Luther warns against making a symbol of something earthly, or of any earthly action. Luther insists that God is the actor and initiator. He fears that when Christ sits in heaven at the right hand and the Lord's Supper is administered on earth, that a separation occurs with the expression "behind" (the bread), with a resulting misinterpretation that only deepens the divide. This should not happen. It is interesting that both sides worried about an aberration during the fight over Holy Communion. Luther intends the activity and the presence of God to combine into the act of administering the bread and wine. He allows for no room in-between. In all circumstances he wants to guard against the idea that the Lord's Supper is merely a symbolic act. Of course, it is a sign; but it is not a symbolic church or religious action that signifies the actual meaning. No, it (the action) must happen in it (the sign). Opponents fear a kind of "magical thinking." The real presence of God could, for example, be understood such that the church does something through its actions, whereby it again would serve in an intermediary role between God and man. Thus, both sides fear the same thing. The intention of both sides is, so to speak, on the one hand anti-Roman Catholic and on the other, anti-heathen. Both sides want to avoid the notion that from the revelation of God in Christ a religion is born that is symbolic, on the one hand, and magical on the other. Both sides of the argument are aware of the weaknesses on the other side: the severing of this-side (earthly) from beyond (heavenly) where Christ sits at the right-hand of God, from action here on earth. And on the other side: the identity of the heavenly with earthly bread. Thus, this fight over the Lord's Supper (between Zwingli and Luther, between "it means" and "it is") represents, to a great extent, the actual problem at issue in the Lord's Supper.

Both sides have done us a favor, however, in that each side, using the sharp eyes of an opponent, can see what the other one is after. Whoever observes the Lord's Supper today only from one side of the debate does not grasp the kernel of the entire debate. In other words, whoever fervently advocates the thesis that Christ sits at the right hand of God and therefore could not be in the bread, and whoever on the other side fervently advocates the thesis of the *manducatio oralis* (whereby Christ's body is eaten in the mouth), erects a "Shibboleth" (symbolic identification, Cf. Ri 12:5f) as the basis for schism. These people do not know that here we have a problem of tremendous depth and import which lies, so to speak, between both of the Protestant theologies. However, if one regards the debate correctly then one will also see that the meaning of "Christ sits at the right hand of God" as it is intended, has a certain validity. Luther tries to explain in another way: whereby God remains a free agent and He does not allow himself to be manipulated by men. The subjectivity of God and the subjectivity of Christ thus, in this case, endure.

The presence of God in the Last Supper therefore remains God's free doing. God binds Himself not to the bread, but to His Word. It is a misunderstanding to understand Luther's intention and the view he represented that God or Christ have bound themselves to the bread in the Lord's Supper. The relationship of the presence of the body and blood of Jesus Christ is determined by the *verbum*. Luther says, using irony: "Or do you want to write against me? So go ahead and write and prove how the Lutherans are so idolatrous as to teach that the Word of God is not in the Last Supper, but only the bread contains the body of Christ. Further, that they have no heart or no soul when they say such words like 'take and eat,' but use only the mouth with which they eat the body of Christ. If you can prove that, then I must admit that your writing about the mass is correct and well founded."[91] The word does not mean to signify "God is in the bread," but because God binds himself to the bread by His word, this word includes the bread and the wine. And so, we are able to take part in the bread and the wine. A division of bread from the *verbum* would mean similarly that Mary would say it is enough that I have the promise of God, I do not need the Word to become flesh.[92] On this point Luther is very clear and says: I will have nothing to do with the real presence of the body and blood of Christ in the bread and the wine if you take the Word away from them. What I care about is that the Word is firm: That *is* my body. In other words: the "is" is constituted through the *verbum*, it is not

---

91. WA 23, 181, 20ff. (Dr.)
92. See also WA 23, 189, 26 f. (Dr.)

simply constituted by the action. Therefore, the Word of God and faith are the most important things in Luther's teaching on the Last Supper.

The Doctrine of Holy Baptism

1. On the Concept of *Res Sacramenti*: The *Promissio*

At the end of his, "The Babylonian Captivity *ecclesiae praeludium* of 1520" Luther says: There are only two sacraments, the sacrament of Holy Baptism and the sacrament of Holy Communion.[93] The first belongs to the beginning of life and the second to the end of life, but both offer us eternal life. "Baptism, which we have for our entire lives, suffices for all the sacraments that we will need in this life. The bread, however, is in truth the sacrament of the dying and leaving, because in it we take part in the transition (*transitus*) of Christ from this world so that we can follow Him. So let us take both sacraments, so that we celebrate baptism at the beginning and throughout the course of our life (*initium*) and the bread at the end to prepare for death. The Christian should be occupied with both of them in this perishable body, until as a completely baptized Christian and thus strengthened, he goes from this world, born to a new and eternal life where He can eat with Christ in the Father's kingdom, as He promised in the Lord's Supper: 'Truly, I say to you, I will not drink of this fruit of the vine from now on until that day when I drink it anew with you in my Father's kingdom,' (Matt 26:29) so that it is clear that the sacrament of the bread is intended for the receiving of the future life. Then, when the matter (the *res*) of both sacraments is fulfilled, and both baptism and the bread will cease."[94] The *res sacramenti* (the matter of the sacraments) is thus that in it the person is taken up and entrusted to eternal life.

Those who, with Luther, emphasis the character of the Word in the sacraments are more correct than those who emphasize their sacramental character. God himself baptizes: "Thus it is for us in Baptism through the hand of a person nothing other than to experience it as Christ himself, yes God himself, who baptizes us with his own hands. It is not a person,

---

93. The Roman Catholic Church recognizes seven sacraments: 1) Baptism; 2) Confirmation; 3) Eucharist; 4) Confession; 5) Marriage; 6) Ordination; 7) Last Rites.

94. WA 6, 572, 23ff. = BoA 1, 511, 5ff. On the important concept of *"transitus"* for Luther's theology we refer to H. Beintker, *Phase Domini*, in the Festschrift for Rudolf Hermann, "Solange es heute heist," 30–41 (J.H.)

but Christ and God who baptize."[95] Baptism is God's activity and only in this sense does it have meaning. It is not a clergy-mediated act of the church for people, but those who conduct a baptism, whoever they are, only lend their hands to something that is God's doing. This is again a sign that the invisible church is the basis for the visible church. The visible church is the one that engages people in the here and now. It follows from an insightful saying: "Be careful that you distinguish in baptism the external workings of men and ascribe the internal workings to God. Both are attributed to God and consider the person who is doing the baptism as nothing other than a tool of God's state (*instrumentum vicarium Dei*), through which the Lord, who sits in heaven, places you in the water of baptism with his own hands and promises to forgive your sins, and in which with the voice of a human being speaks to you through the mouth of his servants."[96] Luther also says that there is no essential difference in the relationship of God here: that God uses the breath of the human mouth, the person's words and thoughts, in order to proclaim the Gospel to you. Analogously, he says in the same connection that the appearance of a person who administers baptism is meaningless for the act itself. It means as little as if a hand, a hammer, or some other tool were used in order to carry out what the person intends to fix at the moment. Nothing more is meant by the term *instrumentum*."[97] It is merely to be interpreted as instrument, or tool. When, however, God himself is the subject and actor in the sacrament, then much more can be understood by it, which is why Luther continually emphasized that here we must always speak in terms of the *promissio*. *Promissio* doesn't mean that we are promised something for the future. Any attempt to understand the promissory nature of the sacraments, in the sense of a sign of chronological human existence, leads to error. *Promissio* is the way in which God's activity comes near to us: it is the way in which He imparts to us His revelation. That is also true of the understanding of the Mass and the Lord's Supper: "So he has in the Mass, given this foremost promise of all, a sign of remembrance (*signum memoriale*) of such a great promise, and affixed his own body and his own blood in the bread and wine, as he said: 'Do this in remembrance of me' (1 Cor 11:24–25). So also, he attaches His Word of promise in Baptism through the sign of being dipped in water. This

---

95. WA 6, 530, 22ff. = BoA 1, 464, 7ff.
96. WA 6, 530, 27ff. = BoA 1, 464, 13ff.
97. See WA 6, 530, 28 = BoA 1, 464, 15.

is how we know that in every promise of God, two things are evident—Word and sign—so that we understand that the Word is the testament and the sacrament is the sign (of it)."[98] When Luther uses the term *promissio*, we must understand that here he means we are dealing with God; just as Abraham dealt with God when he received God's *promissio*, and likewise when Mary dealt with God when she received God's *promissio*.[99] One cannot deal with God in any other way than through His *promissio*. The fact that the *promissio* comes first and is prior to whatever occurs, is correct, but it also comes before the fulfillment of it, which is why it is termed *pro-missio* (prior to sending). It does not point to the future but rather to God's Word which precedes His action. And whoever has His Word, finds His works. Others may receive his works, but they are blind to them: "Surely the Lord God does nothing without revealing his secret to his servants the prophets." (Amos 3:7). In this sense the sacrament is a sign of portending: a sign that God works in us such that he makes us guarantors (of it) so that we can remain faithful to Him and rely on Him. So, we have only the *res sacramenti*. This also means, however, that we are not able to receive anything at all in the *res sacramenti* without having first received God's own assurance. *Promissio* means God has arranged things so that whatever He wants to give you, you cannot have if you don't want Him–if you do not allow God to be God, the Lord of your life and the Lord of the covenant, the covenant of Baptism, in which he envelops you in His promise. You cannot say when you take the sacrament 'I have it.' You cannot 'have it' since the *res sacramenti* is encased in the *promissio*. You only 'have it' because the *promissio* has made that possible for you. Only when God is and remains the Giver can we truly receive the sacraments. And each individual must receive the sacrament for themselves. Just as each person must make the Mass fruitful for themselves and for their own faith,"[100] so also "the priest cannot serve the sacrament but must serve to each individual person."[101] In its entirety, this reveals how Luther's teaching on the sacraments diverges from the Scholastics on the *res sacramenti*. In place of the Scholastic order of *res* and *signum*, from which the Scholastics interpret their teaching on the sacraments, Luther uses the term covenant, and from there he intends

---

98. WA 6, 518, 10ff. = BoA 1, 449, 36ff.

99. See for examples WA 23, 187, 23ff. (That this word of Christ "This is my body..." 1527., Dr.) among others (on Abraham) and also 201, 2ff. among others (on Maria).

100. See the citation IV, p. 262 (n. 71).

101. WA 6, 521, 25ff. (*De captivitate...*) = BoA 1, 453, 36ff.

the meaning of the *promissio* and also the notion of personal faith. With this he eliminates any false subjectivity in faith: faith is a personal gift from God: "They do not hear and do not see that Baptism is not a human work, not based in my faith as my own gift, but is based on God's power and truth."[102] In other words, in the area of God's covenant, the priority must be in terms of God's decision. Whoever attributes faith to the nature of man's creative activity drags the realm of heathen religions into the area of God's covenant. That is heathenism. To elicit something through the personal activity of an alleged faith is religion, but it is not faith. Faith means reception: "Faith should be based on God's Word, not the word of God on faith."[103] In the moment when I create a circle out of faith and God's Word, assuming a correlation between faith and the word of God, in that moment I am no longer able to distinguish what is *apriori* in the relationship. Whenever I attempt to work with the concept of a correlation (mutual interrelationship) then I never know if I'm working with faith or with the word of God. Luther does not drop the issue of covenant or Testament. Here he does not emphasize the objectivity of the sacrament apart from the Testament (covenant) but emphasizes it from within the Testament. And that is the law of the testament: that *fides* is based on the *verbum* and not the *verbum* on *fides*. That is the internal law of life in God's Covenant of Grace. However, for Satan, "the Word is the enemy, and he wants to separate them (i.e., sign and word in baptism). But "we mean to unite them (*nos volumus coniungere*)."[104] And "God binds himself in the water. Here I am, I command it—eternal wisdom and might—when you baptize in the name of the Father, etc., thus you have the forgiveness of sins."[105] Here we come upon the present moment. The words: "Here I am" are remarkable. I might have God in mind, in my thoughts and in spirit, but that does not mean He is present. At the end of the day, everything for Luther hinges on whether Jesus Christ is present. He is present—not just in the water, but always in His Word. To that extent the sign that I see is not the presence, but is a sign of the presence: "So God binds himself in Baptism, which means salvation through His Word, that Word which together with the external thing is there for

---

102. WA 46, 154, 1ff. (Sermon for January 27, 1538, for the third Sunday after Epiphany).

103. WA 27, 44, 8–9 (Sermon of 1528, on Baptism)

104. WA 20, 387, 1–2 (Sermon of 1526, Ascension Day)

105. WA 20, 387, 1–2 n. 6ff.

the affirmation of faith."[106] Similarly, Luther says of the sacrament of the Lord's Supper: "Therefore, this sacrament is established to strengthen faith, that you learn the words that give you the forgiveness of sins."[107]

From all of this we must conclude that, according to Luther, the order of *promissio* or *verbum* and *fides* as it pertains to the covenant of God is not to be reversed, and that faith never arises on its own. Faith depends on Christ and Christ is always thus in the flesh. Whoever denies that Christ took on human flesh is the anti-Christ. Whoever makes of faith in Christ a kind of pneumatic Christology (Christian spirituality) and say that as a believer I have the *pneuma Christi* (spirit of Christ), has already lost faith (*pistis*). Rather, it must be stated clearly that in the area of the covenant of God the *apriori* nature of the Word is asserted for the Word to have become flesh. That Word has not become flesh because I believe, but it is flesh *per se*.

2. The Meaning of Baptism for Life

For Luther, baptism extends over the entire life of the person. In his early work, "A Sermon on the Sacrament of Baptism, 1519" he says: "It's all the same: from Baptism something nimble occurs. But the meaning, the spiritual birth, the increase of grace and righteousness, surely continues in baptism, but also until death, yes even until the Day of Judgment. Then the meaning of Baptism is fulfilled: we will rise from death, from sin, from all evil, pure in body and soul, and live eternally. There we will be rightly raised through our baptism."[108] Conversely, in connection to Baptism, Luther says of death: "The sacrament or sign of Baptism occurs such that we see with our eyes; but the meaning, the spiritual baptism, the drowning of sin, endures as long as we live and when we come to die. There the person is literally immersed into baptism; and what baptism means is realized. Therefore, this entire life is nothing other than a spiritual baptism without intermission, until death."[109] Or baptism is understood by him like a flood: "Now Baptism is a broad and greater flood of any (at the time of Noah) that occurred before. For it is not a flood that lasts a year, but Baptism

---

106. WA 20, 387, 1-2 nn. 34-35. "*Sic cum baptism, qui est salutiferus propter verbum, verbum quod alligat Deus externae rei ad confirmandam fidem*." Trans. H. J. Iwand.

107. WA 30/1, 55/ 1-2 (Sermons on the Catechism: The Lord's Supper)

108. WA 2, 728, 30ff. (On the Fifth) = BoA 1, 186, 40ff.

109. WA 2, 728, 12ff. (On the Fourth) = BoA 1, 186, 21ff.

floods the entire world from the day of Christ's birth until the Judgment Day, flooding all kinds of people. It is a flood of grace, while the previous flood was one of wrath."[110] Therefore: "As much as the sign of the sacrament (of Baptism) has meaning, so the sins of the people are already dead and they are risen; and the sacrament itself is also finished, but the work of the sacrament is still not completely finished, that is, death and the resurrection at the Judgment Day is still to come."[111] Further, Luther says: "Now you are defined by drowning through death and resurrection on the Last Day. St. Paul also laments (Rom 7:18) and all the saints with him, that they are sinners and by nature sinful, although they are baptized and holy."[112] Accordingly, Luther responds to those espousing re-baptism by emphasizing the one-time event of Baptism. In his lectures on Romans, he placed great significance on the one-time validity of Baptism. He wanted Baptism to display a qualitative difference from all other activities that we undertake, such as penance, atonement, turning from wrong-doing and vice, failing and trying again. All these things are repeatable. "A righteous man can fall seven times and get back up again." (Prov 24:16) A person's entire life is one of constant falling and getting up again, in constant repetition. But what is repeated here? Baptism is so that we do not have to go around in circles in an everlasting repetition of the same thing (Cf. Acts 3:21). As the precondition for all repetition and everything that is in the past, going back to the very beginning, Baptism is qualitatively different than penance. Penance can be repeated. And thus, penance is also assumed in the sacrament of Baptism, and arguably one of the greatest accomplishments of Luther in his teaching on Baptism. Luther includes penance in Baptism and says: "You can only do proper penance when you know where you came from, when you go back to the "once" that God has set in your life and from which you can always draw upon. There is no *naufragium baptismi*—no fracturing baptism. That would be the same thing as to say you could fracture a covenant, a *naurfragium testamenti*.[113] As if God's covenant could be broken! Resurrection means a return to the covenant of God, to connection with God. Resurrection is not about "dying and

---

110. WA 2, 729, 12ff. (On the Sixth) = BoA 1, 187, 21ff.
111. WA 2, 729, 34ff. (On the Seventh) = BoA 1, 188, 5ff.
112. WA 2, 730, 13ff. (On the Eighth) = BoA 1, 188, 21ff.
113. See the famous place in "*De captivitate...*" in which Luther refers to the sacrament of confession as the "second plank after the shipwreck" ("*secunda tabula post naufragium*"): WA 6, 529, 22 = BoA 1, 463, 2.

becoming," but is a return to the life-giving covenant with God.[114] Whoever correctly understands Baptism understands what is meant by the Christian existence. The Christian cannot understand themselves from out of their own existence but must understand their life in relationship to the covenant of Baptism, in the sense that God wills that we die in order to live. Luther says: A Christian is a Baptized person, that is, someone who only lives in order to die; a person who carries their death in their life. That is why Baptism endures throughout life: "Here you must again see that the Sacrament of Baptism is not just a sign for the moment, but something continual. Although the service of Baptism is short, the event that it signifies endures (*re ipsa significate*) until death, even to the resurrection of the dead on Judgment Day."[115] In Baptism a nascent becoming of the person is introduced, something different from what Goethe describes in his writings. Rather, in Baptism, the person is prepared for battle, a battle against sin that ends only when they die: "So long as we live here, we attempt what Baptism signifies: we die, and we rise again. I say die, not only by way of internal affect (*affectus*) and spiritually, in that we abstain from sin and vanities of this world, but we begin to really leave behind this physical life and take hold of the future life so that it is, as we say, a real and physical bridge from this world to the Father (*ut sit realis, quod dicunt, et corporalis quoque transitus ex hoc mundo ad patrem*)."[116] In his teaching on Baptism, Luther regards death as a tool for life, as does St. Paul. For Luther, even death is folded into the nascent becoming. My life is practice for dying, day after day. That is what is meant by the *signum* of Baptism when the person is immersed in water. In other words: the new person is not evident, is not there, but indeed is there. And as new people we are confronted with the same situation as is the church: the *signa* are there, but one cannot see them, and the *signa* of the new people are there also and given in Baptism as they are the signs of the cross and of suffering. It is a very significant fact that the practice inherent in Baptism is not one of works, but of suffering and death: "It follows, that Baptism utilizes all suffering and, remarkably, death, as tools and aids in service of it to kill sin. For nothing else is possible: whoever will live in their Baptism and be free of sin, must die. But sin does not die easily, that is why death is so bitter and horrible. But God is merciful and mighty, so that sin, which brings death,

---

114. See Goethe, "The West-Eastern Divan." Artemisausgabe, DTV 5, 15: "Selige Sehnsucht" (blessed longing), V. 5

115. WA 6, 534, 31ff. = BoA 1, 468, 40ff.

116. WA 6, 534, 34ff. = BoA 1, 469, 3ff.

is by its own doing (i.e., death) again banished. One finds many people who want to live because they were pious and speak of themselves as if they were pious. However, there is no easy means or way through Baptism and its work, which is suffering and death."[117] In Baptism we learn to die, we learn to suffer and to endure, and we are empowered to fulfill our duty and to do our own work. So, it is not the case that the baptized do not do works, but their works are born from their dying and rising, their doubts and their faith, that in this way, so long as they live, they are in the process of becoming and that in the retro-grasp of their Baptism they can never be a finished being, but always one who is in the process of becoming. And when we perform this retro-grasp of Baptism, we are always reminded of the *initium* (beginning) by which we were taken into the covenant of God. At the beginning of this journey through life is the immersion, the dying, the suffering, and perishing, so that thus God says to us in such signs also today and now: Why do you wonder that life is invested with death? This is because your life of death, suffering, and failure is ratified and justified by the life of your not-sinful-self through Baptism. This all must be if you are to be my child.

From this we can conclude that there is, of course, a form to Christian existence, but it is not the visible form of our existence. The saints are only represented by the signs of Baptism, and this signifying is the same for all Christians. Through Baptism we become part of the most modest, simple, human existence, in the existence of our Lord and Master Jesus, in his humanity and in His path that He took on earth in His humanity, which every day involved another bit of death; a bit of drinking from the cup that God gave Him to drink (cf. Matt 20:22; John 18:11). That is Baptism. Is that not a kind of unparalleled freedom? Baptism makes us truly human. And this true person is invisible and seen only by God. We see the person only as they are in the process of becoming, falling, and getting up again: hoping and believing, atheists and church goers, heretics and orthodox. This process of becoming truly human encompasses both extremes, but in the end leaves one of them behind. We are conquerors through faith. We are conquerors over sin and over death. Why? Not by themselves. If left to ourselves, we would more likely remember our defeats rather than our victories. However, because God's covenant hides the victory, because God through Baptism has made us His allies, then Baptism is the basis for

---

117. WA 2, 734, 14ff. (A Sermon on the Holy Sacrament of Baptism. 1519, "On the Sixteenth") = BoA 1, 192, 21ff.

all understanding of Christian existence, but Christian existence is not the starting point for an understanding of Baptism.

3. The Work of the Holy Spirit and Infant Baptism

Is Baptism connected to the outpouring of the Spirit? This question by "congregations" who constantly ask this question is the result of starting from the point of Christian existence when trying to understand Baptism. It is basically a Catholic question because it is a question about whether or not Baptism has power. If today, here and there, we constantly go to confession, then we have the sense that eventually we can replace Baptism with the Sacrament of Confession and that it is a kind of aid, or compromise, that the official church must make if they do not want to lose the church. However, it is not the case that Baptism is responsible for founding the church. Interestingly, for Luther the Doctrine of Baptism is always connected to *infant baptism*. That is extraordinary, because he continually advocated the thesis that without faith there is no Baptism, and that any Baptism without faith is a disaster. The mere doing of the sacramental act is not Baptism. On the other hand, he maintains the authenticity of infant baptism and perhaps the primary and most decisive point for him is this: He says that is it the only sacrament that has not been twisted by the Papacy. In his often quoted writing, *"De captivitate"* he begins the paragraph on the Sacrament of Baptism with the song of praise: "'Praise be to God and the Father of our Lord Jesus Christ' (Eph 1:3), 'in accordance with the riches of his grace;' (Eph 1:7) who has at least preserved this single sacrament of the church unimpaired and unsullied by the laws of men and made it available to people of all walks of life. He did not tolerate its oppression by either the hideousness of financial profiteering or the godless machinations of superstition, but the idea that small children, who are yet not capable of avarice and superstition, are christened through it and are sanctified with the simplest faith in His Word."[118] Baptism is the answer to the question of the character of life. In Baptism we are told that to be a Christian means to follow in Christ's suffering. The Christian fights his entire life with himself and therefore is one who is a suffering and dying person. But in Baptism we begin the way to new life. For through Baptism death is robbed of its devilish power and kingdom. Everything that the baptized experience and encounter

---

118. WA 6, 526, 35ff. = BoA 1, 459, 37ff.

during their lives serves for their good (Rom 8:28). Death is subsumed in the becoming of the Christian. The decisive thing appears to me that through this understanding of Baptism the Christian now (as opposed to the Middle Ages), so to speak, approaches death on the road of life as a task that he has already accomplished in this life. So, there is now in our petty existence in this world nothing more that is not open to us.

4. The Uniqueness of Baptism

God's covenant, to which everything earthly is tied, is the foundation of the Doctrine on the Sacraments. Thus, in Baptism we learn the priorities of the covenant for our life and actions. We are only born into this life, but through Baptism we are included in this covenant and the covenant gives our lives meaning. In his teaching on Baptism, the early Luther worked mainly with the concepts of covenant and partnership, though the idea of covenant is lost most representations of Luther's teaching on Baptism. Luther says in the "Sermon on the Sacrament of Baptism," "The reverent sacrament of Baptism helps you in that God binds Himself to you in it and is united with you in a gracious and comforting covenant."[119] And: "Accordingly, whether bad thoughts or doubts plague you, whether you sometimes sin and err, so can you again stand back up again and enter into the covenant, because you are already included in its membership by the power of the sacrament."[120] This idea, that the Christian through faith is again able to enter into the covenant—that each act of faith is also a repetition of the first covenant that God made with men—is therefore significant, because here the person is not shunned due to their mistakes and their falls and sent fleeing into the future by promising to be better. It is self-evident that Luther gives Baptism priority over confession. For Luther, Baptism is the door by which at any time we have access to God's covenant of grace. The uniqueness of Baptism (once only) means that the door never closes: "Therefore must one hold audaciously and freely to Baptism and hold against all sin and anxiety and say humbly: 'I know that I am not capable of any pure work. But I've been baptized, whereby God, who cannot lie, has bound Himself to me and will not count my sins

---

119. WA 2, 730, 20ff. (A sermon on the sacrament. . . of baptism. 1519. On the Ninth.) = BoA 1, 188, 28ff.

120. WA 2, 731, 8ff. (On the tenth) = BoA 1, 189, 14ff.

against me, but has destroyed and demolished my sin.'"[121] The Covenant of God is not an institution, but is constituted through His promise that at all times empowers me when I call upon it, and that is always there when I need it. God's grace means that His covenant should empower me as I live my life out in it.

The interesting thing about the covenant is that I can disempower it. We come across this idea often in Luther that I can make God a liar, though on the other hand I cannot make God truthful; for the possibility that God is lying is not part of the covenant or the truth. Truth and lies regarding God are not in a relationship like light and dark. To make God into a liar is to make Him something that He is not. To make God a liar is rather the creative task of man. If God were indeed not the truth, then there would be no possibility for men to make him into a liar. When I make God into a liar, I *statuiere* (place) or posit a reality that is not there. I replace it with my own existence and with my absolute reality. Just as one person cannot be accused of murdering another person if he is alone by himself, so also can men God also not make out as a liar if God isn't there. If I want to murder, then I create a situation that would never occur if "I" were not there. As someone who hates, I make God into a liar, which means I supplant a reality that does not exist. I make my reality absolute— exactly as in murder—and thereby deny the covenant, and I do this as if my life were on the same level as God's covenant: "For, as already stated, when a person falls into sin, then he thinks most readily on his Baptism, and how God has bound Himself to the person, to forgive all sins, and to fight against sin until his death. One should joyously rely on this same truth and bond of God. And so, the heart is again at peace and happy and the Baptized go about their work and efforts not by their own works or good deeds but by virtue of God's mercy which is promised to them in Baptism, to keep them forever."[122] To make God a liar means to view God's covenant as lacking and to propose a new, self-made covenant with God, a works-righteousness covenant that we ourselves have designed.

If one observes how strongly, in his teaching on Baptism, Luther has incorporated Paul's teaching on Baptism, including his ideas on the covenant, then it is also clear that the Pauline teaching on Baptism with its incorporation in the covenant receives an entirely new meaning. So, it is settled: God made His covenant with mankind who is filled with sin,

---

121. WA 2, 732, 19ff. (On the twelfth) = BoA 1, 190, 28ff.
122. WA 2, 733, 16ff. (On the Fourteenth) = BoA 1, 191, 23ff.

but Baptism does not make one sinless. Luther says, "So nobody should be upset when he feels evil lusts and desires, and should not despair when he feels these things, but should think on their Baptism, and be comforted happily by it, that God has bound himself to you in order to defeat your sin and not condemn you to hell, so that it (sin) does not eagerly or internally remain."[123] And in the same connection he says: "Then you understand how a person is not guilty, but is pure and without sin through Baptism, yet still remains full of horrible inclinations, and that they cannot otherwise be called pure, except that they have begun to become pure and through the same purity have a sign and covenant, and will become more and more pure, for whose sake God has set His seal (earlier, Cf. BoA). The decision not to count our sins against us and moreover to consider the person half pure is the result of God's graciousness out of His purity, as the Prophet says in Psalm 32: "Blessed are those, whose sins are forgiven."[124] And another citation from the *"De captivitate:"* "This truth of God's, say I, will keep you, so that, when all others break, this one, if you believe it, will not forsake you. For through it you have something that you can use against your mortal enemies and against all sin when it troubles your thoughts, when you are terrified of dying and of the law, you have finally, in all struggles and doubts a comfort which is this truth, that says: 'God is faithful in His promises, the sign of which you have in your Baptism. If God is for me, who can be against me!'" (Cf Ps 33:4 and Rom 8:31).[125]

5. The Constant Covenant

The Covenant of Grace in Baptism is and remains: "Christ doesn't count my transgressions from his mercy seat. He is always merciful, let us only not flee from Him and make demands of him."[126] In the covenant that Christ has made with us we find comfort and peace, which Luther describes in an especially beautiful passage: "But now that is the correct view of Baptism, that it is an eternal covenant that Christ has made with us. Christ is our protection, our cover, our shadow, our brooding hen

---

123. WA 2, 731, 29ff. (On the Eleventh) = BoA 1, 189, 37ff.
124. WA 2, 732, 9ff. (On the Twelfth) = BoA 1, 190, 17ff.
125. WA 6, 528, 28ff. (*De captivitate. . .*) = BoA 1, 462, 5ff.
126. WA 46, 199, 36ff. (Sermon in 1538. Last Sermon on Baptism, given on Quinquagesima Sunday).

under whose wings we live. He is our intermediary to God, as Paul says (1 Tim 2:5). He is our advocate who represents us as John says (1 John 2:1). Baptism is a Covenant of grace and mercy and of the delight of God."[127]

There are two paradoxes concerning baptism in 2 Cor that must be clarified: Christians are "known, yet regarded as unknown; dying, and yet we live on; beaten, and yet not killed" (2 Cor 6:9). The *simul* (at the same time) here must be correctly understood that death and life exist together at the same time; the new life that we encounter is not a life in the hereafter, as if we could eschew this life here and now. The new life is much more a life from beyond, just as the reign of Christ, the *regnum fidei* (Kingdom of Faith), is the invisible-yet-present kingdom of God. And again: Christian existence is based in God's Covenant of Grace. It is constituted by and founded upon the promise of God—in His Word. This transcends our existence and points us, the baptized, back to our Baptism for our entire life, as something inescapable: "You can never get away from the fact that you are guilty and must return to the Covenant (*ad pactum*). When you have fallen, think 'through grace I was baptized, and I can return to grace.' For Baptism is an eternal covenant, from which we cannot escape and therefore must remain in our Baptism or be damned for eternity."[128] Baptism is forever. I cannot escape it. It is the heavenly grace of God by which I make my journey in the world; though I cannot feel it, through faith I live in this heaven. Sermons on the word of God should always remind me of my Baptism and its promise: "For once God's word of promise is pronounced over us in Baptism, its truth remains for our entire lives. And so also our faith in it should never waiver but continue to be fed and strengthened until our death by remembering this promise that was made to us in our Baptism. For even if we want to be released from our sins or atone for them, we are doing nothing more than going back to the power of Baptism and faith, from which we have fallen away, and once more must go to the past promise made to us, which we abandoned in our sinning."[129] The repentant see the outstretched arms of the Father who waits to receive him (Luke 15:11ff.).

Atonement means repentance in the sense that I once again turn my face to God's call; that I do not turn my face toward my transgressions, but toward the "Yes" of God, that has been spoken over my entire life. The involvement of life means that everyone's life—and how they live

---

127. WA 46, 201, 18ff.

128. WA 37, 280, 26ff. (Sermon on 1534. Fourth sermon on Baptism for Candlemas).

129. WA 6, 528, 10ff. (*De captivitate...*) = BoA 1, 461, 22ff.

it—is resolved by their Baptism, just as it unfolds. Despite our fears that we didn't want our life to go a certain way or intend it to—exactly this is living in one's Baptism. We must have such confidence in our Baptism that the life that we lead is transformed through the words of grace. The actual life we lead is a baptized one, not an ideal one. It is not the case that through Baptism a seed of purity is sown in us that either grows or doesn't grow, a seed of goodness that is sown and that I must water over and over again through regret and atonement. This understanding of the "higher power" is an idealistic misnomer. Your true and actual life is now incorporated in God. The law has been fulfilled for your life so that you can transform it. I will close this section with a quote from Luther: "This is what the entire Papacy teaches every day: 'When you sin, go, and take (holy) orders, in order to be newly baptized.' This crab had so ingrained itself in my heart that I took the pains and worked to get rid of it, and for thirty years thought my Baptism eluded me. But when you hear such things, ask yourself if God has promised it, because if God did not promise it, then you should not let it burden you."[130]

Church and State in Luther

1. The Doctrine of the Two Kingdoms

Luther's position on authority gained new form and insight through his disagreements with the "Fanatics" (Karlstadt, Müntzer, et al), but also with Zwingli. As a result, his teaching on the sacraments, especially on the Last Supper, but also on Holy Baptism, became more assertive. During his stay in the Wartburg (1521/22), a populace movement led by Andreas Bodenstein (aka Karlstadt)[131] took place in 1522 in Wittenberg, railing against maintaining images of apostles and saints in churches (*iconoclasm*). In August 1524, Luther engaged in a religious discussion with the council of the city of Orla Munde, in which a shoemaker said: "I have often removed my hat in front of images and on my journeys. That is idolatry and dishonors God and does damage to the poor people. That is why we should not have any images." Martin Luther responded: "If everything can be misused, then you must also kill all the women and give

---

130. WA 47, 643, 35ff. (Sermon on 1539. Sermon on Epiphany).
131. See III, 210 (n. 174).

up wine."[132] Here we see Luther's definition of the relationship between church and state as described in his Doctrine of the Two Kingdoms. Through his teaching on the ubiquity of God in the sacraments, which also contain the Lutheran "is," we hear echoes of the relationship between "internal" (*internum*) and "external" (*externum*). Luther maintains that Karlstadt internalized everything that God wants to keep external, and externalized what should be kept internal. Luther understood the course of God's word, and the course of the Reformation very differently from the Fanatics. Thus, he understands Luke 17:20ff: "The Kingdom of God is among you" as "the kingdom of God is inwardly among you." Accordingly, Luther wanted the Christian state to support church reform. One must understand it in this context, that he would soon turn against a certain authority while promoting a different kind of authority in its place. In any case, it is not correct to say that Luther turned against authority because of the Anabaptists. It is more accurate to say this: He fundamentally supported authority and based it on a very particular, centuries-long relationship of church and state.

We have two examples in statements by Luther after the Edict of Worms (1521), which placed an imperial ban on him and all of his followers: "My dear Lords and men, you hasten to put this poor person to death, and if that happens, you will have won. If you have ears to hear, then I will tell you something strange: How, if Luther's life was worth so much to God, that, if he did not live, you would be certain of your own life or lordship, and that the death of you all would be a misfortune? God is not to be played with, go ahead, choke and burn, I will not recant, if God wills: Here I stand. . .God has not given me (as I see it) to deal with rational people, but German beasts all kill me I (if I am worth it) just as if wolves or sows tear at me."[133] And in an Afterword to the same letter he says: "Finally, I ask that all dear Christians would help pray to God for such miserable blinded princes, with whom, no doubt, God has plagued us in great wrath, that we do not follow, to rage against or yield to the Turks. Since the Turk is ten times cleverer and more devout than you princes are. How should such fools succeed against the Turks who tempt and blaspheme God so greatly? For here you see how he, poor , mortal,

---

132. WA 15, 345, 29ff. (Item *die Handlung Doctor Marini Luthers mit dem Rath und Gemeine der Stadt Orlamund.* 1524) See also the ever important writing by Harald (!) Diem: *Luthers Lehre von den zwei Reichen*, esp. 113ff.

133. WA 15, 254, 26ff. (*Zwei kaiserliche uneinige und widerwartige Gebote den Luther betreffend.* 1524).

red-billed woodpecker, the Kaiser, who is not one moment certain of his life, boasts shamefully that he is the true, highest protector of Christian faith. The scripture says that Christian faith is a rock, too strong for the devil, death and every power (Matt 16 (vs. 8)), and a divine power, (Rom 1 [v. 16]) . . . Thus also the king of England boasts he is a protector of the Christian churches and faith. Yes, the Hungarians boast they are God's protector . . . Oh, that is something a king or a prince would be, were he the protector of Christ, and there another who protects the Spirit, then I think the Holy Trinity and Christ together with faith would preserve me from evil. From the bottom of my heart, I complain to all such pious Christians to have mercy with me on such stunning, clownish, mindless, raging, crazy fools. God deliver us from them and give the grace to other regents."[134]

We must also see that in this situation, in which he is formulating his teaching on the state and the sacraments, Luther does not let go of this theme: he does not give it up, even though it tosses him around a bit. If, however, we realize that here a movement of dramatic and Biblical proportions is attacking Luther, then we can understand why the business carries Luther away. It does not allow him a steady, permanent position. He is building the church and the state. The Lutherans of the previous generations have viewed the foundation of the church and state as containing something of what is genuinely Lutheran. As a result, they have involved a counter-revolutionary aspect in their theology from which the Restoration period in the Lutheran church (in Germany) received its power. The Enlightenment appeared where previously in Luther's time there had been the Anabaptists, and so the stance toward the sacraments and the state evolved into a kind of proving ground for people, allowing them to fall easy prey to the conservativism of the "Third Reich." All of this can be found in the relationship between the sacraments and the state. Therefore, we need an entirely new way to think about Luther's fight with the Fanatics (German: *Schwärmer*). What is remarkable in Luther, however, is that he establishes his teaching on the sacraments in the same way that he establishes his thinking on the state. Whoever does not recognize Baptism, does not recognize the state, since the condition for Baptism is also the condition for authority. Let us listen to what Luther says in his "Letter to the Evangelical-Lutheran Churches:" "Therefore be resolute that Baptism always remains valid in its full sense, even though

---

134. WA 15, 277, 21ff.

only one man was baptized and believed to have behaved rightly. For God's ordinance and Word do not allow it to be changed by men nor by others. But they, the Fanatics, are so blinded that they do not see God's word and command, and do not regard baptism and the authority for it more than water in the brook and pots, or as belonging to another man in whom, because they see no faith nor obedience, it is of no worth to that person himself. That is a sneaky, rebellious devil who gladly would tear the crown from the authority, so that later one tramples on it, distorting God's ordinances and treating them as if they were nothing. Then we must be brave and readied and not let ourselves be pointed away or turn from the Word, so that we do not make Baptism merely into a sign, as the Fanatics envision."[135]

From this, we must understand that Luther called upon the authorities to throw the Fanatics out of the country because whoever viewed Baptism incorrectly also took a wrong view of authority—and so the Revolution began. It is therefore not from faith, but from the concept of the sacraments that we take our view of the relationship between church and state. Here, in his zeal during the fight over authority, Luther had imprudently assigned authority to the church, while the Fanatics said: "We must acquire affiliation to the church from the point of view of the spirit," and, "We must evaluate the nobles according to their Christian standpoint." So, according to Luther's teaching, the affiliation to the church must be considered in terms of his stance toward the sacraments. And thus, according to Luther, even a bad noble retains his power as *instiutio Dei*. That is the problem of church and state in Luther. And that is also the problem with the Lutheran "is."

2. Pairing of "Inner" and "Outer"

Alongside the formulation of Luther's teaching on the relationship between state and church, which emerged from his concept of the sacraments, the question of "external" and "internal" keeps emerging because with it the Doctrine of the Two Kingdoms, and therefore also the teaching on the state, come into focus. I cite here a few citations from Luther's writings against Karlstadt: "So now God has let his holy Gospel go forth; he deals with us in two ways, one eternally, the other time inwardly. He

---

135. *The Confessional Writings of the Evangelical Lutheran Church*, Vol. 2, 703, Z. 34ff. = WA 30/1, 220, 1ff. (*The Large Catechism*, 1529, On the Sacrament of Baptism) = BoA 4, 86, 31ff.

deals externally with us through the oral word of the Gospel and through bodily signs, such as Baptism and the sacrament. He deals inwardly with us through the Holy Spirit and faith, together with other gifts."[136] Of the Fanatics in Wittenberg, however, he says, they are of the opinion: "So should a handful of water make me pure from sin? The Spirit, the Spirit, the Spirit must do it inwardly. Should bread and wine help me? No, no, one must eat Christ's flesh spiritually."[137] And Luther continues: "The Wittenberger's don't know anything; they abstract faith from the letters of the alphabet."[138] The Fanatics made spiritual experience the norm as the way of determining if someone truly could speak about the word of God. Experience thus was the starting point from which a person could understand the Word. But Luther judged differently: ". . . just as they invent their own internal spirit, they also erect their own external ordinance."[139]

Here we come across an idea that is new in this context; namely, that interiority is an "invention of the self." But it is not the interiority that God gives and creates—in which he gives the spirit in one's heart—but is a creation of the individual self. Thus, just as the person creates their own interiority, they also necessarily must create their own external order: "Now so much is said to indicate that you know in what way it is this spirit's way directly to drive a perverted way against God's ordinance: namely, what God has ordered of inward faith and spirit they make into a human work. And again: what God orders of the external word and signs and works, they make into an internal spirit."[140] Whatever God produces internally—faith and a new heart in which Christ lives through faith—cannot be represented externally. One might also say that it cannot be substantiated. Luther repeatedly said of the Fanatics: they wanted to go beyond the Word; they wanted more. As we have already seen, the Fanatics thought that there must be something more (i.e., than the Word). Or, we could also say that everything that the Fanatics wanted to substantiate is only what is already contained in and under faith. We cannot externalize what God has in mind because it immediately loses its quality; namely, its essence. In that case, the nature of faith would again turn to works and a life under the law. One would then judge people whether they had a religious image in their room or not, but one cannot

---

136. WA 18, 136, 9ff. (Wider die himmlischen Propheten . . . 1525).
137. WA 18, 136, 9ff. nn. 31ff.
138. WA 18, 137, 1–2.
139. WA 18, 137, 1–2 nn. 21–22.
140. WA 18, 139, 1ff.

say anything about it since that does not make a person a Christian. How often you take communion is not a sign of your new life because Luther came to the realization that the internal life of the Christian cannot be exteriorized—that there is no transcending the internal to the external—and that is why he needed the state. The state was therefore the only possibility of realization for Luther. To the state belonged status, society, the family, and everything that is included in society and what we have in family. This is all allocated by the state for Luther, not the church. It is a hallmark of the order of church and society that in the context of Lutheranism all social problems should be handled by the state. Basically, there is no social doctrine, since society is immediately connected with the church, or where the church itself is the *societas*, or social arena. This still only occurs in Anglo-Saxon areas and North American areas, or in sects. The church cannot be directly associated with society because there is no Christian social organization. If so, then it would fall under the auspices of the state. The state is the transgression of the internal over into the external. It is therefore the kingdom of God on the left; that is the core of this teaching. The state also realizes—rather, it alone realizes—God's reign over external things, but in the sense that it has allowed itself to be realized on earth while remaining invisible (*incognito*) in a lesser sense, as for example, in rare cases when a noble might serve heaven by the shedding of blood.

In this way, we can understand what Luther meant in his letter "To the Christian Nobility of the German Nation" of 1520 when he says: "Christ does not have two, or a double kind of body; one worldly and the other spiritual. He has one head and one body."[141] And: "Since worldly rule has become a member of the Christian body, and though it has a bodily work, it is yet a spiritual estate, therefore its work should go free, unhindered in all the members of the whole body, punish and drive, where debt deserves it or necessity requires it, irrespective of pope, bishop, priests, they threaten or ban as they will."[142] Luther also says, "Worldly rule is an image, shadow, and figure of the rule of Christ."[143] Even if Christ allowed the world to fall apart when he became man, He is still Lord of the world. Otherwise, Luther could not speak of the worldly kingdom with the assumption that he is advising Christians how to handle power, the sword,

---

141. WA 6, 408, 33ff. = BoA 1, 368, 17–18.

142. WA 6, 410, 3ff. = BoA 1, 369, 22ff.

143. WA 30/2, 554, 11–12. (A Sermon That One Should Send Children to School. 1529?)

punishment, and wrath: "Now we will separate the spiritual and worldly kingdoms of Christ. Christ has the earthly kingdom in the children of Israel, used for Moses up to Jesus, that he gave them laws, as in clothing, eating, drinking, ceremonies, and other things. But since Christ has become man, he has actually assumed that and let the worldly fall away. Not that he will no longer be lord over it, but that he has set princes, emperors, and officials to do something about going faithfully around with the poor people. And he will likewise rule that and be lord over it."[144]

One can also see that it is not the case with Luther that there are places where we find the worldly kingdom standing under Christ's rule; where the worldly powers, nobles, and kings, are his servants. It is entirely false if one takes it completely apart later on and makes a dualism out of it. I cannot at this point say exactly how or why that is. There are naturally such dualistic places. However, perhaps the dualistic interpretation occurred so that the entire Doctrine of the Two Kingdoms could be very strongly included in the schema of Law and Gospel. But this was not Luther's primary intent. In the many Psalms about which Luther writes on the worldly order in detail, such as in Psalm 2, he always says that Christ reigns through the world's nobles. But they rule it on the left, and indeed so that the realization of the Lordship of Christ is not a worldly one in the sense that one can actually see the kingdom of God. It is a realization *in incognito*. In the same way, the Christian existence in only understandable as a realization *in incognito*. I am not recognizable as a Christian because I am a father, or a judge. My status does not make it so. Externally, I am "any man." Accordingly, Luther was not successful in giving the church an external representation, not because he couldn't, but because he was basically of the opinion that it wouldn't work because we always tend to pervert what is internal when making it external.

3. The Correct Understanding of "Political" Worship

As previously stated, the state is God's kingdom on the left, yet it is still God's Kingdom! But this kingdom is the *externum*, the external kingdom of God. The activities of God's word in this realm do not seek faith and cannot instruct people, but seek equity, diligence, virtue, etc., all ethical concepts that Luther appropriated from Aristotle in the latter's teaching on status (Aristotle wrote several books on the state in his *Politika*). They

---

144. WA 10/3, 371, 19ff. (Sermon on October 24, 1522, Sunday after Trinity).

are not an expression of faith, but of moral living. This concept of "internal" and "external" is uniquely Protestant. There is no Christian social hierarchy and no Christian state in Luther. If one misses this point, and during a political "change of government," is not able to anticipate the resulting consequences from it, then one is simply stupid. Even intellectuals are not shielded from stupidity; they can support another camp without knowing what they are doing. To be able to see and to know what one is doing is important. For Luther, the state does not just include the area of the law, and the clergy only the area of preaching. If that were the case, then one would literally have thrown out "the law of the Ten Commandments from the church," relegated them to the courthouse, and the Gospel would be merely serve as a comfort blanket for the conscience.[145] Luther expands on this in his "Lecture on Psalm 82" (1530): "Yes, where then is God? Or how will we be certain that God exists, who scolds and punishes? Answer: You indeed hear that he is in the community. Here there is his community, there you shall find him. For this very thing he has ordained his priests and preachers. To whom he has ordained the office, that they should teach, warn, punish, comfort, and in summary, urge the word of God. Now where God's word is ordered, there is God's office to punish. But how the word of God in all the world and in every place is ordered to be preached, that I (need) not tell here. But note that such a preacher by which God punishes the godless, should be in the community. He should "stand," that is, be found safe, upright, and honest in dealing with them. And in the community; that is, in public, free before God and men. In this way two blasphemies are averted. The first is called unfaithful, for now. There are many bishops and preachers who are in the preaching office. But they do not stand and do not serve God faithfully but lie comfortably or otherwise continue their joke with it. These are now the lazy and useless preachers, who do not tell their princes and lords of their blasphemy, some because they do not regard them as such . . . But some pretend and flatter and strengthen the evil gods in their willfulness . . . Some fear for their skin and worry that they might lose body and possessions over it. All these do not stand and are not faithful to Christ."[146] And Luther continues: "The laity is over all the world and in every corner full of those who accuse their gods of evil, that

---

145. See WA 50, 468, 6 f. (*Against the Antinomians*, 1539). For an understanding of the citations, see the Introduction by O. Clemen and O. Brenner on the writings, esp. 461ff., and more by H. J. Iwand, NW IV, 304-8.

146. WA 31/1, 196, 4ff.

is, their princes and lords, every now and then, curse and scold them, but not yet freely in public, with their mobs (sects, heretics)."[147]

Here Luther places the law inside of the implementation of the office of preaching: "My command and my word makes and orders you to gods, and maintains you in it, not your word, wisdom, or might. You are made gods by my word as all creatures, and not yourselves gods or born gods as I. If had not said or commanded, then none of you would not be God ... Mine is all such power, authority, possession, honor, land and people and everything which belongs thereto. I have given it to you. You yourselves have neither acquired it nor won it."[148] Later on, Luther holds up a kind of mirror to the nobles in his "Lecture on Psalm 82." He outlines three tasks for the nobility: 1. To look for a good preacher. That is the task of the nobles. This is how Luther understands the protection of pure teaching. 2. They must protect, support and care for orphans, widows, the poor, and the weak. 3. They must protect and guard against wickedness and power; namely, they must create peace. The promotion of peace (see Matt 5:9 in the Greek) is tantamount to heaven. Thus, in his "Lecture on Psalm 82" he says: "And in summary, according to the gospel or spiritual office there is no better jewel on earth, no greater treasure, no dearer alms, no more certain home, no finer possession than (an) authority which creates and has the right. These are fairly called gods. Such great virtue, needs, fruits, and good works God has laid in this estate. For he has not called them gods in vain, also does not will that there be a lazy, unattached (emptier, more useless), more idle estate, in which one seeks only honor, power, wantonness or self-interest and willfulness. But he will have them full of greater, innumerable, inexpressible good works, that they should with him be truly of divine majesty and help him to do sheer divine, super-human works."[149] In his lectures on Psalm 82 we have a clear idea of what Luther meant by a political sermon. It is the political worship service that he described. God will have it so that Christianity should move and work in the world.

---

147. WA 31/1, 196, 4ff. nn. 35ff.
148. WA 31/1, 216, 5ff.
149. WA 31/1, 201, 16ff.

4. The Question of "Resistance"

The authorities lose their right to their authority when they become the face of the devil. The question of resistance against a perversion of authority is still unclear and stands in contrast to the command to be obedient to authority (Rom 13:1, ff).[150] According to the hierarchy of Middle Ages, the church determined to what extent an individual was subject to authority. The new "order," in which the Christian lives today does not allow for a general ruling, as was usual in the Middle Ages. With Luther, the primacy of the church over the state was discontinued. The state has—from God—just as much right over people as does the church. The undervaluing of the state is demonic. State and church are both treated the same in the 4th Commandment. Luther's teaching on the state did not allow for any comparison of people in the state with the status of people in the church. In fact, Luther elevated the state by giving it the same value as coming from God; namely, from His ordinance. Only from this vantage point can we understand Luther's views on authority, and only from this point can we understand why he said what he did about insurrection against authority. The same Word of God founds the church and the state. Luther said there is no basic establishment of the status of people within the state, although the office of the clergy meant much more to him than a princedom. Fundamentally, the Christian congregation protects the functions of authority, even when they push that authority to its limits. When the state ventures into matters of faith, then it steps into God's territory. In that case, Christians have not only the right to passive resistance, but also to upheaval, whereby upheaval is understood here as resistance against legitimate law and not in the sense of "I-Want to-Be-In Charge." He says, "When it comes to war, God preserve us, then I want that part that resists the murderous and bloodthirsty papists, who have not been scolded for being rebellious, nor allowed it. But I will let it go and happen, that they mean self-defense and for that will point them to what is right and to the jurists. For in such a case when the murderers and bloodhounds want to wage war and murder, then it is in truth no uproar to oppose and resist them. Not that I thereby would push anyone or awaken to such resistance nor justify it, for a that is not my office,

---

150. These and the following statements in the lectures (aside from the lines by Luther) come, by all appearances, from one or more private correspondence on these sections. H. J. Iwand has in NW II, 230–242 given an extensive section on "The theological basis for resisting state power."

much less my right or judgment. A Christian knows well what he should do; that he gives to God what is God's, and to the emperor also what is the emperor's (Matt 22:21), but not to the bloodhounds what is not theirs. However, that I make a distinction between rebellion and other deeds and will not allow the bloodhounds covering for their shame, that they should boast as if they got it over against rebellious people and had good authority by worldly and divine rights, just as the kitten would happily wash and beautify itself. I intend the same to the people not to let their conscience be burdened with danger and care, as if their defense were rebellious; for such a title is too mean and too harsh in such a case. They should have another name by which the law will find them."[151]

Here Luther justifies active resistance against those who conduct a religious war by picking a fight. He says that one should let people be, instead of joining in such an unjust war. That is why one should resist rulers who enjoin people to wage war against the Protestants. Luther wants to expose the authorities who do not have a command from God to lead a war against the Protestants. He views an unjust war as one in which the state undertakes to force a certain confession of faith through the use of power. Thus, Luther secularizes the state and goes through what Ockham recommended in his teaching on the state: namely, a strong division between what is external (the state) and what is internal (the church).[152]

For Luther, resistance is essentially something that arises out of God's Word. When he secretly left the Wartburg to visit friends in Wittenberg in December 1521, he heard that shortly before his visit unruly students and several citizens had disrupted the early Mass taking place in the City Church. On the basis of this and similar incidences, he composed an important writing with the title "A staunch admonition to all Christians, that they refrain from upheaval and revolt" (1522): "I am certain that my word is not mine, but is Christ's word, so my mouth must be one who speaks His word. So, you must not desire physical uproar. Christ himself has already begun one with His mouth, which will be all too much for the Pope, so let us follow the same and continue. It is not our work going out now into the world. It is not possible that a man should begin on his own and advance such an existence. It has also come this far without my

---

151. WA 30/3, 282, 22ff. (A Warning to My Dear Germans, 1531).

152. Wilhelm von Ockham (1330–1350), an Englishman, reformer of nominalism, espoused the view that it is the "pure job of the state to uphold the common good (*bonum commune*). If a ruler neglects this duty, then the people have the right to overthrow the tyrant." (See K. Vorlander, *Philosophie des Mittelalters*, rde 193/194, 106).

concern and advice. It should also go on without my counsel and the gates of hell shall not hinder it. It is another man who drives the wheel, whom the papists do not see, and then puts the blame on us. He must be destroyed without the hand and only with the mouth; nothing else helps. There."[153] The correction of wrong happens by way of God's word. It is fine to translate what is internal as the word of God to the external. Through this Word much more is overthrown than can be overthrown by external actions. The old always remains. It is always the case that when one today overthrows the old forms by revolution, the old ghosts simply remain in new forms. The old gods must be extracted by their roots, then they will die on their own: "He must be destroyed without the hand and only with the mouth; nothing else helps. There."[154] It is Christ's own words that make trouble for the Pope. The truth comes out of the mouths of Christians. That is also true even for rebels and fanatics: "As soon as the lie is known, no blow is longer needed, it falls and disappears by itself with all the disgraces."[155] Because a lie amounts to nothing you cannot fight it externally, but only by exposing it with the truth. Whoever rails against a lie (which is nothingness) using force simply gives it more power than it deserves. Thus, Luther is against rebellion on principle: "But we do not teach that and do not bring such truth among the people, that such a thing be taken from the heart; thus, the pope will remain before us, though we begin a thousand rebellions against him. See what it has done only this single year that we have urged and described such a truth, how for the papists the covering has become so short and narrow . . . What will be where such a mouth of Christ will thresh two hears with his Spirit? Such a game the devil would gladly hinder with physical uproar. But let it be our way to thank God for his holy word and freshly open our mouth for this blessed uproar."[156]

Luther's warning against rebellion is to hold the field open for God's upheaval, so that the word of God can move freely and have room to spread. The word of God is not a blessing on the *status quo*; it does not justify the order of the world but engages it and cleanses it. The freedom of the Word is established by the subordination of Christians to the state. Even here there is a certain order of internal and external. Thus, the fog is lifted, a delusion vanishes, and the view of God's truth becomes sharp,

---

153. WA 8, 683, 15ff. = BoA 2, 306, 20ff.
154. WA 8, 683, 32–33 = BoA 2, 306, 36–37.
155. WA 8, 678, 9–10 = BoA 2, 301, 30–31.
156. WA 8, 684, 6–7 = BoA 2, 307, 8–9.

5. Luther's Doctrine of the Three Estates

In conclusion to this last section of a presentation of "Luther's Theology," the question might arise, whether Luther said something generally valid about human society. However, we must remember that during Luther's time, the entire view of social life was still determined by the idea that a city or a state could not exist without a preacher. Luther did not intend that the office of the clergy should have special status. When he thought about the office of preaching, he did not mean that there should be ranking among people in the sense of a divine order. In his later writing "On the Council and the Churches" (1539) he said: "The school must be next to the Church, since in it one begets young preachers and pastors, after which it puts them in the burial ground. The Burgher's house is next to the school since one must get pupils from it. Next, the city hall and castle which must protect the burgers, so they produce children for the school and raise school children to be pastors."[157] And then later: "But God must be the highest and the nearest, who retains such a ring of circle (or protection) against the devil and does everything at all levels, indeed, in all creatures. Thus says Psalm 27, that on earth are only two bodily regimes, city, and house: 'Where the Lord does not build the house, 'again;'" where the Lord does not protect the city.' The first is the house: here we have people. The second is the city: that is, land, people, princes, and lords (which we call the earthly authority). All of it is given, child, possessions, field, beast, etc. The house must be built, the city must care for them, protect, and defend. Next comes the third: God's own house and city, that is the Church, which must have persons from the house and protection covering from the city."[158] Luther says later on that these "three estates are ordained by God and we don't need any others; we have enough and more than enough to do to live in these three against the devil."[159]

The external life in which my Christian existence appears is, in view of the passing world, determined through the social status to which I belong. Luther clearly intends that the office of clergy, everything that

---

157. WA 50, 652, 1ff.
158. WA 50, 652, 1ff. nn. 7ff.
159. WA 50, 652, 1ff. nn. 18ff.

has to do with family, and finally with the rule of authority, are the three situations, or estates, in which people live, whenever they would do a work that is pleasing to God. Anyone in their position in life does not live on the basis of doing good works according to that position, but they live because their position pleases God. And so, Luther says that God has stapled His Word to this position, as a sign and seal, so that the person, on the basis of the promise born of faith, can follow God's signpost and can be certain of it and sure that his works are pleasing to God.

What does Luther actually mean by the word "estate?" When he speaks of father and mother as an estate, of marriage as an estate, or of authority as an estate, what does he mean by it? He developed his teaching on the "estates" in relationship to the idea that no one can remove themselves from the world. He constantly reiterated this. It is his antithesis to the monastic-aesthetic life. The "Yes" to the world is, for him, given in one's position or estate. What does that mean? That could mean—and I believe, it does—that over faith and for faith, there are instances in the world, positions, or estates in which a Christian can be certain that they are pleasing to God. You must, my dear readers, always understand, however, that Luther never proposed a way in which the internal life of a Christian could be truly externally represented. The life of the Christian is hidden (Col 3:3: "Your life is hidden with Christ in God."). As Luther says, "So, he will not have such saints who run from the people, to which it should apply that one would not need the Ten Commandments over all. For if I am cut off from all the people in the desert, then no one will congratulate me that I did not commit adultery, kill, or steal, and yet think meanwhile that I am holy and have escaped the Ten Commandments set by God that he teach us how we should rightly to live in the world toward our neighbor."[160] Here we see that the world is clearly the estate in which it is only possible to fulfill God's laws, and a "position" or "situation" must be connected with it. In another place Luther says, "See, thus must the whole Christian life be and remain hidden and hardly arrive at any fame, or show, or have respect before the world. So let it happen, and do not take care whether it is hidden and covered and buried, that no one sees nor values it. It is enough for you that your Father in heaven sees it, who has sharp eyes and can see far into the distance, whether it is overcast with large, dark clouds and crowded deep in the earth, so that the life of

---

160. WA 32, 370, 33ff. (Weekly sermon on Matt 5–7. 1530/2. Printed 1532. Matt 5:27–29).

all Christians is directed to God's eyes alone."[161] And on a smaller similar verse in Matt 5:29: "When your right eye offends you, pluck it out and throw it from you . . ." Luther says these words of Jesus, "are only spoken of spiritual life and existence, since one does not externally on the body before the world, but in the heart before God throws eye and hand from oneself, disowns and abandons oneself and all things. For he does not teach that we use the fist or the sword, nor to rule life and goods with a rod, but only the heart and conscience before God. So, we must not enter his words in the book of laws or worldly regime."[162]

In this short introduction to Luther's teaching on the three estates, which should have something to say to us about his understanding of society, I would like to finish with a citation that is at the same time of particular significance for our life, especially for our Christian life in today's world, when understood correctly:

> *Summa*: Whoever will be a Christian must be so clever that he does not do or omit to do any good work for the people's sake, but does it only through his office, estate, money, possessions or whatever he has, in order to serve God and do him honor as he can, though he on earth would never receive any thanks for it. For it is impossible that a devout man would be rewarded for even the tiniest work he does, even if one were to crown him with gold and give him an entire kingdom. So, he should not think about anything else than taking food and drink from the world and expect no reward from it, as if it should pay for or reward such a good work, or that it should recognize and honor a real Christian, whether or not it knows him right off because he is so pious and would thank him. It is not thus for their sake, nor is it omitted for their sake, but is commanded by God who will richly repay it, not secretly, but openly before the whole world and all the angels.[163]

---

161. WA 32, 435, 1ff. (Matt 6:16–18)
162. WA 32, 374, 25ff. (Matt 5:27–29).
163. WA 32, 412, 19ff. (Matt 6:1–4).

Appendix

Supplemental Literature

IN HIS FOREWORD THE editor, Johannes Haar, explains that this book is comprised of lectures given by Hans Joachim Iwand used in an effort to compile his unfinished book on Luther. In the footnotes, Johannes Haar has referenced additional studies of Luther by Iwand which are outlined below.

Chapter 2: Luther's Doctrine of Justification

- The Fundamental Meaning of the Doctrine of the Bound Will for Faith (1930) in: Iwand's Collected Works (CW) I, 13–30.
- Studies on the Problem of the Bound Will (1930) in: CW I, 31–61.
- The Freedom of the Christian and the Bound Will (1957) in: CW I, 247–68.
- Theological Introduction and Explanations (1941) in: Martin Luther, "Free Will Does Not Exist," Munich, Vol. I (1962), 253–315.
- Luther's Life and Doctrine and the Forgotten Treasure of His Theology in: Papers from the Luther House in Königsberg, 1931.
- The Fight over the Legacy of the Reformation (1932) in: CW II, 126–44.
- Sermons on the Law (1934) in: CW II, 145–70.
- Law and Gospel (1937) in: Posthumous Works (PW) 4, 11–230.

- Law and Gospel (1950/51) in: PW 4, 231–401.
- Counterpoint to G. Wingren: Between Barth and Luther (1950) in: PW 2, 401–5.
- Law and Gospel in Luther's Commentary on Galatians of 1531/35 in: PH 4, 404–40.
- Gospel and Law in: PW 4, 441–51.
- *The Righteousness of Faith according to Luther* (1941) in: CW II, 11–125. Trans. R. Lundell, OR: Wipf & Stock, 2008.
- "*Sed Originale per hominem unum.*" Commentary on Anthropology (1943/46) in: CW II, 171–93.
- On Christian Freedom (Afterword to Martin Luther's "On the Freedom of the Christian") 1953 in: CW II, 194–97.

Chapter 3: Christology

- Doctrine of Justification and Faith in Christ (1931 & 1961) and Theology of the Cross (1959) in: PW 2, 381–98.

Chapter 4: Church, State, and Society

- On the Origins of Luther's Concept of the Church. A critical treatment of an article by Karl Holl on the same topic (1957) in: CW II, 198–239.
- The Right of Christians to Resist in the Teachings of the Reformation (1952/53) in: PW 2, 193–229.
- On the Theological Basis for Resistance against the State (1953) in: PW 2, 230–242.
- Outline for an Evaluation of the Question of Resistance in Protestant Teachings (together with Ernst Wolf) in: JK 1952, 192–99.
- The Estates and the Sacraments (1957) in: CW II, 240–264.

Bibliography

Primary Sources

Aland, Kurt. *Luther Deutsch: Die Werke Martin Luthers in neuer Auswahl für die Gegenwart.* Göttingen Vandenhoeck & Ruprecht, 1958.
Aquinas, Thomas von. *Summa Theologica,* . Rome: Leonina, 1923.
Die Bekenntnisschriften der evangelisch-lutherischen Kirche. 2 vols. Göttingen: Vandenhoeck & Ruprecht, 1930.
Borcherdt H. H. and G. Merz, eds. *Martin Luther Ausgewählte Werke* (Münchner Ausgabe) including: B. Jordahn, trans. *Vom unfreieen Willen,* 1. Ergänzungsband, 1954; E. Ellwein, *Vorlesung über den Römerbreif* 1515/1516. 2. Ergänzungsband, 1965; R. Frick, trans., *Wider den Löwener Theologen Latomus,* 6. Ergänzungsband. Darmstadt: Wissenschaftliche Buchgesellschaft, 1960.
Clemen, Otto, ed. *Luthers Werke in Auswahl.* 8 vols. ("Bonner Ausgabe" = BoA). Berlin: de Gruyter, 1950.
Ficker, Johannes, ed. *Anfänge reformatorischer Bibelauslegung.* Vol. 1: Luthers Vorlesung über den Römerbrief 1515/1516 (Glossen—Scholien), Leipzig: Dieterich, 1908 (Fi)
———, ed. and trans. *Vorlesung über den Römerbrief 1515/1516.* Latin/German edition. 2 vols. Darmstadt: Wissenschaftliche Buchgesellschaft, 1960.
Lombardus, Petrus. *Sententiarum IV.* In Migne, Patrologiae cursus completes series Latina (MPL), Vol. 192.
Luther, Martin. *Werke.* Kritische Gesamtausgabe (=Weimarer Ausgabe), 1883 (WA)
———. *Die Deutsche Bibel,* 1906ff. (WA DB)
———. *Tischreden,* 1912. Ff (WA Ti)
———. *Briefwechsel,* 1930ff (WA Br)
Schröder, Rudof Alexander, trans. *Theologia Deutsch.* Anonym. 1516 von M. Luther in Deutscher Sprache veröffentlicht. Gütersloh: Bertelsmann, 1947.

Secondary Sources

Aquinas, Thomas. *Summa Theologica*. Notre Dame: Christian Classics, 1948.
Boehmer, Heinrich, and H. Bornkamm, ed. *Der Junge Luther*. Stuttgart: Kohler & Amelang, 1951.
Brenz, Johannes. *Catechismus: Pia et utili explicantione illustratus*. Frankfurt (Lindau): Brubach, 1551. German translator Hartmann Beyer, 1554.
Capelle, Wilhelm, ed. *Die Vorsokratiker*. Kröners Taschenausgabe 119. Stuttgart: Kröner, 1963.
Dempf, Alois. *Metaphysik des Mittelalters*. Berlin: Oldenbourg, 1930.
Denifle, Heinrich. *Luther und Luthertum in der ersten Entwicklung quellenmäßig darge-stellt*. Annotated by A. M. Weiss. 2 vols. in supplementary 4 vols. Mainz: Kirchheim, 1904–1909.
Descartes, René. *Meditations on First Philosophy* (1641). Indianapolis: Hackett, 1993.
Diem, Harald. *Luthers Lehre von den zwei Reichen* (BEvTh5), 1938.
Dostoyevsky, Fyodor. "The Grand Inquisitor." *Brothers Karamazov*. New York: Penguin, 2003.
Elert, W. *Morphologie des Luthertums*, Vol. 1: Theologie und Welanschauung des Luthertums. Munich: Beck, 1931 (1952).
Frick, R. ed. *Martin Luther, Ausgewählte Werke*. Ergänzungsreihe 6. Munich, 1961.
Goethe, Johann Wolfgang. *Collected Works*. Berlin: Suhrkamp, 1983.
Gollwitzer, Helmut. *Coena Domini: Die altlutherische Abendmahlslehre in ihrer Auseinandersetzung mit dem Calvinismus dargestellt an der lutherischen Frühorthodoxie*. Munich: Beck, 1937.
Haar, Johann. *Initium creaturae Dei*. Gütersloh: Kaiser, 1939.
Harnack, Th. *Luthers Theologie mit besonderer Beziehung auf seine Versöhnungs- und Erlösungslehre*. 2 vols. 1862/86. Newer ed. Munich: Kaiser, 1926/27.
Heidegger, Martin. *Being and Time*. Translated by John MacQuarrie and Edward Robinson. New York: Harper & Row, 1962.
Hermann, Rudolf. "Luthers These 'Gerecht und Sünder zugleich,' und 'Solange es heute heist.'" In *Solange es "heute" heisst: Festgabe für Rudolf Hermann zum 70. Geburtstag*. Berlin: Beck, 1957.
Holl, Karl. *Gesammelte Aufsätze zur Kirchengeschichte*, vol. 1: *Luther*. Tübingen: Mohr Siebeck, 1927.
Hollatz, David. *Examen theologicum*. Leipzig: Schreiber, 1750.
Hunzinger, A.W. *Lutherstudien*. I. *Luthers Neuplatonismus in der Psalmenvorlesung von 1513–1516*. Leipzig: Deichert, 1906.
Iwand, Hans Joachim. *Nachgelassene Werke* (NW). Vol. 1: H. Gollwitzer, ed. *Glauben und Wissen*, Munich, 1962. Vol. 2: *Vorträge und Aufsätze*, ed. D. Schellong and K. G. Steck, Munich 1966. Vol. 3: *Ausgewählte Predigten*, ed. H. H. Esser and H. Gollwitzer, Munich 1963. Vol. 4: *Gesetz und Evangelium*, ed. W. Kreck, Munich 1964. Vol. 6: *Briefe an Rudolf Hermann*, ed. and with an introduction by K. G. Steck, Munich: Beck, 1964.
———. *Rechtfertigungslehre und Christusglaube*. Leipzig: Hinrich, 1930. Reprint, Darmstadt, 1966.
Jacob, Günter. *Der Gewissensbegriff in der Theologie Luthers*. Tübingen: 1929. Reprint, Liechtenstein: Nendeln, 1966.
Kant, Immanuel. *Collected Works*. Vol. 1. Indianapolis: Hackett, 2002.

Köhler, Walther. *Zwingli und Luther: Ihr Streit über das Abendmahl nach seinen politischen und religiösen Beziehungen.* Vol. 1, 1924. Vol. 2, ed. E. Kohlmeyer and H. Bornkamm. Quellen und Forschungen zur Reformationsgeschichte 6–7. Gütersloh: Kaiser, 1953.

Köstlin, Julius. *Luthers Theologie in ihrer geschichtlichen Entwicklung und ihrem inneren Zusammenhang dargestellt,* 2nd ed. Stuttgart: Steinkopf, 1901.

Lortz, Joseph. *Die Reformation in Deutschland.* 2 vols. Freiburg.: Herder, 1939 (1963).

Luther, Martin. *Luther's Works.* Vol. 25. St. Louis: Concordia, 1972.

———. *The Small Catechism.* Minneapolis: Fortress, 1996.

Merz, Georg, and H. H. Borcherdt, eds. *Martin Luther, Ausgewählte Werke,* Erganzungsreihe 1. Munich: Kaiser, 1954.

Möhler, Johann Adam. *Symbolik.* Edited by J. R. Geiselmann. New ed. Cologne: Hegner, 1958.

Nietzsche, Friedrich. *On the Genealogy of Morals.* New York: Penguin Classics, 2014.

———. *Thus Spoke Zarathustra.* Cambridge: Cambridge University Press, 2006.

Plato. *Phaedo.* Oxford: Oxford University Press, 2009.

Ritschl, Albrecht. *Die christliche Lehre von der Rechtfertigung und Versöhnung.* 3 vols. Bonn: Marcus, 1882.

Scheler, Max. *Das Ewige im Menschen.* Vol. 1. Leipzig: Schreiber, 1921.

———. *On the Eternal in Man.* New York: Routledge, 2009.

Schweitzer, Albert. *Geschichte der Leben-Jesus-Forschung.* Siebenstern Taschenbuch, 1972.

———. *The Quest for the Historical Jesus.* New York: Dover, 2005.

Schopenhauer, Arthur. *The World as Will and Representation.* 2 vols. New York: Dover, 1966.

Schröder, Erich Chr. *Meditationen über die erste Philosophie* Philosophische Bibliothek 250. Hamburg: Meiner, 1956.

Seeberg, Reinhold. "Dogmengeschichte des Mittelalters." In *Lehrbuch der Dogmengeschichte.* Vol. 3. Leipzig: Deichert, 1930. Reprint, Darmstadt: Wissenschaftliche Buchgesellschaft, 1959.

———. "Die Lehre Luthers." In *Lehrbuch der Dogmengeschichte* 4/1. Leipzig: Deichert, 1933. Reprint, Darmstadt: Wissenschaftliche Buchgesellschaft, 1959.

———. *Luthers Theologie: Motive und Ideen.* Vol. 1: *Die Göttesanschauung,* Göttingen: Vandenhoeck & Ruprecht, 1929. Vol. 2: *Christus: Wirklichkeit und Urbild.* Stuttgart: Kohlhammer, 1937.

Sellin, Ernst, and Leonhard Rost. *Einleitung in das Alte Testament.* Heidelberg: Quelle & Meyer, 1959.

Shakespeare, William. *Complete Works.* New York: Random House Modern Library, 2022.

Spengler, Oswald. *The Decline of the West: Form and Actuality.* Translated by Charles Francis Atkinson. 1926. Reprint, Oxford: Oxford University Press, 1991.

Stange, Carl, ed. *Die ältesten ethischen Disputationen Luthers.* Quellenschriften zur Geschichte des Protestantismus 1. Leipzig: Deichert, 1904.

Steck, Karl Gerhard. *Lehre und Kirche bei Luther.* Forschungen zur Geschichte und Lehre des Protestantismus 10/27. Munich: Kaiser, 1963.

———. *Luther für Katholiken.* Munich: Kaiser, 1969.

Tauler, Johannes, *Theologia Deutsch.* Edited by R. A. Schröder, Gütersloh: Kaiser, 1947.

Theunissen, M. *Der Andre.* Berlin: Beck, 1965.

Thieme, Karl. *Die sittliche Triebkraft des Glaubens: Eine Untersuchung zu Luthers Theologie*. Leipzig: Dörffling & Franke, 1895.
Ueberweg, Friedrich. *Grundriß der Geschichte der Philosophie*, Vol. II: *Die patristische und scholastische Philosophie*. Edited by B. Geyer, Darmstadt: Wissenschaftliche Buchgesellschaft, 1967.
Vorländer, Karl. *Philosophie des Mittelalters*. Berlin: Rowohlt, 1964.
Weber, Max. *Gesammelte Aufsätze zur Religionssoziologie*, Vol. 1, 1920. Tübingen: Mohr Siebeck, 1920.
Wellhausen, Julius. *Israelitische und jüdische Geschichte*. Berlin: Beck, 1895.

Reference Works

Bauer, Walter. *Griechisch-deutsches Wörterbuch zu den Schriften des Neuen Testaments und der übrigen urchristlichen Literatur*. Berlin: Töpelmann, 1958.
Galling, Kurt, ed. *Die Religion in Geschichte und Gegenwart* (RGG). 3rd ed. Tübingen: Mohr Siebeck, 1957–1965.
Kluge, Friedrich, and A. Götze. *Etymologisches Wörterbuch der Deutschen Sprache*. Berlin: de Gruyter 1957.

Name Index

Aland, Kurt, 13n23, 28n55
Althaus, Paul, 16
Amsdorf, Nikolaus von, 4, 4n4
Aristotle, 192, 220
Augustine, 6, 14, 23, 35

Barth, Karl, 18, 24, 144n157, 230
Beintker, Horst, 201n94
Bernhard of Clairvaux, 9
Biel, Gabriel, 7, 7n14, 21
Bodenstein, Andreas. *See* Karlstadt (Andreas Bodenstein)
Boehmer, H., 28n55
Böhme, Jakob, 21
Bonaventura, 23
Bornkamm, H., 28n55
Braun, Johann, 28
Brenner, O., 221n145
Brenz, Johannes, 193n75
Brunstad, Friedrich, 16
Buber, Martin, 115n93
Bultmann, Rudolf, 18

Capelle, Wilhelm, 70n6
Clemen, Otto, 221n145
Cruciger, C., 140n147

Dempf, Alois, 25n43
Denifle, Heinrich Suso, 22, 22n41, 24–26, 25nn44–46
Descartes, René, 160n204
Diem, Harald, 215
Dilthey, Wilhelm, 4

Dostoyevsky, Fyodor, 81n26
Duns Scotus, 5, 23, 110

Eck, Johann, 28, 28n55
Eckehart, 94n47
Elert, Werner, 4, 15, 15n26, 16n28, 19
Ellwin, Eduard, 3n2
Empedocles, 70n6
Epictetus, 169n16
Erasmus of Rotterdam, 11, 21, 29, 29n60, 50, 51, 52

Feuerbach, Ludwig, 84
Fichte, Johann Gottlieb, 130n130
Ficker, Johannes, 2, 3n2
Flex, Walter, 149n173
Freud, Sigmund, 128, 128n123
Frick, R., 34n12, 37nn22–24
Friedrich of Saxony, 189

Gerhardt, Paul, 9
Goethe, Johann Wolfgang, 47n55, 70n6, 129, 130n127, 207, 207n114
Gogarten, Friedrich, 18, 115n93
Gollwitzer, Helmut, 193n75
Götze, A., 163n4
Griesbach, Eberhard, 115n93
Gunter, Jacob, 130n130

Haar, Johann, 35n15, 85, 153n184, 229
Halesius, Alexander, 192n73
Harnack, Adolf von, 18

NAME INDEX

Harnack, Theodosius, 13, 13n25, 14, 15, 19, 76n16
Hegel, G. W. F., 10, 84, 165
Heidegger, Martin, 108, 108n76, 115n93, 130n130, 136, 137
Heim, Karl, 16
Heimann, Eduard, 118n96
Hermann, Nikolaus, 36
Hermann, Rudolf, 11n22, 60, 60n83, 196n82, 201n94
Herrmann, Wilhelm, 16
Hohlwein, H., 163n1
Holl, Karl, 2, 5, 17, 17n32, 18, 18n34, 19, 20, 21, 21n37, 23, 25n47, 53n71, 86, 87n35, 117, 118n95, 122, 123, 123nn106–107, 124, 170, 170n18, 170n20, 171n21, 230
Hollatz, David, 148n170
Hunzinger, A. W., 171, 171n22
Husserl, Edmund, 82n27

Innocent III, 192n73

Johann of Saxony, 134
Jonas of Coburg, 47
Jordahn, B., 52n70

Kant, Immanuel, 20, 47n55, 82n27, 87, 87n35, 88, 88n37, 90, 130n130, 164
Karlstadt (Andreas Bodenstein), 149, 149n174, 149n175, 150, 151, 214, 215, 217
Kierkegaard, S. A;, 115n93
Kluge, Friedrich, 163n4
Köstlin, Julius, 13, 13n24
Kutter, H., 118n96

Lau, F., 4n4
Leo X, 33
Lessing, Gotthold Ephraim, 162, 162n2
Lombard, Peter, 171n21
Lombardus, Petrus, 78n21, 190n66
Lortz, Joseph, 22, 23, 23n42, 26–27, 27nn52–53

Mann, O., 163n2

Marcus Aurelius, 169n16
Marx, Karl, 84
Melanchthon, Ph., 19, 19n36, 20, 120, 121
Merz, Georg, 14, 52n70
Michelangelo, Buonarroti, 12
Möhler, Johann Adam, 98n55
Müntzer, Thomas, 214

Nietzsche, Friedrich W., 6, 6n9, 84, 128, 128n122

Ockham, Wilhelm von. *See* William of Ockham
Origen, 70

Plato, 141, 141n151, 171n13
Poliander, John, 152n181, 154n185

Ragaz, L., 118n96
Ritschl, Albrect, 14, 15, 20, 21, 83, 83n32
Rörer, G., 162n4
Rost, L., 172n24

Scheler, Max, 82, 82n27
Schlaginhuafen, Johann, 43, 43n39
Schleiermacher, Friedrich, 82
Schopenhauer, Arthur, 51, 51n68
Schröder, E. Chr., 160n204
Schweitzer, Albert, 82n29
Seeberg, Erich, 21, 21n40
Seeberg, Reinhold, 4, 5, 21, 21n39
Sellin, Ernst, 172n24
Semler, Johann Salomo, 163, 163n1
Seneca, 169n16
Shakespeare, William, 129, 129n124
Spalatin, Georg, 78, 78n21
Spengler, Oswald, 15, 15n27
Stange, Carl, 2, 2n1
Steck, Karl Gerhard, 4n3, 175n31
Strauss, David Friedrich, 84

Tauler, Johannes, 53n71, 61n85
Tetzel, Johann, 22
Theunissen, Michael, 115n93
Thieme, Karl, 95, 95n48

Thomas Aquinas, 5, 6, 9, 21, 23, 31, 31n1, 32, 110
Tillich, Paul, 118n96
Troeltsch, Ernst, 4, 18

Vogelsang, Erich, 3n2
Vorlander, Karl, 224n152

Weber, Max, 165, 165n8

Wellhausen, Julius, 82, 82n28
William of Ockham, 5, 23, 24, 25, 224n152
Wingren, Gustaf, 230
Wolf, Ernst, 4n5, 22n41, 99n57, 175n31, 230

Zinzendorf, Nicolaus, 9
Zwingli, Ulrich, 196, 199, 214

Ancient Document Index

OLD TESTAMENT

Genesis

	130n129
2:7	77
3:1	159
4:14	130
16	159n198
22:14	58
32:11	191
43:9–22	127

Exodus

13:21–22	119

Leviticus

6:36	118
26:36	129

Numbers

10	134
22ff	128

Psalms

	119n97, 178
22	68, 68n5, 70
27	226
31:9b	117
31:10	117
32	58, 212
32 (31)	172
33:4	212
34:16	58
45:8	185
73 (72):16	172
82	221, 222
90	136n142
110	148, 157n192, 191n70
117	90n41
118	88n38, 113n87, 138n145, 143n156
118:5	112
119:72	158
119:98	108
119:105	103, 158
142:2	112
142:3	112

Proverbs

24:16	206

Ecclesiastes

10:7	50

Isaiah

9:1	67
42:3	67
46:8	173
53	74
54:13	185
55:10–11	178

Jeremiah

17:16	158n195

Hosea

6:3–4	158

Amos

3:7	203

Jonah

	125

DEUTEROCANONICAL BOOKS

Tobit

4:16	101n63

NEW TESTAMENT (IN LUTHER BIBLE ORDER)

Matthew

3	41n31
5–7	124n113, 227n160
5:4	67
5:9	222
5:16	102
5:27–29	227n160, 228n162
5:29	228
6:1–4	228n163
6:16–18	228n161
7:12	101n63
7:13–14	124n113
7:14	140
9:18–26	91n43
11:2–10	89n39
11:27	82
11:28	67, 74
13:33	39
15	49
15:21–28	144
16:8	216
16:16ff	182
16:18	178, 182, 192
16:19	183n48
18:18	183n48
20:22	208
22:21	224
22:32	138
22:34ff	130n128
23:37	154
26:29	201

Mark

4:35–41	128
7	49
14:66–72	128
16:16	191

Luke

1:38	178
1:67ff	104n66
2:34	67
6:20	67
6:31	101n63
7:36ff	111
10:28	88
13:34	154
15:11–32	195
15:11ff	111, 213
17:20ff	215
17:21	173n29
18:9–14	102
18:9ff	111, 114
18:11	90n42
19:41ff	63
23:35	73

John

	83
1	160n202
1:1–14	84n33
1:1	157
1:13	97
1:14	138
1:29	121
4:47ff	161n207
5:41	197
6:32	155
6:45	185
8:46ff	152n181

8:51	142	3:9	168
14	41n32	3:22ff	184
15	41n32	10:16–17	174
15:2	120	10:17	189
15:16	57	11:24–25	193, 202
16:21	141	13:3	103
18:11	208	13:12	12
20:23	183n48	15	146, 146n162, 147
21:19–24	166	15:12–15	138n144
		15:21	135
Acts		15:24	171
3:21	206	15:25	141
15:9	104	15:43ff	134
		15:51ff	134n134
		15:52	133
Romans		45:15	9n20
	2, 17, 29, 38, 97n51, 109n78, 176	**2 Corinthians**	
1	142		213
1:16	143, 216	3:6	70
1:17	11	3:18	160
1:19ff	153	4:6	119
3:4	147	6:9	213
3:20b	45		
3:25	15	**Galatians**	
4:23	100		42, 76, 110n80, 114n88, 123, 124n113, 126, 131n131, 146n163, 160n205, 169n15
5:3ff	119		
5:5	119		
5:14	135		
5:18	135		
6:3–11	140n147	1:8	138
6:13	168	3:22	59
6:19	132	3:23–29	93n46
7:7–8	45	3:23ff	44n44
7:18	206	3:27	93
8:26	61	3:28	185, 188
8:28	6, 210	4:3	49
8:31	142, 212	5:16	38
13:1ff	223	6:2	74, 194
13:1	165		
14:8	189	**Ephesians**	
15:4–13	114n91	1:3	209
		1:7	209
1 Corinthians		4:5	180
1:19	9n20	5:32	189
2:6	59	6:5	96
2:16	172	6:17	158

Colossians

2:3	76
2:8	49
3:3	227

1 Thessalonians

4:13–14	135n137
4:15ff	133

2 Thessalonians

2:3f	185

1 Timothy

1:5–7	95
2:5	213

2 Timothy

1:13	24

Titus

2:1	24
2:13	105n68, 134n136
3:4–7	110n83

Philemon

1:21	189

1 Peter

2:9	185

2 Peter

3:13	121
4:10	134

1 John

2:1	213
5:4–5	178n36

Hebrews

1:1	152
1:3	158
4:12	158
9:5	15
11:1	11, 172

James

1:12	108
1:13	155
1:18	35, 145n161, 153, 176, 177n35, 178n36, 182, 185
1:20	178n36
1:22	103
1:26ff	178n36
5:7	158

GREEK AND ROMAN LITERATURE

Aristotle

Politika	220

Empedocles

Porentheorie (*Theory of Elements*)	70n6

Plato

The Republic "Theory of Forms"	141n151

MEDIEVAL CHRISTIAN WRITINGS

Thomas Aquinas

Summa Theologica	31
II/1, 55, 4	31n1
II/1, 71	32
II/1, 71, 4	32n6
II/1, 71, 4 ad 3	32n4

www.ingramcontent.com/pod-product-compliance
Lightning Source LLC
Chambersburg PA
CBHW050845230426
43667CB00012B/2150